Michael Bentine grew u... the ethos of the North D... his family in their resea... studied paranormal phe... a scriptwriter is found... clairvoyant, as he explai...

His television series include *The Bumblies*, *It's a Square World*, *The Golden Silents*, *After Hours* and *Potty Time*.

He is the author of *The Long Banana Skin*, *Madame's Girls*, *The Door Marked Summer* and *The Best of Bentine* (both the book and the radio series).

MICHAEL BENTINE

The Door Marked Summer

Doors of the Mind

GRAFTON BOOKS

A Division of the Collins Publishing Group

LONDON GLASGOW
TORONTO SYDNEY AUCKLAND

Grafton Books
A Division of the Collins Publishing Group
8 Grafton Street, London W1X 3LA

This omnibus edition
published by Grafton Books 1987

The Door Marked Summer
First published in Great Britain by
Granada Publishing Ltd 1981

Doors of the Mind
First published in Great Britain by
Granada Publishing Ltd 1984

Copyright © Michael Bentine 1981, 1984, 1987

ISBN 0-586-20016-9

Printed and bound in Great Britain by
Collins, Glasgow

Set in Times

The Door Marked Summer

In my life I have found myself facing many doors. Some I have opened, only to shut them in terror. Others have opened for me, and I have seen much sorrow and pain.

Some I have never yet had the courage to open.

But there is one which, when it opens, spills a great blaze of golden light into my life. Beyond it I can see the smiling faces of all the people that I love, who have preceded me through the door.

This is my favourite—
the door marked 'Summer'.

Michael Bentine

Contents

Author's Note

In 1975 I wrote a potted autobiography called *The Long Banana Skin*. In it I devoted two chapters to my experiences of the paranormal. Since then, many readers have written to me saying they would like to know more about my involvement with the occult.

This book is as honest and as truthful an account of those experiences as I can make it. I may not have got the exact details of times and dates right but wherever possible I have checked the accuracy of the material with my family, and they all agree that these things happened as I have described them.

Foreword

In matters of science there are topics that are 'respectable' and topics that are not. That scientists, some of whom would claim to be seeking the Truth, have avenues they refuse to explore is an anomaly. In the 1930s, when there were just four *fundamental* bits of matter – protons, neutrons, electrons and positrons – physics was as tidy as it was for the Ancients with *their* four fundamentals of earth, fire, air and water. There was a general atmosphere of: 'just around the next corner and we shall know *all* of it'. The rush to discover new particles in the 1940s and 1950s was not unlike the rush for gold in the Klondike. 'Get yourself a new particle and a Nobel Prize goes with it' was a common attitude among researchers. Then the nucleus of the sacred atom was smashed into sub-atomic particles. There were neutrons, held together with gluons (the Goons were infiltrating physics, surely?). There were quarks and different types of quarks. The Lords of Science even ran out of names and resorted to such words as 'charm', 'beauty', 'up', 'down' and other equally unimaginative words. But at least there was a refreshing breeze of open-mindedness which dismissed the idea that, where scientific knowledge was concerned, we were 'nearly there'.

And yet, even within such a healthy age of pioneering, the respectable scientist was not to be found in the dark attic of the paranormal. Even to peep through the keyhole could be the end of a promising career. Undoubtedly one of the causes of this fear of the sixth sense, or whatever name one gives it, was the vigour with which 'evidence' was produced by the un-learned. It was the easiest thing in the world to fake. Magicians had a field day, aided and abetted by the communications media, and the truly unrespectable and the fraudulent grew fat on mankind's ever-present fear of death and of the 'great beyond'. To the older topics of Mesmerism (which eventually found acceptance by the Establishment), ghosts and poltergeists were added UFOs and the other products of modern science fiction, and the 'man in the middle', i.e. the majority of us, became more confused than ever.

I have known Michael Bentine for many years. Most people associate him with comedy alone, but he is a man of many talents who could have chosen any one of half a dozen widely-differing careers and been counted among the nobility of each. The fact that he did some of each, including comedy, is a blessing to us all.

Whilst each one of us can rightly claim that our life is unique, Michael's is both unique and *very* special. His scientific knowledge is first rate – yet he dares to think about and to question all aspects of human experience. 'We invented time' is a typical example of his lateral thinking. He worries about the human race more than most of us and, perhaps misguidedly, takes its problems on to his own broad shoulders, but he does it always in the utmost sincerity and always with profound humility. 'This is as honest a book as I can write,' he says, and it is just that.

He has the courage to set down all his experiences that science cannot dismiss with its 'rational' explanations. I think most of us have shared in at least some of such experiences but most of us keep them to ourselves lest we be thought even slightly 'odd'.

Michael has met disaster, has been to the limits of fear and seen the ultimate Evil. His assault on Hitlerism is relentless. He knows the loneliness of being 'out in front' whether it be on a stage or in thought. I am tremendously impressed in that this great thinker comes so near, in this book, to the same conclusions as did Arnold Toynbee and Daisaku Ikeda in their dialogue *Choose Life*.

The suggestion is that there is a Life Force, almost identical to the Force of Science Fiction as expressed so well in the film *Star Wars*. The 'Dark Side' of the Force is with us in the real world as well as in fiction, but then, is not today's science fiction tomorrow's science fact and has it not long been so, as witness the writings of H. G. Wells and others?

Michael Bentine, we, who dare to think, salute you. You turned the key in the door of the dark attic where conventional science is afraid to go – and you found that it was not dark, inside. You had indeed found the door marked 'Summer'.

E. R. Laithwaite
January 1981

1 Night Visitors

I don't know if my father, Adam Michael Bentin (the 'e' was added by me for professional reasons) was the seventh son of a seventh son, but that he was 'psychic' is undeniable, for, during the course of his seventy-seven years on this planet, he was to touch the lives of many people.

Pop arrived in England from Peru at the age of thirteen, having been sent there by his eldest brother, Ricardo, to be educated under the British system. Already he had a number of elder brothers at one or other of the major universities of the world, such as Heidelberg, Madrid, the Sorbonne, Harvard and Milan, in accordance with the wishes of my grandfather, Don Antonio Bentin Palamerro. Grandad had died at the early age of fifty-five, after eight years as Vice-President of the Republic, and was buried, as President-elect, with full honours. This good man, who did a lot for the under-privileged of Peru, wished to see his sons educated in the widest possible sense, so that they could bring back much of the storehouse of modern technology to their emergent country. When he died his eldest son had become head of the family at the age of twenty-five, and he continued to carry out his father's wishes.

The great difference between Uncle Ricardo's age and that of my infant father did not prevent Pop from adoring him, because 'Tio Ricardo' took the place of his lost father.

Pop's mother died a short time after he was born, and his upbringing was left to his beautiful Indian nurse, Angelica, who loved him dearly.

By the time my father was seven years old, my
grandfather had also passed over, and Pop was duly given
even more loving attention by all his elder brothers and
such sisters-in-law as he had. In other words he was
'spoiled rotten' by the whole family, so that, by the age of
thirteen, he was, by his own admission, a pain in the neck
and a real problem-child for Uncle Ricardo.

His eldest brother was, by then, Vice-President of the
Republic and the Mayor of Lima as well, so he was far too
busy to cope with his difficult youngest brother. A family
council-of-war was held, and it was decided to send Pop to
England, to stay with a close family friend – Mrs Southery,
who had lived in Peru and spoke Spanish.

This marvellous lady, whom Pop always referred to as
'Granny Southery' and whom he adored, took the place of
his lost mother, and she brought up my father as one of her
own family. Moreover, William, her son by her first
marriage to a Mr Hope-Jones, became my father's closest
friend and remained so throughout his life.

Pop arrived in Britain unable to speak more than a few
words of English and was immediately enfolded in the
warm embrace of the Southery/Hope-Jones family. This
affectionate and highly intelligent ménage ran a large
guest house for foreign students in Holland Park Road.

There, among some twenty other bright youngsters from
all over the world, my father learned to speak a number of
languages and to think as an international. He often told
me about those early days in England, far from his much-
loved family in Peru, and his glowing face as he reminisced
about those times was indisputable evidence that they had
been some of the happiest days of his life. That marvellously eccentric family and their friends frequently opened
his door marked summer.

William Hope-Jones – or, as I was later to know him, Uncle
Billy – was tall, immensely strong and gentle, a Rowing
Blue and a great all-round athlete and scholar. Pop was

small, wiry and compactly energetic, a fine cricketer, crack shot and Olympic-class horseman and fencer.

My father, being from South America, where self-reliance is a way of life, had little appreciation of team-work outside his own family, and no idea of sportsmanship whatsoever. At one school where he was initiated into the mysterious sport of boxing, the gym instructor had tried to get the puzzled Peruvian boy to put on the gloves and enter the ring to fight another lad. Pop was reluctant to do so, because, as he attempted to point out, he had no quarrel with the other boy, whom he didn't even know.

The boxing instructor lost his temper and called Pop a Dago coward and, though Pop didn't understand the words, the contemptuous tone of the instructor's voice was enough to convey the general idea. He promptly picked up an Indian club and cleared the gym in two minutes flat. He then held out inside the building, in a state of siege, for over an hour, until a Spanish-speaking member of the school staff could be found to explain the situation to him, which he did through a cautiously-opened window. Later Pop became an enthusiastic amateur boxer and loved the sport till the end of his days.

Slowly, and with infinite patience, Uncle Billy taught my father the meaning and virtues of the British concepts of sportsmanship and 'team spirit' and by the time Pop had been launched into the brutal world of early twentieth-century British school life, he had grasped enough of these principles to survive the hell of being a foreigner in Britain. My father overcame that particular obstacle, which my elder brother and I encountered in the twenties and thirties, by quickly learning to outdo the opposition in sport.

When my father was eighteen, he experienced his first direct contact with the paranormal. It was during a weekend house party in the British countryside.

Before the 1914-18 war, when road transport was in its infancy and the railway was king, such weekend gatherings were very popular among the young. This particular house party took place during a long, hot summer, when Pop and a number of 'Granny' Southery's foreign students had been invited down to the country to meet a large British family and their friends.

In all, Pop reckoned that they must have numbered twenty or more, most of them in their late teens and about to go up to university. Certainly they all had their wits about them, and were in the pink of physical condition. The whole of Saturday was taken up with tennis and the other usual lawn games. In the evening, the hosts laid on a buffet supper and various other friends turned up to swell their numbers to around forty or so youngsters.

The strongest drink available to them would have been a mild punch; lemonade and other soft drinks were the usual thirst-quenchers for these energetically singing, dancing and games-playing young guests.

The evening was absolutely clear: the long daylight hours had melted into a white twilight and, eventually, when night fell, it was brightly lit by the full moon.

Quite suddenly, in the middle of this happy normality, one of the girls gave a loud scream at the sight of a gaunt white face staring in at the window. She was obviously terrified, and the young lads were naturally only too eager to show off by leaping out into the garden in hot pursuit of the intruder.

Pop found himself with four others searching the bushes round the croquet lawn, when quite clearly in the bright moonlight they simultaneously spotted their quarry – a tall, unnaturally thin, dark figure.

They raised the hue and cry and gave chase. Being at the peak of their physical condition, they were somewhat surprised to find their quarry keeping its distance ahead of them.

By this time the chase had been joined by most of the rest of the eager young men, and the hunt was on. The gaunt, dark figure still, somehow, easily outdistanced them until, more by luck than judgement, the youngsters got the intruder surrounded on the tennis court.

All of them saw clearly what happened next.

As they closed in on the sinister stranger, they all experienced an odd reluctance to come to grips with him. The stark white face and long shadowy body looked horribly unearthly, and something seemed to hold them back.

Then, with shocking suddenness, the trapped intruder appeared to dissolve and vanish.

Shaken out of the natural arrogance of their young confident manhood, they rushed in to seize what they all hoped would prove to be some trick dummy or ingenious, grisly practical joke – but to their horror found nothing.

The brightest youngsters among them instinctively grasped the significance of the peculiar ending to the chase and agreed, then and there, not to spoil the rest of the weekend by frightening the girls.

My father never had any doubt as to the authenticity of the phenomenon and often gave it as an example of an elemental haunting by an earthbound entity, conjured up by the natural animal energy of the young people in puberty at the weekend gathering.

Carl Jung gives examples of mass hallucination, but I have not found a parallel to this occurrence among the phenomena that he describes.

'A trick of the light' is too glib an explanation, because it did not occur as a single phenomenon in one particular spot, but was clearly seen by many witnesses moving rapidly across the large garden.

The young men who were chasing the supposed intruder had no idea that they were hunting anything other than a burglar and were in a cheerful and positive mood from their party games, so 'overwrought imagination' doesn't apply, either; and the consumption of alcohol had been virtually nil.

The night was cloudless and brilliantly lit by the moon. The whole scene was windless and warm, far more conducive to young romance than stark terror. Moreover,

all the young men involved felt the same shock of horror at
the final disappearance of their surrounded and unearthly
quarry.

Light collapsible dummies on fishing lines would not fit
the bill either, because of the rapidity with which their
quarry kept ahead of the chase, and anyway some traces of
the practical joke would have been found by the eager
searchers, who all desperately wanted to find a comforting,
natural explanation for the phenomenon.

Between them they cooked up some plausible story to tell
the girls and their hosts, but for the rest of the weekend it
was a very subdued house party.

Shortly after this experience Uncle Billy had an even
more extraordinary and terrifying encounter with paranormal forces. He had gone up to Cambridge, where he was
busily engaged in reading mathematics and becoming a
Rowing Blue. The experience that was to convince his fine
analytical mind of the physical existence of paranormal
forces occurred in his third year.

One of Bill's undergraduate friends approached him
one day to ask his help and advice in dealing with the
problem of a young Divinity student. Apparently, this
young man, during the course of his theological studies,
had become fascinated by ritual magic. This was a practice
that was not unheard of at either Oxford or Cambridge; in
fact, the existence of 'Black Magic' covens at these
universities is definitively covered in the *Encyclopaedia of
Aberrations,* a weighty and eminently respectable scientific medical tome produced in the United States.

Bill Hope-Jones agreed to help the Divinity student, and
felt no qualms about his ability to cope with the problem.
His friend also believed that, between them, they could
easily handle any unpleasantness that might manifest
during their efforts to help the young amateur magician to
free himself from the negative aura that surrounded him.

They found him to be in a very bad way, his nerves shot
to pieces, and absolutely terrified of the state into which the

'Dark Forces' of his mind had led him.

They were also concerned that the Divinity faculty might well send him down for indulging in such practices by citing, as grounds for such action, suspect mental health.

It was with a good heart and infinite faith, based on a happy childhood and sound Christian principles, that Bill and his friend undertook to get the unhappy student back to normality. In the event they both felt that they were fortunate not to have suffered lasting damage themselves – physically or mentally.

I have sometimes found that people who have dabbled in the occult after only minimal preparatory study and the scantest of precautions may fall victim to elemental forces, and to the dark, coarse power of the lower levels of the mind. They then find that disentanglement from the manifesting 'mind entity' is impossible without outside help.

The scene of the struggle for the possession of the Divinity student's mind was in his room in college, a small study-cum-bedroom. The time was the night after Bill was first asked to help.

The plan was to spend the night watching beside the bed of the victim, and to pass the time in prayer and concentration, with the object of ridding him of the obsessing presence which disturbed his mind. Neither of the two young men knew anything about classical exorcism and pinned their faith solely on their own fitness in mind and body, and on the simple faith that their families had bestowed on them.

At first everything seemed to go well. The young 'dabbler in magick' was comforted and encouraged to rest, stretched out on his bed while Bill and his friend kept their long vigil.

Sleep had become a prime necessity if the young man was to avoid a complete nervous collapse, because in his terror of losing consciousness and allowing a takeover of his personality, he had already passed two nights awake.

It proved to be an uneasy slumber, disturbed by restless and involuntary twitching of his limbs and obvious distress - but at least he was asleep. About midnight he seemed to relax completely and to fall into a *deep* sleep which bordered on a trance.

Bill Hope-Jones's description of what follows was simple and dramatic. The room became depressingly cold and a sensation of unpleasant prickling started to affect the skin of the two watchers by the bed. The shadows in the corners of the small, compact study now seemed to increase and grow dense and then, in rapid succession, a number of changes took place.

The energy-sapping chill suddenly switched to a hot, stifling humidity redolent of a tropical rain forest. The air became heavy and foul, with the sour stench of decay, and the unpleasant prickling sensation increased alarmingly, so that their skin itched unbearably and they both wanted to throw off their clothes to relieve the smarting stings that seemed to be biting into them.

All this took place rather more quickly than it takes to describe.

The gaslight had been lowered to facilitate the sleep of the Divinity student, who started to thrash around wildly in the foetid darkness. Both Bill and his friend were now thoroughly alarmed, but they kept their nerve and prayed aloud as they struggled to restrain the deeply disturbed student convulsed on the bed.

At this point, the hot stinging darkness seemed to solidify into a definite shape and, giving off a dreadful smell, it formed into a powerful, moving and gyrating spiral of force, like a dark purple-coloured tornado.

Remember that both these undergraduates were powerfully built young men with cool nerves, confident courage and total faith in their ability to deal with the situation. But now they were literally being physically attacked and thrown around the room by the mini-tornado, as though they were being set upon by a gang of toughs.

Bill's principal memory, he told my father, was of being punched and pummelled while he fought back desperately against that hot, stinking cloud of whirling shadows. During the struggle every stick of furniture in the room was caught up and smashed to pieces, while china and ornaments were shattered against the walls.

The raging vortex of black force, which they were now fighting with all their physical strength, seemed to have joined onto the threshing body of the Divinity student, as he tossed and writhed on the bed. By a tremendous effort of will, Bill managed to gasp out the words of prayers which seemed to be impressed on his mind, and by the sheer strength of their youth, the two of them forced their way to the door of the study.

The dark presence seemed to sense their desire to summon aid and increased its attack on them. At last they forced open the door and spilled out onto the floor of the passage beyond. This was rapidly filling with amazed undergraduates who had hurried there to find out what all the row was about.

The milling throng outside the study door naturally thought that Bill and his friend had been fighting, for both of them were bruised and bleeding profusely as they lay, panting breathlessly, on the floor of the passage. Neither of them could, or in fact would, explain the situation for fear of involving the Divinity student and causing him to be sent down from Cambridge.

The bursting open of the door, and the presence of the other undergraduates had broken the chain of events that had generated the power for the manifesting force, and apart from the lingering smell there was no sign of its appalling presence. Windows were hurriedly opened and some of the other undergraduates assisted in clearing up the mess of broken furniture, smashed crockery and glass.

Bill and his friend fobbed them off with explanations of an amateur chemistry experiment going wrong, or some such hurriedly cooked up excuse, but they avoided specifics, as both of them hated lying.

On examination, although they were badly bruised and had bleeding noses and the odd missing tooth, neither of them was seriously injured; and they both got a bawling out for brawling in their friend's study. However, as they were both known to be reliable and undoubtedly first-class students, their Master-in-college realized there was much more to the whole unpleasant business than they would admit and, after making enquiries, soon reached a sound conclusion.

Although neither Bill nor his friend would confirm his suspicions, the Divinity student himself finally owned up to the truth and gave them both his heartfelt thanks for having released him from his overshadowing dark forces.

He was not sent down and eventually he received his degree, while Bill and his co-sufferer in the night's ordeal went on to graduate themselves.

These manifestations of paranormal phenomena were the first either my father or Uncle Billy had experienced, and neither of them could explain the phenomena by any of the means then known to physical sciences.

These men, my father and Uncle Billy, were to be two of the most important influences on my attitude of mind, my method of thinking and, indeed, my whole approach to life. I have been very fortunate to have known them.

2 *There was a Young Lady in Bolton*

The other major influence in my life was my mother. Though she passed over in 1949, my mother's common sense still makes itself heard from time to time among the emotional surges of my life as a writer and artist. Born in Westcliff-on-Sea and named Florence, she was the youngest of the five children who made up the Dawkins family. Her father, James Dawkins, worked for the Water Board in the Essex area, and was all the things that the social structure of that day expected of him – he was a master mason, a pillar of the local church and a stout member of the town's urban district council. He was also a living double for Charles Dickens and had a great sense of humour, which he passed on to each of his children, and especially to my mother.

Ma was a 'card', with her lively, attractive and good-humoured face always ready to burst into a radiant smile, and her irresistibly contagious laugh. Furthermore, when she wanted to she could charm the birds off the trees. I have seen her face the wrath of some self-righteous bully and, within minutes, have him dancing to whatever tune she wished to play. She was also a mimic of considerable talent, and had the happy knack of capturing exactly the essence of a person in an impromptu impersonation that was deadly accurate and yet never malicious.

Her upbringing in a happy and united Essex family couldn't have been more conventional but as she had lost her mother at an early age, she was brought up by her elder sister Mary, whom she adored.

She was an extremely sensitive person and very much a perfectionist, which could account for the appalling migraines that turned her, in a few minutes, from a happy and gregarious person into a pain-racked and incoherent recluse. But she never lost her courage during these crippling attacks, nor throughout the long suffering from abdominal cancer that eventually took her life.

Having had a large number of violent 'classical' migraines in my own life, I have some idea of what she went through, and I know from having seen them that her attacks were far worse than the ones I have had to put up with. Mediumship - sensitivity, paranormal awareness or whatever you like to label it - seems to have an inevitable price tag attached to it, be it migraine, asthma, hay fever, urticaria or any other psychosomatically induced malfunction of the human body.

With Ma it was migraine; with Pop it was viciously crippling asthma and with me it was both, though to a lesser degree, thank God!

These two diametrically-opposed individuals became my parents. Ma, with her happy, outgoing personality, and Pop, with his introspective, deeply analytical and stormy Latin American emotions only held in check by the discipline of his British upbringing, met and married, within a few weeks. The year was 1915.

My mother had been engaged to a young soldier from Westcliff, who had been a childhood friend and who had been killed in the trenches of the Western front. To work out her grief, she had come up to London to help a family whose father had gone to France. Meanwhile my father, who was busily engaged on secret work in aeronautical engineering, had also come up to London, only because his work had briefly taken him there. Was it then just a chance meeting?

By 1912 my father had an impressive array of qualifications. He was an associate member of the Institutes of Electrical, Mechanical and Constructional and Civil

Engineering and had some years' practical experience of heavy engineering in the railway shops of Darlington and across the border in Scotland. Here, while building giant dynamos and generating plant, he had first turned his attention to flight and became interested in the infant science of aerodynamics.

Yet at the outbreak of war my father's Peruvian nationality prevented his enlistment in the Royal Flying Corps. The newly founded Aeronautical Inspection Department (AID), however, welcomed the bright young engineer with open arms.

So Pop went to war with a slide rule and a drawing board rather than a rifle and bayonet, and designed and built seaplanes for Vickers Supermarine mainly at Hythe on the Solent. But even though he hadn't made it to the trenches or the Western Front, he led a hairy life, because he insisted on testing his products personally.

My father patented, and handed over without royalty a number of ingenious gadgets, one of which, the spring-balance for tensioning flying wires on biplanes, is still used today on vintage machines. He tuned the wires with this device because he had an ear like a brick wall when it came to music, and the current official method of rigging was to use a tuning fork, matching the pitch of the fork with that of the tensioned wire.

My parents were married in London and their honeymoon was spent moving into furnished lodgings in Calshot, on Southampton Water, where Pop was now engaged on building the latest secret 'Fleet-spotting' seaplane.

My father often told me how he visualized the aircraft he designed and the safety features that he had developed for the AID. The method that he used was obviously subjective clairvoyance. Like Nicola Tesla, the great Hungarian-born inventor and electrical engineer, whom the Establishment treated so shabbily when he refused the Nobel Prize in 1912, my father was able to visualize clearly or, if you like, 'imagine' each of his inventions and designs as a coloured

three-dimensional model projected on the inner screen of his
mind.

Tesla describes how, when a boy, he was so deeply troubled
and inconvenienced by the clarity and solidity of his visions
that he made a tremendous mental effort to wipe them out
for ever. He actually succeeded in controlling their manifestations so that, from the age of twelve onwards, he could
either totally suppress their appearance or summon them up
instantly by a small effort of will.

Pop had precisely the same experience, even to the strange
ability, which these two sensitive men shared, of being able
to 'test run' machines in the mind and thereby 'see' where
the points of wear or weakness would be. Like my father,
Tesla worked from sketches and notes, and as both of them
were fine applied mathematicians, they were able to
visualize these mental measurements to the accuracy of a
10,000th of an inch.

Knowing my father's abilities and his unquestioning
loyalty, my mother used to become incensed at the
authorities' treatment of Pop. Although he was privy to
highly secret information Pop had to report to the country
police station in every district in which he lived or worked,
and this infuriated my mother. Like her, I have never been
able to suffer fools gladly and having suffered from petty
officialdom for most of my life, I know how she felt. But my
father tolerated this kind of small-minded bureaucracy with
amazing patience.

By 1916 my elder brother, Tony, had arrived, and the three
of them wandered about the country, from aircraft factories
at Hythe to those at Felixstowe, with no more permanent
home than the lodgings they lived in en route.

When the Armistice came, Pop decided to accept an offer
from the Peruvian Government to build their Air Force,
which then consisted of a few worn-out early wartime
machines, and in 1920 my father, mother and four-year-old
brother set out on the SS *Ortega* for a much delayed second
honeymoon, in South America.

It was there, in Peru, that I was conceived and later born in Watford, Hertfordshire, on their return to England, which Ma had insisted on, in order to ensure that I, like my brother, was a British-born citizen.

The date was 26 January 1922 and on that day I became entitled to two passports and dual nationality, British because I had been born in Britain and Peruvian because, under the laws of the Republic of Peru, if a father is a Peruvian his children are too, and his sons are liable for military service in the Peruvian Army. So you can see that for that innocent, new-born baby, life would never be uncomplicated.

When I was a year old my family moved to Folkestone. All the concentrated academic study, the long hours in the factories, the field trials and flying had resulted in my father being constantly assailed by vicious attacks of asthma and bronchitis, and he was forced to retire at the age of thirty-two. The bracing Folkestone air had been some chest specialist's recommendation. My family settled there in 1923 and I lived there for the next eighteen years of my life.

A naturally energetic man who loathed social functions of any kind, Pop was highly accomplished as a craftsman, and loved to work with his hands to fine tolerances. The idea of retirement from industrial life was anathema to him and a great worry to Ma, who knew that a busy Pop was a happy Pop and that enforced idleness in a town where bridge and gossip were the mainstays of social life would be sheer hell for him.

So Ma persuaded my father to take up golf. This he did, with the same single-minded thoroughness which he applied to any other undertaking. He played golf six days a week, starting at eight thirty in the morning in nearly all weathers, and finishing as the sun went down, and all the time that he maintained this intensive physical programme his asthma was kept in check.

His skill on the golf course was partly due to his now excellent physical condition, partly to his power of total

concentration, and partly to his experience in aerodynamics, which had given him an instant ability to
visualize the parabolic flight of the ball. He virtually made
that tricky, windy golf course play golf *for* him; and I well
remember his making accurate scale models of the greens
and then spending hours working out the best approach
shots and putting lines.

All this may seem irrelevant, but it does give some idea of
the painstaking approach that was so typical of my father.
Whether it was electrical engineering, pioneer radio
research, golf or model aeroplane design and construction,
my father never did anything by halves; and this was his
attitude of mind when he eventually became involved in
paranormal research.

Ma had a particular talent – playing bridge. This she did
every afternoon (except at weekends, which she devoted to
the family) from three thirty till seven, when Pop, on his way
home from golf, would pick her up in the car, always a few
bob richer, for my mother played bridge expertly, and for
money as well as pleasure.

Though much more gregarious than my father, Ma was,
like Pop, uninterested in gossip for its own sake; but
anything really interesting in conversation, such as
people's true experiences in life, intrigued and fascinated
her.

These were the two people who made up the oddly
constrasting but well-balanced team which would eventually
investigate and assess the paranormal phenomena that we
experienced as a family during my childhood, youth and
early manhood.

My father undertook the research because he felt strongly
impelled to do so and was utterly convinced of its
importance, and my mother joined him in it because she
loved him and, on the principle of 'whither thou goest, I will
go', gave him her full support and co-operation.

I will briefly outline my childhood before going on to discuss the paranormal experiences I shared with my family. I should explain that my recall is reasonably good and that I have a very clear memory of having my tonsils out, at the age of two, lying on the kitchen table at Elysée Mansions in Westcliff Gardens, Folkestone.

I can still smell the sickly sweet odour of chloroform, which was administered from a bottle with two thin projecting spouts in its rubber-corked top. I seem to remember that I had to sniff it while it was poured out, drop by drop, onto cotton gauze covering what looked like a tea strainer.

It was a traumatically unpleasant experience and the extensive scar tissue in my naso-pharynx still bears witness to the savagery of that tonsillectomy. I often wonder whether my subsequent handicap of a dreadful stammer does not spring from that primitive home surgery.

At the age of four I neatly pulled over a large, heavy, stone garden urn so that it crushed my right foot and badly bruised my left one, leaving me, to use Ma's words, with 'cheap feet' and strong suspicions about the stability of garden ornaments.

Shortly afterwards I contracted acute appendicitis. My appendix was whipped out in the local nursing home, and once again I experienced that revolting, primitive method of administering anaesthetics. I seem to recall it was *ether* this time, dripping down onto the tea strainer mask. I woke up and was so violently sick that I burst some of my stitches. Forty-eight hours later, I contracted whooping cough, and broke the rest of them.

As soon as I was convalescent I went to a Folkestone school which took dayboys and a limited number of boarders and was housed in a tall, sombre Victorian pile with extensive playing fields attached, which we shared, albeit rigidly segregated, with brown-pinafored, long-plaited girls from the convent school two houses up the road.

There I stayed, unhappily, for seven years, under the tuition of a highly-strung headmaster of fierce demeanour who was the living personification of Carl Giles' brilliant cartoon schoolmaster 'Chalky'.

A gaunt, craggy man, who had been a good athlete, he terrified me with his sudden, apparently violent moods, yet when he was relaxed, he used to read to us with a marvellous compelling voice, and he drew superbly well. His only unbending contact with me was when he found out that, owing to my elder brother's patient and skilled teaching, I could draw with some ability and was a competent spin-bowler at cricket.

There were probably domestic reasons, and some financial ones, for his constant tenseness, but it certainly didn't help my stammer, which, when he stood me on my desk seat and hit the calves of my legs with a ruler, became totally incoherent.

Today he would not be allowed to express his pent-up tensions in such a way, and it is the general feeling among the few surviving members of that school who weren't massacred in the war that he should have been more restrained. He was, however, such a charmer and had about him such a scholastic and healthy air of normality, outside the frustrations of the classroom, that our parents, and mine among them, thought we were exaggerating when we bitterly complained.

Just as my prep school had been an unhappy experience, my stay at Eton was the reverse. The reason my brother and I went to Eton had nothing to do with snobbery, but was the logical outcome of the great friendship and affection between my father and Uncle Billy.

When Uncle Billy and Pop were boys they had made a pact that, if Bill became a schoolmaster, which was his sole ambition, Pop would send his sons to be educated by him, wherever he happened to be teaching. As it happened, he became a housemaster (tutor) at Eton College, and so Tony and I went there; and neither of us ever regretted the outcome of that odd pact made at the turn of the century. My mother's bridge winnings were a considerable help in paying the heavy fees!

Uncle Billy, or m'tutor, as I still think of him, gave us the benefit of his humorous wisdom and his love of learning, for which neither of us can ever thank him enough.

In 1932, Pop was persuaded by a friend of my Mother's, Miss Purse, to attend a spiritualist meeting at a small bungalow near Westenhanger, on the top of the downs just across the way from Hawkinge airfield. It belonged to the widow of a flying officer in the RAF. She claimed that she regularly communicated with him and, because of this experience, had become a spiritualist. As there was no established spiritualist church in the district or the immediate vicinity, she had started to hold meetings at her home.

Pop was reluctant to accompany Miss Purse on what he suspected might prove to be a wild goose chase, and I remember my mother encouraging him to go. However, it was more to please Ma than for any other reason that he took Miss Purse along with him in the car, and soon found himself sitting in the front parlour of the Westenhanger bungalow, one of a small group of people, mainly women. Since none of them seemed to be mentally disturbed or otherwise abnormal, Pop began to take a polite interest in the proceedings.

The medium was a woman friend of the bungalow owner, and had come over from Canterbury. Gramophone records of a suitably solemn nature were played and the medium led them in a short prayer, then went into a light trance from which she gave them an address. She acted as an unconscious channel for an entity who had apparently taken control in order to deliver a short homily on life beyond the veil.

This seemed harmless enough in its content, which was a mixture of simple religious philosophy and a reassurance that life continued beyond the grave. There was nothing in it that smacked of charlatanry, or self-indulgence, and Pop continued to take a mild interest in the proceedings. Indeed he was impressed by the simple straightforwardness of it all.

I have since heard many such trance addresses, ranging
from the downright charlatanry of well-worn clichés and
mixed-up misquotations, through appalling potted poetry
of the greetings card type, to genuinely inspiring
addresses, delivered without hesitation in a most lucid style,
and conveying the impression of a highly developed
personality quite unlike that of the medium through whom
the address was being communicated.

Then, after a preliminary explanation of what clairvoyance was about, the medium gave a demonstration of
clairvoyance which included various messages to different
members of the small gathering.

The content of these communications seemed so ordinary
and prosaic, and were personalized to such a degree that, to
Pop, they were completely incomprehensible; but the
different recipients of each 'message' seemed delighted with
it, and obviously grateful as they thanked the medium and
the professed entity that was giving her the information.

Nothing that had happened so far had prepared my father
for the extraordinary experience that followed. According to
Pop it went something like this:

MEDIUM:	I wish to come to you, sir! (She indicated Pop, who wasn't too keen to be singled out.)
MEDIUM:	Yes, you sir, the gentleman at the back – I have a young lady here who has a message for you.
POP (shyly):	Thank you.
MEDIUM:	This young lady gives me the name Bolton. Does that mean anything to you?
POP (politely):	No – I'm sorry – I don't know anyone of that name.
MEDIUM:	Wait a minute – she's saying that Bolton is the name of a *place* – the town where she saw you last.

| | (Pop was now the centre of attention and was loathing every minute of it.) |
| POP: | No. I'm sorry. Bolton means nothing to me. |

Had the medium chosen Lima – Paris – Berlin – Madrid – Heidelberg – New York or a hundred and one other places which Pop knew, she would have been nearer the mark.

MEDIUM (patiently):	I can't understand it. This young lady keeps saying 'Bolton'. Ah! Now she is showing me a stage – like in a theatre – are you connected with the theatre or perhaps you knew a theatre in Bolton?
	(Pop, by this time, was wishing that he was in some other place – even Bolton!)
POP:	No. I'm very sorry. I'm afraid not. Are you sure the message is for me?
MEDIUM (emphatically):	Absolutely, wait! Now she is telling me that you will surely remember a theatre in Bolton – many years ago, when you were a young man – she says: this will refresh your memory – she is showing me an *auction* – yes! an *auction* – and she says: 'Remember the *auction,* on the stage at Bolton.'

Pop told us that he suddenly saw it quite clearly in his mind.

POP:	Good Lord! Yes! I do remember – that auction – on the stage at that theatre in Bolton. It's so long ago – I'd forgotten – I'm sorry.
MEDIUM:	She's very excited – this young lady. She's giving me her name [here the medium gave a Christian name which I have forgotten]. She is

> telling me that she is very grateful
> for what you did for her.

At these words, the whole meeting had swung round to get a
good look at the man who had done things for a young lady
of Bolton - on a stage, by holding an auction in a theatre.
Pop, however, didn't even notice their riveted interest, as
the medium continued:

MEDIUM: She's telling me - that this message
                 is going to open up a whole new world
                 for you. She is so happy that she has
                 been chosen to be the instrument that
                 will alter your whole life! Do you
                 understand that, sir?

POP: Well, I certainly understand the
                 Bolton auction - but the second part
                 of the message I can't make head nor
                 tail of!

MEDIUM: Well, I'll leave the message with you,
                 sir. The young lady is very excited
                 and so happy she has contacted you.
                 She tells me that from now on, your
                 whole life will change. God bless you!

Pop thanked her and could hardly wait to drive home and
tell us all this strange story.

I can see him now, explaining this curious experience to
my mother, my brother and my fascinated ten-year-old self.

When Pop was a student, aged eighteen or so, he was
studying electrical engineering at Faraday House in
Charing Cross Road - a building now long ago demolished.
There, with another South American friend, he had met and
fallen under the spell of a young actress. She was about to
embark on a tour of the provinces, and as the summer
holidays loomed ahead they had both been caught up in the
excitement of it and joined her touring company. They
worked as assistant stage managers and had small walk-on

roles to play. They were practically unpaid and had a whale
of a time.

In 1905 or thereabouts, to go on the stage was the height of
decadent adventure, or the last resort of desperate people,
according to the way you looked at it. For two young
engineering students to do so was unusual to say the least.

Pop remembered very little about the plays that the
company alternated in their repertoire on this mini-tour of
the north of England, but he recalled that one of them was a
thriller in which he came on in the first half as a silent
villain, and that he had two words to say as a policeman in
the last act of another.

The tour was a disaster, and eventually ground to a halt at
Bolton, where – as they say in show business – 'the public
stayed away in thousands'. The manager slipped out of
town with what funds they had left, leaving the company
stranded and flat broke on the Friday 'when the ghost
walked' (i.e. when they should have been paid).

The actors had an emergency meeting at the theatre, and
the local management kindly offered to hold an auction of
all their scenery, costumes and theatrical props on the stage
of the Bolton theatre that Saturday morning.

They had to sell everything and be out of the theatre by the
Saturday night, as the next production was due to move in
on the Sunday.

Meanwhile, Pop and his friend had telegraphed home for
emergency funds. (My father cabled Granny Southery.)
These they collected on the Saturday morning, as soon as
the post office opened – which shows how marvellously
efficient the GPO was in those days.

Armed with some ten pounds between them – a lot of
money at that time – and being too shy to go to the auction
and bid, they gave a stage hand half the money and
instructed him to buy back all the personal things belonging
to the young actress. They also left her a note, together with
her fare to London, and left Bolton by the next train.

That, in a nutshell, is what had happened some twenty-six

years before the meeting in that bungalow at Westenhanger.

Pop put it to us like this: the name Bolton, as a town, would
be an unlikely shot in the dark to form a link with an
unknown sitter. The information about the theatre was an
even more unlikely probe for information, if that is what it
was. The additional piece of information about the auction
being held on the stage made the chances of a 'lucky hit'
about as remote as you can get. Being a mathematician of
great skill, my father calculated the odds, and found them to
be millions to one against.

An alternative explanation – that the medium somehow
knew the story, and my father's part in it – is so far-fetched as
to be dismissed immediately. Firstly, she didn't know my
father from a cake of soap, and secondly she couldn't have
got the story locally because Pop hadn't even told my mother
about this odd incident from his youthful past.

My father thought about the whole business very
carefully, in that painstakingly thorough way of his, and
then told us that he was convinced the evidence was genuine
and that this was some form of contact with a discarnate
entity. He rejected the possibility of thought transference
because the memory of those particular events was so deeply
buried in his subconscious that at first he didn't even recognize the name Bolton. He also told us – at a family council-
of-war – that he now intended to devote his time and efforts
to investigating the field of paranormal phenomena.

My parents' habit of letting the two of us in on family
plans was a good one, and probably a remnant of Pop's
upbringing in Peru where, to this day, any important Bentin
family event is discussed by the whole Bentin tribe, about
fifty-eight in all.

My mother backed up Pop in every way, though inwardly
her heart must have missed a beat or two when she
considered the attitude of the snobbish middle-class
Folkestone society – i.e. the bridge club – to an investigation
of the 'occult' and their instant disapproval of anyone who

believed in psychic phenomena.

These narrow-minded, complacent bigots would soon turn their backs on my mother, and though she kept a few loyal friends she became virtually a social outcast, which worried her only because she was gregarious by nature. As she herself said: 'What have they got to be snobbish about?' It didn't worry my father, but being the wife of 'that Peruvian nut' did give my mother some unhappy moments.

Even at school I got some of the backlash, but it didn't bother me too much, even though it was an unpleasant new twist to the usual Dago ragging. My stammer had prevented me from making friends easily and only three other boys ever became really close chums: Kit Rusack, the son of a brilliant X-ray specialist, David Phillimore, a born naturalist and the son of a retired admiral, and Paul Tomlinson, brother of David who was to become a well-known actor.

My elder brother kept mum about Pop's activities at Eton, and m'tutor was much too wise a man to interfere. Besides, he had, himself, good reason to know that such phenomena existed.

Our South American family at first regarded Pop's investigations into the 'occult' with undisguised horror, for the *familia Bentin* was staunch *Catholica* down to the newest born babe. Aunt Rosa, Uncle Ricardo's widow, was particularly disturbed by my father's latest activities and told him bluntly, on her next visit to Britain, that she thought that her beloved brother-in-law had been hoodwinked by the Devil. However, as Pop didn't burst into flames at the touch of a crucifix, or disappear in a puff of smoke at the surreptitious sprinkling of a small phial of holy water, it came as a great relief to Aunt Rosa to realize that my father hadn't *actually* signed the Faustian pact with Mephistopheles, at least not yet!

As the field of paranormal research became my father's speciality he soon learned where to look for the tricks of the trade. Ma's shrewd and perceptive judgement of character helped enormously and, working as a team of observers on both the scientific and practical levels of research, they achieved great success.

Experimental research in this area of human experience is far more dangerous than anything else I know. To give you some idea of how vulnerable the researcher into the paranormal becomes, imagine the investigator as a person standing naked on the shores of a great lake, with the intention of exploring the depths below it and the heights above it to the limit of man's ability.

As he takes his first paddling steps into the dark waters he realizes that he must learn to swim or drown. Once he has mastered swimming on the surface, and dipping his head below it, he then equips himself with a snorkel and dives down a few metres lower. Fascinated by what he sees he now learns to use a sub-aqua-lung and descends deeper.

At a comparatively shallow depth he finds himself in danger from the 'rapture' of nitrogen poisoning and disorientation of the mind. Should he require to go deeper into the unknown, he must equip himself with heavy diving gear and a back-up team on the surface to monitor his dive. If his researches require still deeper dives he must use a submersible armoured diving suit and, finally, a stoutly-built submarine for exploring the great depths. All this takes years of study and practice and the dedicated assistance of a skilled team of associates.

Conversely, if he decides to explore the heavens above, he will have to learn to fly, at first a glider or light training-plane, then an aeroplane capable of higher altitudes, till he graduates, after years of training and experience, to a pressurized high-altitude jet plane. Continuing onwards and upwards our intrepid investigator will be trained for orbital flight, then lunar explorations and, finally, after long and intensive research and training, and with supreme physical fitness, he will one day perhaps journey to the planets.

Apply these similes to paranormal research, inwards into the mind's inner space, or outwards to the heights of mental projection, and you will have some idea why so many would-be investigators, totally unprepared physically or mentally, end up permanently impaired in health and all too often in the psychiatric ward. Plunging headlong into paranormal research without adequate training or precautions, and frequently artificially boosted by the use of hallucinogenic drugs, it is small wonder that they become quickly disorientated and subsequently dangerously deranged.

Just to ram the point home, if someone was intending to become an Olympic athlete he would automatically accept the long and increasingly hard years of training; he would refrain from smoking or drinking except in minimum amounts, and if he was wise he would refuse the use of booster drugs like anabolic steroids to build up his muscular power or, in the case of girl gymnasts, puberty inhibitors to retain the suppleness of childhood in their bodies.

Nature requires payment for favours granted, and athletes who have resorted, under some totalitarian regimes, to artificial aids to athletic attainment age rapidly as a result of their use. The investigation of the paranormal is akin to mental athletics of an Olympian kind, and an exactly similar attitude is required if the investigator is to succeed and survive.

All these considerations were carefully weighed by my parents and only when they were sure of their ground was a course of action formulated. Both my brother and I were often party to these planning sessions.

Pop had a good trick up his sleeve when it came to dealing with charlatanry, because he was a very knowledgeable and adroit conjuror. Moreover, in Folkestone there were two members of the Inner Magic Circle, that splendid London-based club which only accepts members who can demonstrate their ability and skill in prestidigitation (lovely word!).

Major Webster, a retired army career officer who had been General French's aide in the First World War, and Arthur Condy, a retired businessman with a nice line in humour, were both always on hand to assist and advise my father with their expert knowledge; for both of them were marvellously skilled in the craft of stage magic.

I fondly recall the Major's beautifully simple and deeply mystifying disappearing and multiplying coin trick, using a black and blue velvet background for the illusion.

Arthur Condy performed his own elegant version of Horace Golding's famous 'Miser's Dream', in which streams of flashing silver and gold coins are produced from 'thin air' and poured resoundingly into a silver jug. This necessitates the magician back-palming at least half-a-dozen metal coins at a time without letting them 'talk', i.e. clink together. Arthur performed it marvellously, and I often watched fascinated as the scintillating streams of metal cascaded down.

Between the three of them they were a formidable tribunal of experts in deception, and succeeded in unmasking a number of phoney mediums. They felt no pangs of conscience when they destroyed the reputation of one of these phonies. Nor did anyone in my family. To help expose this sort of evil fraud by confidence tricksters perpetrating their wicked deception for profit on innocent dupes is a necessary act and very much a part of the investigation into paranormal phenomena.

This then, was the setting for what was to become my parents' mission in life, and they would make many sacrifices to accomplish their task, before eventually their own doors marked summer opened for the last time.

3 *The Breakthrough*

The first medium I remember was a plump jolly woman who lived in Seabrook. Her bungalow was set back from the main road which ran along the top of the sea wall between Folkestone and Hythe. Her garden fell in a series of rocky terraces to the road below and was covered with clumps of the green succulents that are about the only plants hardy enough to grow in that wind-blown salty environment.

As we sat in her sunny parlour, looking out over the grey-green rolling water of the Channel, she struck me as being such a normal sort of common-sense person that my boyish apprehension at being in the presence of a 'witch', as I had thought of her, quickly faded away. I am grateful that my first curious introduction to paranormal phenomena was so sun-filled and unalarming.

This medium was an automatic writer. Her pencil raced over the pages of a school exercise book, at which she never looked once, and at the same time she chatted away to us about everything under the sun. She asked me where I went to school, whether I liked it, had I enjoyed the long summer holidays, and all the time that pencil rushed along.

I remember that she had a small pot of ready-sharpened pencils beside her and as she used up one she would change to another, pause for a second or two, and then off her hand would go, filling page after page as she chattered on.

At last the book was full and the time had come to read it back to us. She did this in a firm unfaltering voice, without any hesitation, and although I can't remember the words after such a long time, I still recall the gist of what she said.

It was a series of prophecies (which later turned out to be remarkably accurate) about my father's future, telling him how important his research work was to be. Even to a ten-year-old boy it was obvious that the jolly woman who had so cheerfully chatted to us that afternoon was not the same person who had composed the words she was now reading out. I can remember that they were very clear and somehow inspiring, and as I write this I can almost hear her homely voice, with its soft Kentish burr, reading them without faltering.

Several people have expressed surprise that my parents should have exposed my brother and me to the sort of dangers that beset the whole field of paranormal investigation, but I am grateful that they did so.

The opportunity they gave us to develop our awareness of other planes of consciousness was well beyond the scope of any system of conventional education or normal religious teaching. This early training gave me a survival mechanism far superior to the much vaunted pragmatism of today's youth, because it opened the doors for creative thought and has been the main reason why I can earn my living as a writer.

The subjective clairvoyance that developed from my exposure to my father's researches has become so integral a part of my life that I can switch it on and off like a computer. Should I over-use it the price is asthma or migraine; but sensible employment of sensitive awareness enables me to earn a living without hurting other people and to be given the opportunity to see a little further and a little clearer into the future.

'As through a glass darkly' is the popular misconception of the process of heightened awareness. It applies only to some fragmentary and rather confused glimpses of future events that tantalizingly fade in and out before the inner vision. When the faculty has been fully awakened and carefully developed over a long period of time – without the use of drugs which only deceive the senses and synthesize a pseudo-experience while exposing the body and mind to the dangers of addiction – the clarity of the images becomes quite startling and the import of their meaning unmistakable.

That first experience with automatic writing showed me a simple manifestation of something outside the normal field of human experience. Later, without me, Pop had long and erudite mathematical discussions with other entities who manifested through the channel of that British housewife. At one sitting with Pop she produced pages and pages of beautifully written German script, using elegant German of a somewhat earlier period, a language my father spoke well.

I remember his bringing the papers home and how impressed he was with the contents. After all, the Seabrook housewife could hardly have been a German scholar of highly educated background and a first-class mathematician as well. He was drawn to the conclusion that the source of these written communications could only be intelligences outside the medium.

He realized that the next step must be to develop his own latent sensitivity and mediumship, for my father believed, and I agree with him, that this ability to extend the frontiers of the mind is common to everyone. Anyone, given the discipline and determination, can, over a long and arduous period of time, acquire the same degree of awareness.

Pop set about inviting a number of reputable mediums and sensitives into our home and listened to their experiences, making notes of useful hints and instructions for developing mediumship. Some of his guests were normal down-to-earth people, while others were as full of mumbo jumbo as a fake witch doctor.

I am not such a good judge of character as my mother was. I'm inclined to give the benefit of the doubt and, like my father, I have been robbed of considerable sums of money because of misplaced trust in friends. But when I concentrate on the field of paranormal research I can immediately tell the phoney, the charlatan, the self-deluded and the self-seeking from the genuine sensitive. I work on a certain set of wavelengths and if I don't find a response on the same frequencies I know that I am up against a manifestation of self-delusion or downright faking on the medium's part.

The phenomena which they produce, or attempt to fake, range from clairvoyance, clairaudience and psychometry through other phenomena like Tarot, I-Ching, crystal gazing and palmistry to the whole physical range of 'paranormal' manifestations such as direct-voice materialization, transfiguration and telekinesis.

The clairvoyants that Pop investigated were divided into *subjectives,* who work on a high-frequency nervous level of symbols and images that they attempt to describe from the fleeting impressions that manifest on the screen of their inner vision, and the *objective* clairvoyants who see images and whole scenarios of action in colour and three dimensions, usually projected externally onto an uncluttered surface such as a wall, or can even see single entities lifesize standing beside the sitter with whom the contact is being made.

Fake practitioners of either kind of clairvoyance are unmistakable by the way that they fish around for corroboratory evidence, trying to lead the sitter into subconsciously giving information in their eagerness to communicate with someone they have lost and are trying to contact.

If these mediums are simply self-deluded they can be forgiven; often their motive is a genuine desire to help and comfort the bereaved. But if the exponent of fake phenomena is doing it for profit or to wield power over other people they should be exposed as soon as possible. Fortunately, with one or two exceptions, they are not too difficult to spot as they are habitually given to over-acting and to a great deal of self-important pomposity.

All the genuine mediums and real sensitives with whom I have sat over the past forty-five years have been modest and genuinely delighted when they got a message home to an enquirer; and the more obscure and evidential the content of the message, the more pleased they are, because it also renews and strengthens their own convictions.

It is of course arguable whether external 'intelligences' are manifestations of your own 'supra-conscious', Overmind, or part of some vast collective unconscious, but from my own experience, it is unarguable that they exist.

In those early months of my family's forays into paranormal investigation, our home was the base for the manifestation of such phenomena. Wellfield was the seventh house in which we had lived since arriving in Folkestone for, apart from bridge, my mother's other hobby was the designing and building of pleasant houses in which we would live happily for a while and then, without advertising the fact that she was willing to sell, she would receive an offer which she 'couldn't refuse' and we would buy or build another.

Wellfield was a simple, double-cube-shaped, whitewashed four-bedroomed family residence with a pleasant garden big enough to bowl a cricket ball in and lined at one end with a complex of aviaries which stretched most of the way across its width.

This was because Pop and Ma were deeply interested in breeding birds of domestic and exotic types; and while Pop looked after some one hundred or so roller and border canaries, my mother bred budgerigars of every colour and hue, some of great beauty, plus a number of assorted rare South American species of parrotlets and parakeets. This collection of some three hundred birds, six Scottie dogs and four cats, plus the inevitable animal smell that must have hung over our home, gave the impression that we were running a private zoo.

Our long-suffering neighbours, who luckily were all animal lovers and kept pets themselves, may have listened to rumours that my parents were indulging in the Black

Arts, but happily dismissed them as nonsense. They, like ourselves, knew that no self-respecting cat or dog, or for that matter any domesticated animal, will remain for more than a few moments where any 'Dabbling with the Devil' or other negative practices are being indulged in, and will rapidly leave the scene of the crime.

I like to have an animal around me when I am opening up to the paranormal field of force, to give me a corroboratory warning of anything negative being attracted to the focus of power that I am tuned in to. This I learned from my parents, who always welcomed the presence of a dog or a cat when conducting their investigations.

Our neighbours' curiosity must have been aroused, however, by the endless stream of weirdos, some complete with flowing robes or even turbans, who arrived at our front door and were ushered inside to be tested and assessed by my parents and fed to bursting by our Irish cook.

When our cook eventually left to get married, we had a succession of lovely lasses who all became fascinated by the 'goings on' as they called them and one of whom became a marvellous hypnotic subject. Occasionally the moans and groans that emanated from the small spare room which was commandeered as the test area for the investigations must have driven one or two of the less courageous lasses to cower under the bedclothes; but on the whole I think they enjoyed their stay with us and, as they all seemed to get happily married, I can only assume that we brought them luck.

Those early days of paranormal investigation were the worst times from my own point of view, because I wasn't allowed to sit in on trance mediumship circles till I was over fourteen. This was probably just as well. The room where the seances were held was next to my bedroom and I could hear a lot of what went on. Sometimes the sounds issuing from the little room were quite alarming.

I should explain that a manifesting entity, whether you accept it as discarnate or as some archetypal personality

from the deep subconscious of the medium, finds that
control of the medium's body is difficult, and the results are
sometimes quite spectacular. The explanation given by
experienced spiritualists is that the discarnate spirit has to
re-live the condition through which it passed out of its body
when it attempts to manifest through a medium for the
first time, i.e. when it re-enters the earth-plane.

This condition, according to a spiritualist, could range
from dying on a battlefield to being trapped in a sunken
submarine, from desperately trying to bail out of a spinning
aircraft to expiring in a wrecked car.

This grim picture is not wholly in accordance with what I
have witnessed on a number of different occasions, but
could be applicable to certain circumstances. I have helped
people to recover from traumatic experiences and their last
memory before losing consciousness is often repeated as
their first reaction on coming round.

This does not mean that they themselves are experiencing
the trauma itself. It is rather a reflex action when they find
themselves back in the body.

The medium, though often thrown about and apparently
convulsed, doesn't appear to suffer any bodily harm; but
it is an experience that has put me off trance mediumship
for life. I decided that no one was going to relive their
passing condition with *my* body. Also I do not like to be
part of any seance involving deep trance mediumship after
dark.

My brother once sent me a marvellous cartoon of a
flooded seance room filled with the floating wreckage of a
sunken ship, to which the 'sitters' are clinging. A nervous
initiate to trance mediumship is being reassured by an
experienced habitué of the circle: 'Don't worry, old man! It's
only Sailor Jack re-living his passing condition.'

That sense of humour, which Ma, Tony and I possessed to
a far greater degree than Pop, undoubtedly helped to
prevent us going round the bend in those early hairy days of
paranormal research.

Pop's sense of humour had been sadly lacking until Uncle Billy awakened it in his youth, and he was finally brought up to British Standards by a process of osmosis with Ma. My father soon found that this priceless gift helped us to keep some sense of proportion and balance, even in the most fraught situations.

Evil or negative forces abhor the sound of genuine laughter, not snide, sarcastic, sneering laughter, but that marvellous deep belly laughter that shakes the solar plexus and rids the soul of darkness.

Hatred, in particular, instantly dissolves in the presence of a good old down-to-earth guffaw.

One day a medium from Tenterden, where there was an active spiritualist centre, came to our house to give a demonstration of table-turning.

As a form of communication this is somewhat cumbersome and apparently needs a physical medium to supply the coarser form of ectoplasm required for the telekinetic part of the exercise. In other words, to lift or levitate and operate the table, 'power' is required. Yet although physical contact with the surface of the table is usual to produce the results, it isn't absolutely necessary once the initial magnetizing of the table has been achieved.

It all sounds like a lot of pseudo-scientific claptrap, but amazingly it does work. I have been present at many table sittings and seen too many fake-proof demonstrations to discard this rather odd method of communication.

Communication with what? is the obvious question – and the answer is largely determined by individual belief. It is the result which determines whether it is some form of projected action-at-a-distance or actual communication with another intelligence.

Pop chose a table with a central pillar. It was round and about two foot six inches in diameter. A typical Victorian piece of solid mahogany and other inlaid woods, it rested on four squat feet which projected from the four corners of the squared-off base of the strong central pillar. It was designed to stand square and firmly, holding tea trays, a large aspidistra pot or perhaps a bracket clock. You couldn't tip it over without exerting considerable effort.

The table sitters positioned themselves round this pleasant example of an occasional table, as I think it was called, seated comfortably and with their hands lightly placed on the surface. Some suitable gramophone record was played to induce a relaxed and reassuringly familiar feeling, usually a family favourite which in Pop's case was 'Oh for the Wings of a Dove' sung by Ernest Lough, a London choirboy with the voice of an angel. Having heard it hundreds of times, together with 'Liebeslied' and, for some odd reason, a rather highbrow recording of the 'Eton Boating Song', I find these three pieces of music difficult to enjoy today. Nevertheless, as an aid to inducing the right conditions for table-turning, those three records did wonders.

We continued our weekly sittings for about three months with little result except for the occasional tremor which seemed to pass through the table. Then, quite suddenly, one evening in mid-'Wings of a Dove', the table moved. It was a sensation I will never forget. The solid Victorian piece of furniture suddenly seemed to come alive under our hands.

Let me get one point quite clear. The pressure of our fingers was so light that the table virtually moved *under* them, sliding below the lightly maintained contact of our fingertips as it tilted and rocked.

At the same time a cold draught started circulating round our feet and, increasing in strength but with no appreciable decrease in temperature, it climbed upwards in a spiralling vortex of force till it seemed to hold its position above our knees and just under the bottom surface of the table-top.

This feeling, though distinctly odd, was not frightening or alarming, and immediately my mother and I found ourselves yawning our heads off. This tended to relax us still more, and a sensation of pleasant anticipation and well-being accompanied the phenomenon.

This yawning is a bit disconcerting to new sitters, who think their colleagues are either bored or tired, but the reaction is impossible to contain, for it is apparently caused by the draining of power from the solar plexus and base of the throat of the physical mediums.

If you politely place a hand in front of your mouth you have to take it off the table top, and that breaks the 'circuit of the sitting'. So to this day I often forget to cover my gaping mouth with a polite hand and, during 'healing', when consciously giving 'power', I yawn away like a member of the House of Commons.

On the first occasion when, at last, that robust example of British tablemaking circled the four of us, Ma, Pop, Tony and me, and leaned momentarily against each of us in a strangely affectionate gesture, it really did seem to be 'alive and well and living in our house in Folkestone'.

It sounds pretty weird, in cold print, but that is *exactly* what it felt like. One moment it was a well-made lump of various woods, the next it was a living entity – until the sitting was over, when it went back to being inanimate.

Why had it taken three months of patient regular sitting before the table eventually took off? What was the significance of the cold draught that circled our feet and then rose rapidly to just below the tabletop; and what about the uncontrollable yawning that accompanied it?

How did a heavy well-balanced, firmly-grounded wooden table move so lightly and agilely in all directions under our fingers if none of us was consciously pressing down on its surface? And how on earth did an inanimate table convey affection?

We had already experimented with Ouija boards and planchettes with rather unpleasant results. These heart-shaped pieces of flat wood, some twelve inches in length and ten inches or so in width at the base, are normally mounted on three sets of ball-bearing runners and are equipped with a pointer or a downward angled pencil at their apex. The

sitters lightly place their fingers on the Ouija board and it
soon starts to move and spell out messages by pointing to an
alphabet of letters and an array of numbers printed on a
large card or arranged individually on the table top. Alter-
natively, if a planchette is used, the pencil at the apex of the
heart writes on large sheets of paper or card.

We tried both and almost immediately got results, which
were erratic, sometimes mindless, and somehow accompanied by an unpleasant feeling of being in contact with a
low degree of elemental intelligence.

It sounds odd and slightly pompous, but that is what
it felt like. My father later told me that, as we had precious
little experience, we had approached the operation in too
earthly a manner, with too much of a 'Let's have a go at
the Ouija board' attitude, and too soon after eating a heavy
meal.

With Ouija we were given a lot of mindless nonsense and
even the sort of vicious messages that one would associate
with a spiteful and mischievous personality. Once, it just
repeated the one word death – till Pop stopped the sitting and
we never tried that method again.

I am appalled to think that you can buy Ouijas and
planchettes anywhere, and was intrigued, when I asked the
BBC prop department for one, to be told quite seriously that
the department was not allowed to keep them in stock.

We conducted the table sittings on a regular, disciplined
basis, refraining from eating or drinking anything other
than water for some hours before the sitting, and approaching the whole business in a more respectful and sober way.
In other words, the motive wasn't just curiosity and thrill-
seeking but a genuine shared sense of purpose and unity of
spirit. Pop would never allow a sitting if there was illness in
the house, if we were unusually tired, or if there had been
some family disharmony – a tiff or quarrel – anything which
would set up a disturbance in the atmosphere of relaxed well-
being and security that gave us our best results.

Our table sittings were a simple form of ritual, as every

seriously researched paranormal phenomenon eventually becomes. Ritual includes the safety precautions we take in our everyday lives, from the well-advertised and wise 'Clunk Click' campaign aimed at fastening one's safety belt, through cooking and eating rituals, to the complex cockpit checks of a jet airliner crew. They are all rituals, and the simpler they are the less chance of making mistakes.

The cumbersome, almost unwieldy method of table-turning seems ponderous and even a bit ridiculous. But it worked well for us and through it we received some remarkable evidence and amazingly accurate prophecies.

The method of communication we used couldn't be simpler, once the table is 'working'. One tilt for No, three tilts for Yes, and the alphabet spelt out by the number of tilts. When we got used to it we would often guess a word halfway through the spelling-out process; but it was really better to be patient and let the table spell out the whole word, because if you made a guess the table had to tilt out yes or no and, if no, continue the word from where you had interrupted it.

The results were astonishing, and to a really astounding degree the information 'passed' through the table turned out to be true. Many of the predictions were of a purely personal nature, and you will have to take my word for it that they were a hundred per cent correct.

The general type of prediction and prophecy, such as the outbreak and outcome of the Spanish Civil War and the events leading up to the Second World War, plus an amazing prediction of an air war in Britain which would be won at great cost by the young British and Allied pilots, were incredibly accurate – even to the information that Germany was working on heavy war rockets to bombard London and experimenting on winged bombs, to fly like robots, all of which was predicted *before* the outbreak of hostilities, when they were only ideas in the minds of their inventors.

But what were the seances like? My father described them as being 'like a crowd of people all trying desperately to get through to their families, and there is only one telephone, i.e.

the medium, or in our case, the table. They're all trying to get their messages over and were it not for a controlling entity, rather like a doorkeeper or a policeman, to keep some sort of order, it would be a shambles.' Other mediums have told me more or less the same thing.

In our circle the other end of the communication system was controlled by an entity who informed us that his name was Tom Shepherd, that he had lived in the eighteenth century, and had been a doctor.

Well now! There's rich pickings for the psychiatrists! I've heard a number of erudite explanations from a few of them already. These include: 'Ah yes! The name Shepherd gives the clue. Obviously a deep psychological need for some sort of order, a need for cosmos out of chaos.' There have been a number of rather odd sexual interpretations from a couple of Freudians and 'an Archetype. Definitely an archetypal entity, which your father concocted, or in fact any or all of you concocted to protect the family. We'll except you, Michael, as you were too young to protect the family – i.e. tribal circle – Shepherd was a ritual gamekeeper in fact, a defence mechanism.'

This fact is the nearest to a sane explanation and, together with the first, leaving out the Freudian ones as 'cranky', provides the alternatives which would be acceptable to a rationalist.

Either way the results were the same. Somehow or other, we had tuned in to a method of predicting future patterns of events with a degree of accuracy way beyond the mathematical laws of chance.

The idea of an entity (archetypal or otherwise) is my favourite, as it was with my parents and my brother. The table seemed to take on a definite personality, for accompanying the phenomenon we had a feeling of 'presence', and this altered noticeably with each 'personality' as it manifested in order to get its messages through.

We all felt Tom Shepherd as a definite personality, quite different from J.W.D., Ma's father, whom she felt very strongly when he manifested as she was the only one there who had known him.

Others gave initials or names, some recognizable, some unknown, but all apparently entities who were attempting to pass a message through to someone inside or outside the circle.

These were interesting because they were evidential and were later corroborated by the people for whom they were intended.

It is not an easy task to go up to someone, whom one knows only slightly, and say: 'I've got a message for you from your brother Charlie, who was killed on the Somme.'

With that sort of an introduction the message has to be pretty evidential. The general sort of cliché that one often gets in sittings, such as: 'Tell Mavis I'm happy. It's lovely here and Dad sends his love' won't get you very far.

However, in these cases, the rest of our message would be of the highly evidential sort, such as 'Tell her I said that she's lost a ring; it was one I gave her, a three-stone diamond and ruby ring with her initials and the word "from" and my initials. Tell her she will find it in a shoe – a brown shoe in her cupboard – where it dropped, etc.'

And sure enough, when just out of curiosity the recipient went to check, there it would be.

That particular example is of course only typical of the sort of message we used to pass on to various people.

Like anything else, table-turning requires discipline. As an example of how *wrong* a table sitting can go, I cite the case of an acquaintance in Folkestone – a very earthy, rich and self-important character who, after a heavy drinking and eating session with some friends, thought he would have a bash at a table sitting.

There was sufficient raw power there, in the shape of two members of this man's family, also somewhat bloated and heavily built, who by their glandular structure could generate the basic 'force' required.

After bawling out a couple of rugger songs to parallel the

preconditioning by music, and then upbraiding and finally insulting the stubbornly inanimate table, the small circle of 'experimenters' got the shock of their lives.

They had generated ideal conditions for a demonstration of an elemental low type of intelligence and sheer brute force; the table became a living vicious manifestation of power without control and chased the terrified gathering round the darkened room, eventually pinning the originator of the experiment hard up against the corner where it physically hurt him.

Needless to say, when one of the experimenters switched on the lights and the manifestation stopped, our ill-advised acquaintances swore never to dabble in the 'occult' again.

'Like attracts like' seems to be one of the ruling laws of this area of the paranormal. Our gate keeper, Tom Shepherd, was always apparently there in control, and we seldom experienced any difficulties or unpleasantness.

The best parallel I can think of is that of having someone on whom you can depend at a family party to keep out gate-crashers and drunks. The more you think about this simile, the more it seems to apply.

All this is difficult to get across in cold print but *anecdotal evidence* is the biggest source of material for paranormal research at the moment. Therefore, you have to be able to trust the person who is giving you the information, or you must feel from the evidence that it is valid.

The lack of written-up experimental research of an empiric, i.e. repeatable, nature is due to two factors. The first is that in any normal physical experiment the subject for analysis is an element, a chemical compound, or a detectable field of force. Therefore, allowing for the normal course of chemical change, you can achieve the *same* laboratory-conditioned results, time after time, once you have an effective operational technique.

With a human being as the 'bio-link' in the experiment, you come up against many obstacles to empiric results. Every one of your subjects will be totally different, even if they are identical twins.

Secondly, you cannot bring back last Thursday week, or whenever it was that the first experiment took place. There are too many changing factors or variants involved, the rapid chemical changes in the human body, the constant decay of brain cells, the emotional state of the subject and a hundred other small factors which are all in a state of flux.

Also our instrumentation is still primitive. The paranormal fields of energy are very weak and many of them are not detectable on the instrumentation in use. Therefore, you can take precautions against fraud of a blatant nature, but the final assessment of the validity of the experiment is, once again, reduced to anecdotal evidence.

To sum up, research into the paranormal is at a stage where it needs new thinking to complement the old methods used by man in one form or another for thousands of years.

A number of so-called 'pragmatic' scientists have recently banded together to drive out the 'heretics' who are attempting to push the frontiers outward from the restrictions imposed by physical science.

Their attitude is best summed up by the lines attributed to the Master of Balliol, Dr Jowett, in the last century:

'I am Master of this College; and what I don't know isn't knowledge.'

Burn the heretic. Destroy his books! Why? What does pragmatic science have to fear? – because *fear* is obviously the motive here. I'm not knocking the scientist. I happen to be the son of one, and a good one at that. I'm knocking the technologist who thumps his textbook in the same way as the nineteenth-century missionary thumped the Bible.

The heretic thinks for himself, therefore he or she becomes a danger. My concept of a radical heretic is not that of a bomb-throwing, sub-machine-gun-carrying member of some terrorist group masquerading as a freedom movement, but that of the 'free thinking' man using his incarnate ability to question his own incarnation.

To quote Professor Eric Laithwaite (from memory): 'If

research into the paranormal was found to have a commercial application, or could be used for military purposes or mass mind-manipulative techniques, the funds available would be unlimited.'

He went on to tell me some fascinating things about his own researches and the strange influences that had become apparent during them.

Here is an honest man, and a fine analytical and creative mind. When I go to ask his advice, as I do with a number of other tolerant scientists and philosophers who accept my amateur status and don't instantly reject my ideas because of it, he sometimes says 'Rubbish', and at other times 'You've got a point there, Michael'. That is what research into the paranormal is all about. Sometimes it is 'rubbish', and sometimes you'll find 'you've got a point there'. That was our state of mind, as a family, by the mid-1930s.

4 From the Paranormal to the Ridiculous

My first indication that Folkestone was to have a spiritualist church was the sight of my father lugging long planks of stout oak into the garage. Although none of my family was a spiritualist by religion, Pop and Ma realized that the proposed church would be a focus for research into the paranormal.

The garage was Pop's workshop and he kept it in a meticulous state. Every chisel, mallet, hammer and screwdriver, saw and plane had its allotted place, and one sure way to get my father's temper up was for one of us to borrow a tool and fail to replace it.

The object of the exercise was for my father to build an altar rail for the new church, which he proceeded to do most beautifully, until the large and impressive oaken structure took up the whole garage. It was made to last several lifetimes, and, for all I know, it is still there in that small meeting hall-cum-church. I often wonder how many mediums have clutched that massive oak rail and derived comfort from its solid security as they waited for the power to manifest through them.

Throughout the mid-1930s, a constant procession of mediums came to our small house in Wellfield Road to give demonstrations of practically every kind of paranormal phenomenon.

My mother, however, drew a firm line at materialization, because it was an alarming form of mediumship and seemed to leave a residual aura behind, similar to that indefinable feeling of depression that hangs around the site of road accidents.

I have noticed on a number of occasions that whenever large quantities of coarse ectoplasm have been present a definite feeling of shock and a sensation of negative 'emptiness' is left behind.

In the case of physical mediumship, as with 'direct voice', some kind of artificial larynx seems to be needed for the voices to manifest; this is presumably constructed from coarse ectoplasm by the manifesting entity.

In full materialization also, this type of ectoplasmic exudation, apparently emanating from the medium's glandular system, is manifestly present and enables the three-dimensional image to 'solidify' in full view of the sitters in the circle. It is a form of mediumship that, while impressive, is, to me anyway, alarming and slightly repulsive; and it is naturally open to various types of fake illusionary effects.

My mother wisely decided to limit the use of our home to research into the sort of phenomena that didn't seem to leave residual effects. Consequently, direct voice, full materialization, etc., were left to other researchers and we concentrated on clairvoyance, clairaudience, psychometry and, above all, the development of healing.

I started to develop clairvoyance in a subjective manner, through concentrating on my ability to project images onto the screen of my inner mind as well as receiving totally unexpected scenarios of 'imagined action' which manifested to my inner senses.

Clairaudience, like clairvoyance, can be divided into subjective and objective modes. *Subjective* clairaudience 'sounds' inside the head and is similar to intuition. *Objective* clairaudience can be 'heard' externally, in the form of 'bells', 'raps', 'knocks' and 'voices', such as those manifested to Joan of Arc.

Actual raps and knocks, which are heard by a number of witnesses, are another manifestation of coarse power

applied to other forms of physical phenomena. That is to say
they are *telekinetic*.

A spirit rap or knock sounds like a .22 blank cartridge
being fired *inside* a piece of furniture, usually a wooden
table, but it can manifest as a definite knock, such as
would be the result of a sharp tap with a hammer. It goes
without saying that to fake the latter is quite simple, but
to simulate the former effect would require very complex
trickery.

I have patiently listened to the usual know-alls who hand
out explanations like: 'It's the house creaking'; 'the
furniture is expanding and contracting' and even: 'mice or
rats'.

Having heard every one of these effects at some time,
especially in old houses, and in some new ones which were
lavishly furnished with unseasoned wood, I can say: 'No, it
is nothing like any of those effects.' Genuine raps or knocks
are unmistakable.

Psychometry is another fascinating study and one my
father developed to a remarkable degree. Essentially, it is
the faculty of being sensitive to objects and their associations; but, taken in a broad sense, a psychometrist is
sensitive to atmosphere and auras, and can translate these
emanations from an object - be it a spectacle case, a piece of
furniture, an ornament or even a house, megalith or
landscape - and transmute them into images, sensations
and symbols.

Psychometrists say something like this: 'This article, I
feel, belongs to an elderly person, associated with academic
work - I am seeing an elderly lady in a blue dress. I can see a
school or college - this person was a headmistress - she was
a very particular, painstaking person - she loved order - she
also loved animals, etc.'

That is a translation of what a psychometrist picks up from
the physical contact of touch. It is essentially a tactile form
of mediumship, or a general sensitivity to atmosphere.
People who have been blind from birth seem to possess

uncanny powers of tactile sensitivity and often make marvellous psychometrists.

Obviously one essential condition for such transference of information is that the object in question has been associated with the person or place for some time, the longer the better.

A blank sheet of notepaper in a person's wallet will give some information if it has been there for a long time; but it is far better if it has been written on, when the ink and physical action of the writing will encapsulate some of the essence of the writer.

The most obviously constructive form of applied medium-ship, apart from the predictive value of precognition, appears to be that of healing. Over the years, I have seen a number of demonstrations but by far the most effective sessions were those conducted by Mrs Doris Collins. Watching Doris work reminds me of my father healing, but in a much more positive way. Doris gives direct healing to the patient and then firmly suggests that the condition has improved. She has effected some extraordinary improvements and does, in fact, work with enlightened physicians.

Like my father, she would never claim that healing is a replacement for conventional medicine; but she does claim, and I agree with her, as I did with Pop, that there is a valid place for the healer working with the physician in contemporary medicine, especially when the patients are children.

The methods of healing seem to vary greatly, from a straightforward transmission of energy from the healer to the patient, to the channelling of energy from some external force and origin through the healer to the recipient.

To me, 'miracle' cures are always suspect. There is too much evidence of spontaneous regression in many condi-tions for that, but who is to know whether healing, in a number of cases, did not trigger off the reaction which brought about the regression.

A genuine straightforward transference of energy is

certain to be beneficial because the condition is bound to worsen if the patient is weak and exhausted. Better morale, a higher level of energy and an increase in the will to live, plus a diminution of fear, all contribute to a better chance of recovery.

At a number of demonstrations of healing, I have felt that a hysterical factor was the main reason behind the 'miracles', when people who had not been able to raise their arms or move their legs find themselves doing so. The deaf apparently hear immediately, and the partially blind 'see'.

The ultimate test has to be one of endurance. For how long do these miracles last? That is the conclusive test.

I have seen some very impressive demonstrations of healing, in which cases of partial paralysis due to shock have been almost immediately remedied or ameliorated, and the recipients of the healing have walked or been able to perform the impaired movements. In many of these cases the improvement has been lasting.

Healing is an art, and great artists in healing are as hard to find as great masters in any other field of the arts. They do exist and I believe Doris Collins is one of them.

Another outstandingly positive person is my friend Mary Rogers, an intelligent and no-nonsense healer who has had excellent results, notably with the cricketer, Colin Cowdrey.

Mary has recently been ill herself, as much a result of overwork as of her condition. Here again is an example of positive healing, in that her own morale, having suffered from the clinical treatment, required building up; other healers responded and gave her an energy transfer which helped her greatly.

Healers such as Parrish and Edwards, whom my father knew in the thirties, and Doris Collins agree that during healing their fingertips and other parts of the tactile sensing system of their hands swell, and contrasting sensations of heat and cold are felt.

Very few healers lay their hands directly on their patient; they often place their hands near the part of the body that requires 'treatment'. All of them claim, and I'm sure they are right, that they can 'feel' the centre of the malfunction of the system by passing their hands over the body.

I have myself experienced remarkable healing in a near-fatal condition which could have resulted in the loss of my left leg; so naturally my viewpoint is biased in favour of genuine healing.

I have nearly died three times – that is to say that I have survived three separate severe illnesses in which I passed into a deep coma. Each time I felt certain sensations which I will discuss later and, apart from anger or regret, once the struggle to survive was over, I found myself more in awe than in fear, and aware of a natural acceptance. Better environmental surroundings, plus a positive and comforting attitude towards people who are dying, are, for me, just as much a priority as the conditions required for painless and secure birth.

Some people have told me: 'Suffering is good for the soul', and: 'Only through suffering can you find God.' They have patently never experienced suffering. I have seen a lot of it and experienced some of it. It is not a prerequisite for enlightenment and too many people make too much money out of far too much of it.

A few moments of real suffering can seem like a lifetime and to prolong it needlessly is inhuman. When all the art of medicine has failed, apart from the gift of the suppression of suffering by the administration of drugs, why not let the genuine healer do his or her bit to help the condition?

Better still, why not call the healer in before the condition becomes terminal?

Neville B. was a friend at my prep school. He was a quiet, reserved Jewish boy whose father was, I think, an accountant. Mr B. was a widower and he and Neville lived alone – looked after by a visiting housekeeper.

When Neville was thirteen years old, in accordance with the Jewish faith, he came of age at his Barmitzvah. As he

was an only child and somewhat lonely, he tried to grow up
as fast as he could, and in the way of the young, tried to show
his newly-acquired 'manhood' by arguing with his father.

Mr B. was distressed and puzzled by his gentle son's
behaviour and, as he knew that my father had a son (me) of
his own lad's age, and another, Tony, six years older, he
came to see him and ask his advice. He discussed the
paranormal with Pop whenever he came to pick up Neville
from a visit to our home. He himself was a rabbinical
scholar, a devout Jew and, as he had a working knowledge of
the Kabbala, the body of esoteric Jewish doctrine, he had
become interested in Pop's researches.

It was a sunny afternoon, in the late summer of 1936, and
Pop and Mr B. were having tea in the drawing-room when I
was asked to join them. Mr B. wanted me to answer a few
questions about Neville, principally whether I had noticed
the change in him.

A boy of fourteen doesn't notice much about a boy of
thirteen, apart from whether he happens to like him or not,
and whether he is fun to be with and joins in the sort of
pursuits that he is interested in - in my case cricket in the
garden, climbing trees, making model aeroplanes and
generally rushing around.

I liked Neville. He was clever, quietly cheerful and, in spite
of his light build, a good cricketer. He also had a lively
imagination and could enter into the spirit of any game that
we devised and, kind lad that he was, didn't make fun of my
permanent stammer.

I told Mr B. that Neville was fine, as far as I was
concerned, taking some time to say so because of that bloody
stammer, and I remember Mr B. asking me to do an
experiment in 'thought transference' with him.

This was something I had done many times with Pop and
Tony, and I was quite experienced at it. We used a number of
cards on which Tony had drawn bold basic symbols - a
snake, a triangle, wavy lines, a circle, etc. - in fact the sort of
cards that Dr Rhine used for telepathic experiments at Duke

University, Carolina. In those days I could 'hit' (i.e. guess) something like ninety per cent of the targets projected mentally across a room, with the transmitting experimenter standing or sitting so that we were back to back.

Mr B. had tried it with marked success at his own home on a number of occasions when I had been to tea with Neville and was much intrigued by the high percentage of correct hits.

To me it was an interesting game rather than an experiment, and Pop would only allow me to do a small number of demonstrations at any one time, because he knew that it was a tiring exercise in intense concentration. Pop agreed to the experiment and I hit around ninety per cent, which delighted Mr B. and, being human, I felt pretty chuffed with myself as well.

At this point in the proceedings my brother Tony came in from cricket practice. He had been bowling energetically at the nets for a couple of hours and was well relaxed - so much so that, after a cup of tea with us he sat back on the sofa and immediately fell asleep.

I was surprised, and a bit embarrassed, that he should fall asleep so suddenly in the presence of Neville's father, but as I went to nudge him awake, my father stopped me and indicated that I should leave him alone.

It was only then I realized that Tony was already going into deep trance. His breathing became deeper and slower until he seemed to be reaching far down to fill his lungs, and he expelled the air in long exhalations. I started to yawn as I watched my brother's body rhythmically moving in his deep breathing, and realized that he was drawing power from me!

Tony had been developing trance mediumship in our family circle, and the signs of the threshold of deep trance were unmistakable.

On previous occasions the manifesting entity had been a bit incoherent, and could well have been some facet of his own personality but in this case it was completely different.

Quite suddenly Tony's eyes opened, but did not appear to see anything, while from his throat came a deep guttural voice, at first speaking slowly and with some effort, and then with growing fluency, as though becoming used to manifesting through my brother's vocal cords.

The language which was used was utterly unlike anything I had ever heard before in my life. Our family was used to foreign languages, and Tony and I both had a good ear for accents and from time to time used to amuse ourselves, and confuse others, by making up mid-European sounding languages of our own. None of these languages, real or false, was now being spoken in the deep throaty tone issuing from my brother as he sat bolt upright in deep trance.

Mr B.'s face was transfixed with wonder. He was a small, neat man, like Pop, but somewhat tubby, with a pleasant round face and button-bright shrewd eyes looking out at the world from behind gold pince-nez.

To our amazement he started to reply to Tony's strange guttural language in what sounded to me to be the same tongue, though, of course, I didn't understand a word of what either of them was saying.

The odd thing was that while whoever or whatever was speaking through my brother was fluent in this strange language, Mr B. was obviously having difficulty remembering words, and stumbled in his phrasing as though speaking a tongue he hadn't used for some time.

He started to cry - the tears rolling down his plump cheeks - but, even to me, they were tears of joy and happiness rather than uncontrolled sadness. This extraordinary dialogue continued for some twenty minutes - Pop quietly sitting there with his hands resting palms upwards on his thighs, giving power, while I yawned my young head off. I could feel the power being drawn from me in waves as I followed my father's example and sat with my hands open on my lap.

Eventually Mr B. became completely overcome with emotion and suddenly seemed to collapse, while he sobbed his heart out. Strangely enough it was neither alarming nor embarrassing and, at this moment, my brother stood up, seeming to radiate power and benevolence, his strong, athletic body appearing taller and broader. With a flow of guttural and yet at the same time musical words, the phrases spoken in a sing-song cadence, he obviously gave the now kneeling Mr B. a blessing.

Then my brother sat back on the sofa and closed his eyes - at the same time seeming to shrink back to his normal size and build. A moment later his eyes flicked open and blinked with embarrassment as he realized that he must have dropped off in front of the guest. He was about to apologize when he suddenly took in the sight of Mr B. rocking back and forth, his whole body racked with sobbing.

My brother was utterly bewildered and still recalls the incident: 'One moment I was having tea and sitting back to relax on the sofa, the next I was confronted by Pop's guest - your mate's father - in the throes of hysteria.' To this day he has no memory whatsoever of *what had happened in between*.

Pop told Tony that he had been in trance and that he should nip upstairs and clear the condition by running cold water over his forearms.

My brother, being an experienced sitter, didn't argue and went off to comply with Pop's instructions - on the way quietly telling me to let him know what happened while he was gone from the room.

Mr B. had now almost got himself under control, and Pop was wiping away the condition by pressing his hands over Mr B.'s head and down his back and arms - this being a standard procedure to clean the aura. Finally Mr B. managed to speak: 'Adam,' he said, 'will you give me your solemn word? Will you swear on your son's life that he does not speak either Hebrew or Yiddish?'

My father smiled: 'I don't have to. I can assure you that no one in this family speaks or has any knowledge of either of those languages.'

Then Mr B. told us: 'That was my rabbi! Forgive me asking you that last question, but I had to be absolutely sure – though really I have no doubt that, through your eldest son, I have spoken to my rabbi! It has been a wonderful experience.'

His face showed his utter sincerity as he spoke, for it was now glowing with happiness. He told us that his rabbi had been a very close friend of his father's, and, when his father had died, had treated him as another son. Mr B. loved him as he had loved his own father, and when his rabbi had died he had mourned him as his closest friend and adviser.

His concern for his son Neville and his future would have been precisely the sort of problem which he would have gone to talk over with his rabbi.

He explained that the reason he had replied with such difficulty was that he was out of touch with Hebrew. He also explained that his interest in the paranormal was due to his rabbi's knowledge of the Kabbala.

Mr B., himself, had been a good Talmudic scholar and had studied Hebrew and Aramaic far deeper than was necessary for him to read a portion of the law, which, he explained, was the task set for each Jewish boy at his Barmitzvah.

His rabbi had discussed some of the aspects of the Kabbala after solemnly warning him that only those qualified by years of scholarship should practise its techniques; but his death had prevented him passing on further knowledge of the paranormal.

Mr B. summed the whole strange business up when he said: 'I have no further worries about Neville. I now know that he and I are in God's hands and are being guided.' He then thanked us most movingly. He was, I remember, a very nice man.

Let us examine the pros and cons of what had taken place. Either Mr B., my father and my brother were in some kind of weird collusion to fake the whole business to impress me – a fourteen-year-old boy – which is a little unlikely, or Mr B., who had not got the world's greatest sense of humour, was playing some strange kind of practical joke on us, which is even more unlikely!

Certainly, my brother wasn't fooling – I know him far too well for that – and Tony, like me, is a shy person and certainly wouldn't behave like that in front of a virtual stranger.

My brother, my father and I had absolutely no knowledge or practice in either Yiddish or Hebrew and the only word I knew in Hebrew was 'Shalom', which Neville had taught me.

The final possibility is that I have made up the whole story, which could of course apply to this whole book.

I assure you that those are the *facts,* as closely as I can recall them, and the words used as clearly as I can remember them. Nearly forty-five years later my brother remembers everything except the part when he was in trance, and, of course, he had my father's, Mr B.'s and my own word for what happened then.

If Neville B., who would recognize these events, is still alive, I should be very happy to hear from him, as I lost contact with him in 1936 and have had no word from him since. Perhaps he has already passed through the door marked summer?

In direct contrast to this convincing and moving experience, I well remember being a terrified witness to one or two highly disturbing manifestations.

I explained earlier that the preliminary part of the threshold of trance states often appears to involve the medium in the manifesting entity's 'passing condition'. As the medium experiences the disengagement of his own psyche from his body, he seems to stand to one side of it while he allows the manifesting entity – or, if you prefer it, some aspect of his own deep subconscious (an 'alien' personality) – to take charge of his body. That, in itself, sounds alarming enough and, if the sanity of the medium is to be preserved, it should be allowed to take place only under strictly controlled circumstances and conditions.

In the strange case of the manifesting rabbi and my
brother, I remember my father keeping a close watch on
every point and move in case he would have to step in and
disengage the contact. After all, he was taking a calculated
risk with my brother's sanity, and could only be guided by
his instincts and by what he had learned in the preceding
four years.

Whether you consider trance mediumship a form of deep
self-hypnosis which allows another facet of the medium's
own personality to manifest and control the body, or
whether you accept the concept of an alien 'discarnate
entity' stepping in to take over, the results are what matter.

Taking as read every possible precaution, both before and
during the sitting, and being constantly vigilant to make
sure that the medium does not lose the vital link with his or
her own body, trance mediumship is an advanced and
deeply researched aspect of paranormal phenomena and, as
such, is as safe as any other physical mediumship.

Without such precaution and vigilance, it is a highly
dangerous practice. I therefore try to impress on the mind of
the researcher that guidance by experienced mediums is
essential in the early stages of development. It goes without
saying that no one with a nervous disposition, or who feels
apprehensive under stress, should even attempt these forms
of mediumship. In fact, paranormal investigation should
remain to them a closed book, as they are particularly open
to a 'take-over'.

In the following example of trance mediumship I hate to
think what the consequences might have been, had my
father not been present.

Alan Dawkins, my elder cousin from Westcliff and Tony's
contemporary, had been staying with us for a couple of
weeks, and we also had, as a house guest, Brian L., a friend of
my brother's from Eton.

The sitting was on a sunny afternoon during the mid-
1930s in a small, airy guest bedroom which had been set

aside for research. It was kept spotlessly clean and sparsely furnished, and its only equipment or furnishing for anything of a paranormal nature was a curtained-off corner of the room which provided a separate alcove 'cabinet' for a medium who required darkness for her particular phenomena.

The cabinet contained a plain wooden table and a cross which Pop had made simply and beautifully of oak. Pop had intended to investigate materialization and direct voice in this cabinet, but at my mother's insistence it had never been used.

The sitters were Pop, Alan, Ma, Tony, Brian and myself, aged fourteen. At first everything seemed quite normal or, rather, normally paranormal, as we sat round the table with the light chintzy curtain drawn to shut out the brightest of the afternoon sunlight, leaving the sitting still in good light without any hint of darkness. Pop said the usual short prayer. We linked hands and Tony put on a suitable record on the portable wind-up gramophone.

Nothing happened for a while. We unlinked our hands, lightly rested them on the table, and waited patiently for it to move.

Ma and I started yawning, followed by Alan, and Pop sat with his eyes closed breathing deeply and slowly. If anyone was to go into a trance we expected it to be Pop.

To our surprise Alan ceased yawning and sat back in his chair. His eyes were shut and he was breathing stertorously – quick heavy gulps of air which became slower and more regular as he went deeper into the trance state. His body started to quiver and vibrate and his breathing became still deeper and more rapid, as though he was hyper-ventilating his system. Then, without warning, with his eyes still closed, he stood up and stretched himself to his full height, which was an inch or so below six feet, from which position he seemed to continue to *grow* in height and to *swell* in proportion.

We all saw it happen, so it is extremely unlikely that the

experience was a subjective one, and, though none of us knew it at the time, this stretching and enlarging (or diminishing and shrinking) of the medium's body is by no means an uncommon occurrence in physical mediumship.

The room had become ice-cold – not the familiar chilly but unalarming draught of power that we were so familiar with in table sittings – but a uniform and uncomfortably severe drop in temperature throughout the whole room. Accompanying this disturbing change in temperature there was a feeling of vibrant power in the air – sheer animal energy of a very powerful and alarming type.

Pop was in trance, breathing steadily and deeply, and the rest of us were speechless with amazement and fear – plain naked funk!

Alan by this time had swollen in size like a huge bullfrog.

Brian cried out: 'For God's sake, Mr Bentin – stop it!' and I could feel that Ma was as frightened as the rest of us.

At that moment, in a loud ringing tone of voice utterly unlike Alan's quiet modulated tone, my cousin, or whatever was manifesting through him, cried out: 'Go into the cabinet.' He indicated my mother, who sat speechless, shaking her head in flat refusal to obey this command.

Brian again pleaded: 'For God's sake don't do it, Mrs Bentin! Please don't!'

'Go into the cabinet!' thundered that strange alien voice, and the little room seemed to shake with the raw power of that awe-inspiring presence.

Ma prayed: 'Lord – please help us!'

Tony was getting ready to tackle the problem physically, for my brother was built on powerful lines and had now got over his first shock at Alan's amazing transformation.

I was praying too – mainly that Pop would wake up and settle it all peacefully, because I had a strong feeling that Tony alone couldn't control our entranced cousin.

Immediately my father came out of his trance and at once sized up the situation. Looking mildly up at the now-towering figure of the commanding colossus, my father said quietly but firmly: 'Thank you, friend! That will be quite enough. If you can speak and give us a message – God bless you! If not – you will leave the medium immediately!'

To our heartfelt relief and no little amazement, the giant entity which had manifested through Alan appeared to shrink down into the normal well-built but by no means giant form of my cousin Alan, who now slumped back into his chair. Pop stood up and, with rapid positive passes of his hands, 'cleared the condition' from his nephew's aura.

Alan sat shaken and sweating, even in the rapidly receding chill of the little room. He was totally unaware that he had been anything but asleep – and apologized for dropping off: 'I've had such a lovely nap, Auntie! I'm sorry if I was rude.'

The understatement of the century.

Thinking back on this episode, I don't remember any feeling of malevolence or evil – only a mind-boggling sense of great power being generated and a very natural shared fear of the unknown.

We all compared notes afterwards over a strong cup of tea, which was my mother's standard remedy for any shock or injury. It applied to every emergency, whether it was failure to pass an exam, a near-fatal car accident or, later, during the war, our dust-covered survival from a near-miss by a large German bomb.

We were all agreed that Alan had grown alarmingly, in both bulk and stature, till he seemed almost to touch the low ceiling; and there was no disagreement either on the paralysing cold and fear which had gripped us all, except the two entranced sitters – Pop and Alan.

Had not my father been there to deal quietly and efficiently with the situation, I think we would all have cut and run for it.

It taught us all a good lesson, and none of us was any the worse for the experience; but it reinforced Ma's determination that no physical phenomena should take place in our home and, to show willing, my father took down the cabinet curtains but left the metal runners up to prove that he was still the *pater familias*.

I dislike sitting in a darkened room while tambourines and megaphone-like trumpets thrash about over my head – it is so open to both fake and fear. I like to see what is happening and to be able to assist in some way if things go wrong.

It is only recently that I've allowed my own children, who are now adults, to 'sit' with my wife and me during a rare healing session or an attempted energy transmission to someone in need.

That is the keynote of an involvement I now have with the paranormal – other than subjective clairvoyance, which is the method I use for writing. Only when the *need* – usually someone else's need – is there do we 'sit' to give positive thoughts (odd though that may sound it works very well) and healing.

I don't believe it is a good thing to practise research into the paranormal field while children are growing up in the home, and I am certain that my father did so only because he was convinced it would be folly not to share his conclusions with his family.

Tony and I were away at Eton during large portions of this research and, knowing my father's mathematical approach to everything, I am sure he counted this absence in his final decision to let us both sit as an aid to our general development.

There is an obvious parallel here with over-exposure to radiation. The body can take a certain amount without harm but over-exposure to radioactivity is highly dangerous and usually fatal.

So it is with this type of research and activity: you over-expose yourself and your family to it at your peril! That is why the dire warnings of the Church – no matter which religion is involved – have been sounded against unguided exposure to these fields of experience.

To lighten the atmosphere a bit, let me tell you about

some of the doom-and-gloom merchants we encountered in the thirties, and about some of the archetypal sitters that we met at various seances.

Many developing mediums go through a 'dark' phase of prophecy, in which all they can see is disaster. Most pass through this phase and emerge into lighter areas of precognitive experience, only occasionally, and then with good reason, receiving prophetic warnings of doom.

One medium who actually revelled in the prediction of dire destruction came to visit us for a test sitting. Almost before she was through the front door, she had fixed a gloomy eye on me. Had I a chest condition? No? Well, I was going to have one – probably fatal.

Had my mother got a breast condition? No? Well, one breast would be off before the year was out.

Had my father a weak heart? No? Well, he'd better watch it!

If I remember, even the dog wasn't going to last the week!

She didn't last long either, because Ma, who had twigged that here was an enthusiastic 'doom spotter' in full spate, turned her round, with her coat half-off, and steered her through the front door.

Ma never did have much time for fools, though with the grief-stricken and genuine searchers, she had infinite patience.

I remember her demolishing one fake (as opposed to self-deluded) medium, in about two minutes flat. This particular individual was a florid and over-bearing female who had openly boasted of extraordinary powers. The proceedings went something like this:

PHONEY MEDIUM (after much
    groaning and thrashing about):   War! War! War!

(This approach was, presumably, a 'come on', in the belief that anyone of my mother's generation was a safe bet to have lost someone during the Great War of 1914–18.)

MOTHER (calmly, having cottoned on immediately):	Yes?
PHONEY MEDIUM (redoubling the over-acting bit):	War! War!
MOTHER (taking up her cue):	Is that you, Obadiah? (This was enough for me, as Obadiah was a family joke name.)
PHONEY MEDIUM (swallowing the bait):	Yes – Obadiah is here! It's Obadiah speaking!
MOTHER (all bright eyes and enthusiasm):	Oh, how lovely to speak to you, Obadiah! It's a miracle!
PHONEY MEDIUM (hamming it up like mad):	Yes, yes! Obadiah is so happy! Such a wonderful miracle through this wonderful channel [i.e. herself] to speak to you, Flo!

(This was a bad mistake! This self-professed prophetess had found out that Ma's name was Florence, but she couldn't have guessed that my mother hated the name 'Flo'!)

MOTHER (her heart now like stone):	Yes! It *is* a miracle to hear you speak, Obadiah [pause and then the *coup de grâce*] especially as you are a dog!

The 'gullibility factor' of some sitters was quite extraordinary, but then there is none so ready to believe as the person who wants to believe.

For example, there were the sitters who claimed that everything was for them, at any sitting.

MEDIUM (indicating a sitter on the left side of the room):	I want to come to you, sir! There is an elderly lady beside you, and she tells me that her name was Samantha – she was your aunt.
CLAIMER (on the opposite side of the room – confidently):	That would be for me – that's my Aunt Elizabeth.
MEDIUM (confused):	No! I'm sorry – this lady says her name was Samantha.
CLAIMER:	That's right! What she means is that her name is really Elizabeth, but I once had a doll called Samantha.
MEDIUM (more confused):	No! She says that's not it at all – she is definitely called Samantha and was the aunt of this gentleman here!
CLAIMER:	Ah yes! – well! she would – that's typical of my Aunt Elizabeth – always getting things muddled up. [Loudly.] Don't you remember Auntie, my *doll's* name was Samantha!
MEDIUM (getting nettled):	Perhaps this will convince you, madam, that the message is not for you. She says her husband's name was Roderick and that she doesn't know you at all. It's this gentleman that she is linked to.
CLAIMER (triumphantly):	Well actually her husband's name was *Bert*. What a card she is, fancy calling him Roderick! God bless you, Auntie, and thank you for coming through to me!

Another popular species found in the seance room is the enthusiastic sitter who is determined to contact a *specific* entity; willy-nilly, they are determined to get their money's worth.

MEDIUM (vaguely):	There is a little girl here.
EAGER SITTER:	That will be my George. Hello, George!
MEDIUM (startled):	No! I think it's a little girl – but then, of course, at that age, it is hard to tell – perhaps he could be a little boy.
EAGER SITTER:	How lovely to speak to you, George. Is Mother there?
MEDIUM (caught off guard):	I don't seem to feel an *elderly* lady here!
EAGER SITTER:	Mum passed over quite young – seventy-eight actually! Hello, Mum! Is Dad there?
MEDIUM (feeling that she's lost the ball):	I'm sorry I can't see a gentleman.
EAGER SITTER:	Hello, Dad! Can I speak to Mary?
MEDIUM (drowning):	Please let me—
EAGER SITTER:	Hello, Mary! Just wanted to tell you that Fred's getting married – but then you probably knew that already. Charlie's got his 'A' levels. Thanks for all your help. Oh! and the cat's better! Shall I go on that holiday to Majorca or not?
MEDIUM (helplessly):	Please . . .
EAGER SITTER:	Oh good! I thought you'd say yes! Bless you dear! – Lovely to have this little chat!

On the other hand you come across the exact opposite – in a form of total resistance to any evidence, no matter how convincing. This type of sitter should never be called for jury service as his or her mind is already made up.

MEDIUM:	I want to come to you, sir. Does the name Quentin Murgatroyd Bellamy mean anything to you?
RELUCTANT SITTER:	Well, perhaps.
MEDIUM:	He says that he was your stepfather by your mother's third marriage – and that her maiden name was Miranda Delgado.
RELUCTANT SITTER (grudgingly):	Mm! What else does this so-called entity say?
MEDIUM (getting annoyed):	He's telling me that your younger brother's name is Aloysius Lawrence, and that he was named after your maternal grandfather, who was a well-known amateur astronomer and an acknowledged authority on asteroids.
RELUCTANT SITTER:	Can he be more specific?
MEDIUM (exasperated):	Yes! He says that he was lost at sea on the *Titanic* and that he left you his collection of butterflies and rare sea shells. He also says you had a dog called Buonaparte, a cat named Hildegarde and a West African parrakeet that could whistle 'Ave Maria'.
RELUCTANT SITTER:	In what key?

During those early years we saw them all!

In many cases it was the medium who was at fault. There was, for example, the unfortunate 'psychic' who had an off day at our local town hall, where the meeting had taken place in cold, draughty surroundings with only a few stony-faced sceptics present.

At last, goaded beyond endurance by the atmosphere, the unhappy 'sensitive' called out: 'Does anyone here tonight know the name Smith? Not necessarily in spirit!'

Another medium looked straight at a sad sitter in the front row with elephantiasis of the lower limbs, which were grotesquely swollen, poor soul. 'I am picking up a leg condition,' she declared triumphantly.

Some of the seances we attended were so unbelievably full of gullible sitters as to defy the law of averages, while the 'discarnate entities' that were supposed to have manifested were what Ma called the 'regulars'. By this my mother meant the archetypal popular misconception of the sort of departed spirit who came through to give the living world proof of survival.

In those days these were Napoleon, who spoke no French; the Kaiser, who spoke no German; Anna Pavlova, who didn't speak at all presumably because she was a ballet dancer; Disraeli who usually sounded like a bad impersonation of a Jewish music-hall comedian and, for some strange reason, Isadora Duncan.

A sitting in which one of the 'regulars' was supposed to manifest would go like this:

DODGY MEDIUM:	Is – Is – Is!
1ST SITTER:	Is who dear?
DODGY MEDIUM:	Is – a – dora Dun – can—
1ST SITTER (excitedly):	Ooh! It's Isadora Duncan!
2ND SITTER (equally chuffed):	Fancy – *the* Isadora Duncan.
3RD SITTER (puzzled):	Who's Isadora Duncan?

1ST SITTER:	You know, dear! That exotic dancer who got killed in her car!
2ND SITTER:	That's right – she was strangled with her own long scarf! It got caught round the back wheel – it was in all the papers.
1ST SITTER (thrilled):	Have you got a message for us, Miss Duncan?
DODGY MEDIUM:	Yes! Don't drive in an open car while wearing a long scarf.

Exaggerated? Not really! At times we did see and hear incredible nonsense like this greeted with 'oohs' and 'ahs' by complacent sitters who thoroughly deserved the rubbish that was doled out to them.

Amazingly, they would go away from the sitting feeling smugly privileged and distinctly honoured by their famous if somewhat dull 'visitors from another world'!

However, the *genuine* evidence given at the sittings which so impressed us and convinced my family of the validity of paranormal phenomena stood out like currants in a rather stodgy cake.

I wouldn't have missed it for anything!

5   *The Remarkable Grocer of Dover*

In the mid-1930s my father met an extraordinary man who
kept a tiny grocer's shop on the outskirts of Dover. Dover,
like Folkestone, is a terminal for ferries to the Continent.
The town itself, apart from the forbidding bulk of its ancient
castle looming high above it, was largely made up of
Victorian terraces, set in rows behind Dover's pride, a line of
villas of eighteenth- and nineteenth-century elegance.

These had become a bit shabby in the 1930s, when Dover
had fallen far behind its posh rival, Folkestone, and was
only patronized by the 'well orf' on their comfortable way to
the Continent.

I used to think of Folkestone as a Victorian matron sitting
on top of the cliffs, gazing out disapprovingly at the immoral
coast of France while dabbling her toes in the sea. A mite
whimsical but oddly appropriate and, if true, then Dover
was the personification of her busy and badly-paid companion.

Dover town also housed military and naval families,
especially in wartime, and the legendary white cliffs -—
actually a grubby grey - were honeycombed by a huge series
of interconnecting tunnels, exactly like a giant version of
Gibraltar.

The narrow winding streets that stretched back towards
the Weald of Kent climbed either side of the town in long
lines of red-brick and peeling-plastered terraces of small
houses two up/two down. Eddie Partridge's minute grocer's
shop served a complex of these modest and compact homes

from its strategic position on a corner.

Eddie was himself, like his wife Biny, small in stature and big in spirit.

A natural psychic from birth and an outstanding healer, this cheery grocer was also one of the best known breeders of racing pigeons in Britain. Years later, when I was being well and truly taken for a ride by a couple of smart operators over a film I was making, I was sitting in despair when I was handed a racing pigeon as part of the props for my role as a London East-Ender.

'It's called Champion Eddie,' the animal trainer said.

In my depression, the name rang a distant, joyful bell. I immediately perked up: 'Anything to do with Eddie Partridge?' I asked hopefully – then remembered that Eddie had passed over long before.

'Blimey!' replied the startled trainer. 'How would you know that? Are you a breeder, mate?'

'No,' I admitted. 'But I knew Eddie well. He bred champions named after him. I was hoping this bird might be one of the line.'

'The best there are, mate! Eddie's name is still famous – and this one is a marvellous example of what Eddie Partridge did for pigeon racing.'

All the worry and anxiety over the unfortunate circumstances vanished as I held that warm little pigeon in my hands, and I felt Eddie say: 'It'll be all right, Michael! These things are just part of learning what life's all about!'

Those years came back to me clearly, especially the day when Pop returned from his first meeting with Eddie – full of enthusiasm and a touch of awe. 'He's such a marvellously simple man! You can feel the goodness – it's a tangible aura. He radiates it round him – simplicity and honesty! And he's got the cheerfulness of a sparrow. He's a grocer – but I've got the strangest feeling that he's like someone a long time ago, only that one was a carpenter!'

My father never exaggerated, in fact he positively disliked over-statement, so a description like that, of someone whom he had only just met made me sit up and take notice.

The Partridge family lived behind and above their small corner shop. Their only son had then recently joined Boots the Chemists, and was already well on his way to becoming the local manager.

Eddie was barely literate. In fact, his son had taught him to read and write. Yet Eddie, 'unaided', never got his accounts wrong. He once told me that, before doing them, he offered up a short prayer; then down would go the figures – which, when finally totalled up, were correct to the nearest halfpenny.

His shop intrigued me, and I can still see it plainly – if you like, clairvoyantly – with its glass-panelled door which, heralded by a tinkling shop bell, opened into a small compact wonderland of glass-topped tin biscuit boxes, dark-painted shelves loaded with tinned goods, Cheshire cheese under glass, a small home-cooked ham on a china stand with a muslin-covered wire cage over it and, to one side, the scrupulously clean counter. This bore old-fashioned scales complete with brass and heavy black cast-iron weights, clumps of paper bags hung up by one corner on strings and a huge roll of brown wrapping paper side by side with an enormous ball of string.

The whole shop smelt of homely things like fresh bread and OK Sauce, boot polish, sugar mice and jam, and somehow managed to contain, in its packed complexity, anything required by the neighbourhood, from a needle to an anchor!

I can see Eddie standing behind his counter or bustling about with a word for everyone, addressing them as duck, mate, dear, Mum or Dad – according to their age and sex.

In the shop he habitually wore a shirt with a celluloid collar and small dark tie. Over his shirt, to the elbow, he had black cotton over-sleeves, and he topped off this archetypal grocer's ensemble with a spotless apron.

Eddie inspired confidence whether as a grocer, a breeder of champion racing pigeons, an avuncular figure for all the neighbourhood kids (who adored 'Uncle Eddie') or, as we came to know him, an extraordinary medium and great healer. Come to think of it, in all the years I knew him, I never saw him down or depressed; *concerned* for someone else, yes, but never negative in any way.

All through the years of depressing peace and grimmer war that little shop seemed to be able to find something for everybody who came to it in need. No one was ever cheated or 'dunned for the money' or went away empty handed. Eddie seemed to manage to keep it all going somehow. All round that little corner shop, and even underneath it, large bombs, parachute mines and naval shells crashed to earth, some to blow up in lethal blasts, others to lie amazingly unexploded. In all that carnage, Eddie's shop remained untouched – without even a pane of glass broken. Coincidence? Perhaps. But a miraculous one! I know, because I visited it in 1944 and saw it for myself. That remarkable man seemed to be able to open his door marked summer at will.

We all had genuine affection for Eddie, even Ma, whose shrewd assessment of character would have soon seen through any false humility or phoney bonhomie. My mother totally accepted and admired Eddie; Pop loved him dearly and called him 'brother' – a form of address he rarely used.

By 1936 Pop had been through four years of concentrated research and had already undergone some extraordinary experiences, but with Eddie Partridge, sitting in that small back parlour behind the little shop, he received some of the most convincing evidence of all.

This tiny room was a warm, fire-lit square, simply furnished and containing a fair-sized table which did service as a solid platform for the Partridge family meals and as a simple place to sit round for paranormal phenomena. The room radiated 'love'. I can't explain it any better than that.

Before she sat with Eddie's small home circle my mother had received a mass of interesting and highly convincing evidence through various clairvoyants and psychometrists, but she had not experienced any physical phenomena involving her personally. But here she was levitated, quite suddenly, in the middle of a sitting in that small back room, straight up from her chair, whisked (her own word) above the table, in full darkness, and deposited, a bit breathless, on the lap of the sitter opposite her.

Ma told me that it all happened so quickly that she didn't have time to feel frightened. But it certainly convinced her of levitation.

I am fully aware of my parents' faults, as I hope my children are well aware of mine. However, honesty and integrity were two of my parents' virtues, and, in recording their impressions of things that happened to them, especially in the field of the paranormal, these qualities were of enormous importance.

When my mother told me of this demonstration – and her transference from one side of that solid table onto the lap of the opposite sitter – I *knew* that it had happened.

Let's look at the factors involved in the levitation of my mother, who tipped the scales at over ten stone.

The other sitters consisted of Eddie, who must have been around nine stone six, Biny, his diminutive wife, who was of the order of eight stone, and Pop, who was always at his fighting weight of ten stone. Besides them was Eddie's brother-in-law, who I think was called Charlie, who weighed in at around ten and a half stone.

It is unlikely that, in pitch darkness, they, individually or collectively, could have lifted up my substantial mother, and, without dropping her, transported her silently and safely over the table and deposited her gently and securely on the lap of, I believe, Charlie.

In full light, all together, it would have been an effort and a hazard to Ma's safety. In total darkness it could not have been done.

Many of the sittings in which physical phenomena manifested were carried out with the Partridge family circle in almost total darkness; but, in all fairness, 'light-tight conditions' are normally obtained only under laboratory conditions; throughout these particular sittings there were still significant amounts of light from chinks in curtained windows or loosely fitted door sills.

Darkness is mandatory for physical phenomena and it does make sense. Firstly, the darkness precludes the possibility of the attention of the sitters being drawn to the objects that, even in a bare room, catch the eye. Secondly, if, as we believed, the generation of the coarser form of ectoplasm required to contain and sustain a tangible field of force sufficient to levitate a human being is ultra-sensitive to light, then, obviously, the absence of light becomes necessary.

I have evidence, and more is available from many other sources, that the sudden switching on of a bright light causes the ectoplasm to rebound and be immediately reabsorbed by the physical medium involved. This obviously causes shock, and consequent physical damage to the nerve centres.

The sudden swallowing of the dense forms of catarrh generated by an asthmatic is a simple parallel to this reaction, which is of course on a far more traumatic scale. As I have nearly choked to death as a result of this simple physical phenomenon, I can well imagine what the sudden, instant reabsorption of a similar physical substance animated by some form of self-generated energy would do to the medium.

A 'know all' who suddenly switched on a powerful torch 'to expose the fraud' for his own personal aggrandisement nearly killed a genuine physical medium under test conditions with my father. It was the last time Pop carried out physical tests without a personally vetted team of investigators under rigorous control.

With Eddie and his small circle, infra-red light and IR photography (then in its infancy) were allowed, and any reasonable course of investigation was welcome. Even Ma, who disliked physical phenomena, especially in deep darkness, felt neither fear nor doubt during these proceedings.

At one of Eddie's sittings with my parents a live pigeon materialized and flew round the room. (According to well-informed researchers this is not an uncommon form of manifestation.)

'Simple,' your sceptic says confidently. 'The man bred racing pigeons.'

A legitimate point, but not a conclusive one, when the same pigeon, having flown round the darkened room, in *red* light, then perched on Eddie's head before dematerializing under the eyes of all the sitters.

If it was an illusion it was a very good one indeed, and one which would have put Eddie Partridge in the front ranks of the world's stage magicians.

I have performed in shows with some of the top magicians who worked with birds, Channing Pollock, 'Cody' Codell and others, and even seen the sleight-of-hand manipulations performed by gulli-gulli men at Port Said, Aden, etc.; and my father knew rather more about prestidigitation than I do. Pop stated categorically that the pigeon materialized, and Ma confirmed that it dematerialized. So I accept their word for it.

Self-hypnosis? Mass hypnosis? Multi-hallucination? All these easily-trotted-out explanations are offered, but never demonstrated by the persons 'explaining it away'. The simplest explanation is that it happened the way my parents told it to me.

The message content of the 'evidence' was, to all of us, the whole *raison d'être* of the operation; and this was amazingly accurate in the prediction of coming events.

This was the period between 1936 and 39, and the content of the messages, which purported to come from discarnate entities identifying themselves as family relatives gave my father and mother more than sufficient evidence to convince them that they were genuine and valid prophecies from well-identified sources.

Some of the predictions about the coming war were extraordinary and horribly accurate, even down to the dreadful evil of the mass murder of civilians and the takeover by Hitler's forces of most of Europe.

Yet all through the messages, which of course weren't all

as doom-laden as these, there was the theme of war fought between good and evil – light and darkness – in which the light would gain the upper hand but only after enormous sacrifice.

My parents, and indeed each of us, were told that we would survive, and that we had a job to do. Tony and I would both serve in the coming war, Tony in the army, and I in the RAF. Not, to my intense disappointment, as a pilot (which was the summit of my pre-war ambition), but I would fly a lot (which is precisely what happened to me).

Even by stretching the mathematical laws of chance to their limit, there isn't much of a 'probability factor' in all those predictions being a hit. Yet they were one hundred per cent correct.

Another of Eddie's remarkable abilities was his great gift of healing. In the final analysis, the determining factor in a successful healing is the basic relationship between the healer and the one in need of healing. After all, if you have no faith in your doctor his chances of healing you are fairly remote, with or without the use of the latest wonder-drugs.

I recall, with great clarity, the day my father returned home from a visit to Eddie Partridge and described as near a miracle as he had ever seen. While Pop and Eddie were chatting in the shop, arranging their next sitting, the door burst open and in rushed a girl of about fourteen, crying hysterically. She was obviously suffering from an acute form of acne, and her face was a mass of angry spots and boils. While Eddie comforted her, she cried out pathetically: 'Look at me, Uncle Eddie! It's horrible! I'm so ugly, I'm going to throw myself over the cliffs!'

My father was certain that she meant it and was very distressed.

Eddie smiled that marvellous grin of his: 'No you're not, dear. Everything is going to be fine. I'll take it away from you.' As he said so, he passed his hand over the girl's face and wiped away the condition. She stopped crying immediately. Eddie told her to go home and lie down – then to come and see him later. The girl left the shop quite calmly, closing the door quietly behind her.

'She'll be all right. You'll see, Adam,' Eddie reassured my father. Then they both said a short prayer.

About an hour later, the shop bell tinkled and the same girl virtually danced into the shop. She rushed over to Eddie and hugged him affectionately. 'Look at me, Uncle Eddie,' she laughed as she spoke, beaming all over her now radiant face.

Pop examined her skin closely, and confirmed the evidence of his amazed eyes. There wasn't a mark on it – no scars, no redness. He told me his sense of wonder was as great as his sense of relief at the outcome of what could have been a tragedy.

Let's take stock of these proceedings. For a start, there was absolutely no doubt about my father's wonder and awe at the healing, for he had come home immediately to tell us about it while it was fresh in his mind.

Years later the suggestion was made that identical twins had been used. A neat theory, if the first sister had been a marvellously accomplished actress. But the girl didn't have a twin.

Several medical friends have made the point that the girl was in puberty and hysterical, and they tell me that such a skin condition is often caused and aggravated by such circumstances. However, a total cure of the symptoms took place in about an hour. Even modern antibiotics and anti-inflammatory preparations such as penicillin and hydrocortisone, need time to work their 'miracle' cures. The most impressive factor in the whole business was the completely unmarked face of the girl on her delighted return.

Eddie's healing power (for which he claimed he was only a channel) seems to have stimulated the natural antibody defences of the girl's system and, by calming the hysteria, to have accelerated the whole tissue regeneration process by an abnormally high factor. That is the explanation one or two close medical friends have offered.

Eddie was shy of his abilities in healing and mediumship, and only discussed them with genuine researchers like my father. He was never on an ego trip.

One day Pop was in the shop when a biscuit salesman breezed in, all beer and bonhomie, a large, cheery extrovert. As he had his order book poised, the largest black cast-iron weight – about ten pounds or so of solid metal – quietly rose straight up in the air from its normal position on the counter, hovered a few inches above the wooden surface then moved across it in a flat trajectory and silently descended onto the other end of the counter. At the same time a bundle of hanging paper-bags whirled round on its retaining string, like a propeller.

'Jesus Christ! What the bloody hell's going on?' yelled the startled salesman.

Eddie was embarrassed by this sudden impromptu display of telekinesis. 'Must be the wind,' he said lamely.

'Wind be buggered! I'm off!' shouted the salesman and, clutching his order book like a protecting talisman, rushed out of the shop.

'He must be a wonderful physical medium,' was Eddie's only comment before he and Pop dissolved into helpless laughter.

The last pre-war experience of the paranormal I had with Eddie Partridge occurred just before the outbreak of hostilities. I have already given an account of it in *The Long Banana Skin,* but it was so outstanding that I'd like to retell it.

The year 1939 had given us a good summer, which was gently fading into a mild autumn with warm, clear nights. We all felt the storm of war gathering over Europe, and I was young enough to feel apprehensive about my chances in the coming holocaust, even though Eddie and other mediums had told me I would survive it.

Eddie sensed my tension on this visit and smilingly reassured me: 'You don't want to worry about that, Michael,' he said, though I hadn't expressed any of my doubts and fears. 'Tell you what, Adam,' he turned to my father, 'will you drive us out into the country? It's not far and there's something I want to show Michael.'

We duly drove out a few miles, into the Weald of Kent - those peaceful sheltered valleys that are one of the most attractive features of the Garden of England. Eddie asked Pop to draw into the side of the country road, then we got out and followed him down a short, narrow track that led to some woods at the foot of the valley.

The night was calm and quite warm, with a few lazy clouds drifting across the moonlit sky. We walked silently in single file through the lush ferns that now rustled round us. The dense underbrush continued as we passed into the thick clumps of trees which made up the small wood. Here the light was considerably reduced, yet Eddie continued to lead the way effortlessly.

Quite unexpectedly, we came out of the clusters of saplings and mature trees into a small clearing, which must have been centrally placed in the wood, and there Eddie stopped. The moon had come out from behind a large billowing cloud and now lit the whole scene almost as brightly as daylight, but with a soft silvery light. You could almost hear the silence.

Eddie turned to me as I stood a few feet behind him just in front of my father. He smiled, and gestured to me to listen. Then he turned and, in a low voice, halfway between a whistle and a word, gave one strange, short, gentle call.

Immediately, from every corner of the wood, the birds, the beasts, even the insects and, I felt, every tree and plant, answered him!

It was a great, joyous, chorus of greeting to a much loved friend.

There was no 'alarm' in that spontaneous answer - just a massive response of nature to nature: like attracting like.

Tears streamed down my face and I could see my father crying too - marvellous natural tears of joy that seemed to wash away the fears and doubts that had assailed me, reaffirming that nature is far stronger than man alone.

I shall never forget that moment!

6 The Possessed Publican and Dragon Power

During the last forty-four years I have met many publicans and inn-keepers and have found most of them to be generous, good-hearted people, of an outgoing and cheerful disposition. Their trade leaves them open to a wealth of human experience and a lot of temptation, but seldom, I should imagine, to the sort of weird experiences that befell L., a publican of Dover.

The outward appearance of this mild, apparently normal man, middle-aged, slight in build and neat in appearance from his carefully polished shoes to his neatly waxed 'snail's horns' moustache, gave no indication of the fury to come.

He was not at all the popular image of a publican. Here was no jolly, beaming 'mine host' with the bright personality and earthy repartee that would make his hostelry a sought-after social rendezvous. Quite the reverse. L. was a man of moderate habits with a retiring personality not leavened with much sense of humour.

Yet his pub became a focus of attention amongst the locals, and invariably seemed to be full. In fact, for a time it was a resounding success, and L. himself was the unlikely reason for the interest.

The building itself was typical of that undistinguished, solidly-built genre of public house that was the mainstay of Victorian brewing enterprises. It was heavily furnished, with dark oak beams, a massive oaken bar equipped with porcelain handles for the beer engines and much pewter and many horse brasses in evidence.

Upstairs was the modest, spotlessly clean apartment where L. and his wife lived, and this, too, was as prosaic as the solid Victorian respectability of the pub beneath. It was rather more modern in its style of decoration, which was in the vogue of the 1930s – with a porcelain-tiled fireplace, ducks on the wall and typical cheerful chintzes.

But L., the landlord, and not the pub, was the attraction, and the reason was that he had developed an extraordinary talent. L. could tell the winner of the 3.30. For that matter, he could, with amazing accuracy, also predict the winners of other horse races – be they the 1.30, 2.30, 4.30 or however many races were being run that day. His 'hit' rate was extraordinary – provided that he didn't bet himself.

Strangely enough I went through a similar phase when I was developing subjective clairvoyance. I did it as an exercise and, provided that I didn't boast about it or show off in any way, I could accurately 'hit' around ninety per cent – about the same accuracy rate that I was getting with thought transference (now called ESP – Extra-Sensory Perception). If I tried to include a profit motive, either in cash, by asking Ma, who enjoyed a flutter, to bet for me or as a demonstration of 'cleverness', it went wrong. With L. it went wrong in a dreadful way.

L. was either a subjective or an objective clairvoyant – I believe it was the former – and his uncanny accuracy in picking winners became an obsession with him. He developed the strange ability in his middle life, and it surprised him as much as it amazed his clientele. If I remember the circumstances correctly, the predictive faculty revealed itself when he took over the public house in Dover, whereupon the pub, which had always done reasonable business because of its convenient location in the town, soon became almost a place of pilgrimage, certainly among the betting fraternity but also among the locals – for after all, few people haven't enjoyed a flutter at some time or other.

Even so the whole thing would probably have petered out
in the normal course of events, had it not been for a character
flaw in L.'s personality. This colourless, prosaic man was
inordinately vain, and the sudden popularity occasioned by
his surprising acquisition of precognitive ability turned his
head. He began to believe he was a great psychic and attracted to himself a low-level 'intelligence' which eventually took
over the unfortunate man's body. It is, of course, debatable
what it was – but that it proved to be monstrous in its sub-
bestiality was demonstrated all too horribly when Eddie
Partridge and four colleagues fought and won a temporary
victory over this appalling manifestation of evil.

In one way, it was reminiscent of the battle fought by
m'tutor, William Hope-Jones, and his friend for the soul of
the Divinity student in Cambridge all those years before.

The take-over of L.'s body began with his determination to
make closer contact with whatever 'intelligences' were
providing the information which had turned him from a dull
publican into a sought-after minor prophet. To further this
aim, L. started sitting in a room over the saloon bar after the
pub closed for lunch.

At first, he used the glass and alphabet method of
communication. The glass quickly responded to these
sittings, and a character emerged which identified itself as
an entity called 'Old Pal'. To these totally inexperienced,
and not-too-well equipped seekers (either spiritually or
intellectually) everything seemed to go well. Predictions of
the outcome of horse and greyhound races and even local
football matches came through with remarkable accuracy,
and soon the pub had achieved an even greater notoriety.

Soon, to facilitate betting, the sittings were extended
beyond the afternoon seances to sessions after closing time.
L. blossomed, preening himself in the local limelight like a
scraggy fowl that suddenly finds itself turned into a
peacock. In short, he became well and truly hooked. Soon, he
could hardly wait for lunchtime and closing time, to get his
fingers on the agile glass.

Then things started to go wrong. It was the sort of nightmare situation which Harold Pinter has built into most of his work – the gradual inexorable take-over of a man's comfortable and seemingly secure life by some weird and powerful personality.

It was the manifestation of some monstrous entity of the id, if that's how you like to think of it, or the possession of a human body by an earthbound and intensely evil discarnate entity.

Dire warnings began to be transmitted through the glass as it darted from letter to letter. L. must '*burn* all the bedding'; 'get rid of the dog' (which, incidentally, refused to enter the room when L. was sitting), etc. All these warnings and threats were of the 'or else' variety.

Slowly, and with no more than a terrified token resistance from L., 'Old Pal' took over the petrified publican's life. It was after L. had, on this monstrous entity's instruction, smashed up a brand new radiogram which was his wife's pride and joy that she decided to plead for help.

A sympathetic friend who knew about Eddie Partridge and his knowledge of psychic phenomena put her in touch with the kindly grocer, and Eddie, after hearing what it was all about, called in my father to assist him in a Rescue Circle. After one contact with L. both of them knew that the only way they could hope to rid the publican of his overshadowing companion was to make the entity manifest itself physically instead of merely communicating through the glass, and then deal with it.

The principle of the Rescue Circle was not a new one. This type of operation, to help discarnate entities who were unaware that they had been through the death change, was the province of experienced mediums and researchers such as Eileen Garrett, Conan Doyle, Oliver Lodge, and a number of others. It requires strong nerves, complete mental discipline and, sometimes, a strong body to restrain the subject of the Rescue, should the manifesting entity become violently disturbed while operating through the medium.

It all sounds like do-it-yourself exorcism, which is sometimes practised by amateurs, with disastrous results. It is not an operation to be undertaken without a great deal of knowledge, faith, courage and preparation.

Whether the Rescue Circle assists a discarnate entity bewildered by its timeless situation to manifest through a medium and, thereby, be contacted in another body – when the situation can be clarified, so that the entity may progress – or the whole operation releases some confused personality locked in the deep subconscious of a possessed person is a matter for argument. What is apparent is that, whatever the explanation, the results seem generally to be helpful and constructive. They are also exhausting for the sitters.

It is, of course, normally the province of the various established churches to perform exorcism. I have met at least two exorcists. One of them is Dom Robert Petitpierre, who is a down-to-earth fundamentalist. He is also a great scholar who deals with his problems in a way which is totally rational, at the same time backed by experienced faith.

The same could be said for my father, Eddie Partridge, the priest involved and Eddie's brother-in-law, although a Rescue Circle is not a form of exorcism as practised by the great religions. It is rather a group therapy of a specialized kind.

Eddie and my father had both, separately and together, assisted at such operations with marked success; otherwise they would never have undertaken L.'s case. A qualified physician was invited, both as an observer and to monitor the proceedings.

After a short prayer following a ritual 'cleansing' of the room – which had already been swept and cleaned and stripped of non-essentials – L. went into a deep trance – something which, so far, had not occurred in his dabbling with the paranormal. He started to breathe deeply and loudly, and then became violently agitated. The room went ice-cold. Suddenly, the whole place reeked of evil, and the sitters, who included L.'s wife, actually gagged at the stench of stale liquor that emanated from the dribbling mouth of the entranced L.

In fact L. was moderate in his drinking habits, and in no way could he have been the source of such a powerful and foetid smell of stale beer and wine.

At the same time, his slight, middle-aged body seemed to expand and grow, as had happened with Alan Dawkins, my cousin. The difference was that although that particular manifestation had been deeply alarming, no actual feeling of evil had been generated – there had been no reason why it should. In L.'s case the manifesting entity was so appallingly sub-bestial and gross that, as it took over L.'s body, it virtually impressed on him its own foul aura and repulsive exudations.

L.'s face, in my father's words, had become a bloated, hideous caricature, swollen and mottled, and his thin lips, normally primly closed, hung open, framing a wet, slobbering mouth. His eyes bulged from his head and seemed to roll horribly – a maniacal glare accentuating their watery bloodshot state.

Had not Eddie, his brother-in-law, Pop, the priest and the doctor been such experienced stalwarts, with complete faith in the ultimate triumph of good over evil, I am sure that they would have made a bolt for the door. Poor Mrs L. was completely overcome and collapsed sobbing. The doctor comforted her but she stoutly refused to leave her husband or whatever it was that had taken his place.

L.'s horribly distorted mouth poured out a stream of the foulest language and abuse, and his breath stank of decay. My father, Eddie and the priest knew that if they didn't prove the stronger the results would be terrible, especially in the damage which would be done to the mind and body of the frail publican.

Had they physically attacked this hideous manifestation, as had Uncle Billy, at Cambridge when he fought that materialized evil, they would all have been badly injured.

For L. would have possessed the physical strength of a raving lunatic.

However, the weapons they used in this struggle for the soul of the publican were far more powerful and effective than mere physical strength. The depth and intensity of their prayers seemed to generate a force-field which literally bound the manifesting entity, enclosing L. and the hideous being that possessed his body inside a 'cage' of power and light.

Gradually, its bullying, mindless, raging fury seemed to wilt and then as suddenly as the dreadful intensity of its being had manifested, it collapsed as though some foul gas which had inflated its victim's whole body had suddenly dissipated, leaving L. a pathetic heap on the floor. The poor man just lay there until they managed to help him back into his chair, from which he threw himself down on his knees, babbling out hysterical thanks for his deliverance.

My father told us that they had all expected a long and strenuous argument with the controlling entity, as had happened at other similar circles; but because the being was so low in intelligence and so brutish in its mentality they scared it off by the power of their own positive thinking. They all felt exhausted, as though drained of power, and as they comforted the weeping publican and his sobbing wife it seemed that a dark shadow had left the room.

They flung open the windows and all traces of the dreadful smells quickly dispersed. Then and there, they undertook a further cleansing of the atmosphere by prayer – charging the aura of the room with positive power. Immediately it recovered its normal cosy atmosphere and seemed to be filled with light and warmth.

While the distraught L. calmed down and his wife regained her composure, the rescuers extracted their solemn promise on the Bible that they would never again dabble in the occult.

L. had been given a second chance and, for a time, he was frightened enough to keep away from anything to do with the paranormal. But his vanity started, once again, to gain the upper hand.

The jeering clients of his pub in Dover pushed him over the brink.

'What's wrong, L.? Can't you do it any more?'

'Lost your power then?'

'I always said it was a trick!'

'Go on, old man, give me just one winner and I'll believe you!'

'Go on, L.! Show us what a bloody wizard you are!'

L. managed to hold out for a time, mainly through terror and his wife's entreaties, but he eventually gave in. He died, raving mad, in the padded cell of a violent ward in a Kent mental hospital.

He was a dreadful example of my father's warning: 'In this area of human behaviour motive is everything.'

The wider the spectrum of the paranormal we experienced, the more firmly convinced my father became that these manifestations were a natural extension of our everyday survival mechanism.

He told me: 'Everyone, to a greater or lesser degree, has this set of faculties and abilities lying dormant in their system, and war, with its enforced survival demands, is one of the channels through which nature awakens this sleeping dragon.'

My father believed that the original concept of 'dragon power', as identified by the Chinese and, later, the Western philosophies, was an allegorical statement of paranormal power in man. In Chinese literature a wealth of identities are given to the various types of dragon, which are, like the sleeping powers in man, normally neutral and quiescent but can be either beneficent or malevolent to man, according to the way in which they are invoked, awakened and used.

The Chinese concept of dragon power is basically the same concept as Britain's own archaic image of the dragon overcome by St George.

The worm, the dragon, the serpent – beneficent or malevolent – all represent the natural primeval force in man, often manifested on a purely physical plane by poltergeist (noisy ghost) phenomena which are usually traceable to the unconscious generation of coarse ectoplasm by young people in puberty. Once awakened it is powerful – and highly dangerous, unless controlled. This is the sort of power that manifested through those two contrasting victims of the darkness – the unfortunate possessed publican and the maniacal Führer of Nazi Germany.

The same basic power – controlled by reason, rationale and motive and carefully released in small potent quantities – can provide the mental climate that gives rise to the great quantum jumps in human knowledge. Jung described these manifestations of the latent power of men's minds as part of 'the collective unconscious', which he defined as a vast contactable reservoir of knowledge and abilities inherited through the ages by succeeding generations of men and women, the *true heritage* of man.

He also stated that there exist, as entities within this incalculably vast field of the collective unconscious, archetypes or living symbols which embody man's highest and lowest characteristics. Extremes of the concept would be the Christ figure of supreme sacrifice and total compassion or the dark destroyers of man's highest values such as Attila, Genghis Khan, Adolf Hitler and Stalin.

In the Chinese and Egyptian civilizations, long before the Christian era, the great natural powers of thunder and lightning, tempest and typhoon, deluge and drought, famine and plague, earthquake and tidal wave, etc., were deified and embodied in a pantheon of god figures. Their hierarchies had a strict pecking order, just as the Judaeo-Christian religion allotted a precise power structure to the thrones, Archangels, Cherubim, Seraphim, Eloihim, Beni Eloihim and Angels, right down to the opposition in the

shape of Satan and his generals and all the rest of the
legions of Hell.

This complex 'battle order' goes right down, in strict order
of rank, through basic elemental powers to undines, the
spirits of water; gnomes and trolls, the spirits of earth;
sylphs, the spirits of air and salamanders, the spirits of fire.
These complex invisible power structures apparently
controlled all aspects of natural phenomena which plagued
or benefited man, and had to be propitiated and properly
respected if the chances of survival were to be kept at a safe
level.

The Chaldeans, Persians, Minoans, Greeks, Romans,
Etruscans *et al,* followed the same pattern in their
pantheons of natural forces. To all of them, the normal and
the paranormal were so totally interwoven as to make the
one indistinguishable from the other, and with minor
alterations this hierarchy still holds the imaginations of
enormous numbers of the population of the earth.

Viewed objectively, and I assure you *without* blasphemous intent, there seems to be little basic difference
between the beautiful concepts of Isis, Osiris and Horus and
the Blessed Virgin, God the Father and God the Son. Both
visions of deity are a trinity. Both are worshipped with great
humility and sincerity and are the highest manifestations
of the human spirit, or, as I have come to think of it, the
'Overmind'.

Throughout mythology and legend these hierarchies of
good and evil reappear in many forms. The court of Osiris,
where he is betrayed by Set, his evil brother, is remarkably
reminiscent of King Arthur and his Knights of the Round
Table - and the betrayal of Arthur by Mordred. The legends
of the South and Central American Indians have similar
parallels, and even Christianity's concept of Jesus and the
twelve disciples has a resemblance that cannot be dismissed
as pure coincidence. For there is a clue in the *table*, at which
Osiris and his court met - and in the Round Table of Arthur,
which could expand and contract to accommodate different

numbers of Knights. There is the table of the last supper, which is represented as much as a focus for a meeting or a sitting as for the mystical meal, and the table at which Odin and the Norse gods sat, in Asgaard, to drink and eat their warriors' fill. All of them seem to represent a *focal point*, a meeting place, a set of order, a religious function of cosmos.

Also, in one way or another, all these legends, myths or religious beliefs are associated with a quest that is indirectly associated with the death of a god. In the case of the Egyptian religion it was the quest by Isis, the sister of Osiris for the dismembered parts of the god's body scattered by Set throughout the land. In the quest for the Holy Grail it is the endless search for the cup that was believed to have caught the blood (the Essence) of Christ on the cross and that can be found only by the peerless knight *'sans peur et sans reproche'*.

In Christianity the circle of Jesus - i.e. His Disciples - were carefully chosen for their devotion to Christ and for their paranormal abilities, for each of them showed these powers of healing and prevision during the period of proselytizing that followed the Crucifixion. Their quest was to spread the word and to build the Church of Christ.

All these circles of disciples, colleagues, knights, etc. seem to be based on the figure twelve plus one: the twelve tribes of Israel plus Moses; the Knights of Arthur plus Arthur; the court of Osiris; and the twelve disciples plus the master, Christ. Could *all* these legends, mythologies and religious beliefs be based on the one awe-inspiring presence which, from the beginning of man's life on earth, has been the untouchable Power beyond?

To me, they are *zodiacal* in their archetypal manifestation; and that is *not* intended in any way as a blasphemous statement - only as a possible set of parameters to contain the essence of the legend. The hierarchical courts of Osiris; the court of Arthur in Avalon, where he and his Knights supposedly lie sleeping; Asgaard, the home of the Norse gods; and Valhalla, the heaven of Heroes; even the heaven of Christianity - all seem to me to be part of one concept - the end of the quest - the ultimate peace - the perfect tranquillity - immutable and eternal.

To man, the earth beneath him is the place of suffering, the base for torment, his struggle for survival - while *above* him he sees the eternal, which, by its seasons, controls his life.

Therefore, around the mysteries of the sun, quickening the corn and bringing the game that he hunts to the plains; and around the moon, lighting the darkness of his fears as he huddles in his cave or his grass hut at night, he weaves a cosmic pattern, an ordered system of worship to comfort him in terms of ordeal and to bring order into his life. This becomes a dogma and a Credo, and, in his quest for cosmos - an *order out of chaos* - he creates his calendars, his predictive computers, positioning marks, rocks and stones in circles and other zodiacal calculators. He tries to bring cosmic order out of chaos and to find a reason for his being other than that dictated by the raw necessities of survival.

I've never been remotely interested in politics, because its very pragmatic attitude seems to me to be destructive. For me, it is the quest that matters, not some materialist result that will justify any means to accomplish it. In fact it seems that closed systems are by their very nature the death of creativity, because they reject heresy, and heretical thinking is the springboard for creative visualization. In a closed totalitarian society the whole system becomes static and no further movement forward is possible because it disturbs the *status quo* of the establishment. In such a system the archetypes of the collective unconscious sleep, like Arthur's Knights, waiting for the call of the human spirit to cry out against its enforced oppression.

Some of these archetypes manifested themselves to our researches in the thirties, in the form of the guides who controlled various mediums that we were sitting with. Zulus, Chinamen, Red Indians and Arab scholars seemed to be favourite choices.

In many cases it proved to be self-delusion – the mumblings and weird chantings that issued from the mediums in trance sounding more like the sort of Hollywood dialogue given to the faithful M'Gombo in African epics shot on some back lot at a studio in Los Angeles: 'You Michael – me M'Gombo. Great Zulu Chief.'

Another favourite was the Red Indian 'guide', who also gave a fair impersonation of any Hollywood actor playing the role of the 'Noble Savage': 'I come from Great White Spirit!'

Chinese 'guides' closely followed the then popular 'Charlie Chan' character: 'My name Po-Hi – Chinese doctor from Imperial Palace', followed by a lot of 'Ls' for 'Rs' and a whole mass of clichés – supposedly direct quotations from Confucius.

On the other hand, a number of guides who came through to control various trance mediums, like Bernard Rodin, Mrs Estelle Roberts, Mrs Helen Hughes, Arthur Badhuri and Joseph Benjamin – all of whom father knew well and sat with many times, often at our home circle – certainly seemed to project entirely different powerful personalities from those of their mediums.

Obviously this area of the paranormal is as fraught with booby traps as a minefield. You simply have to use your loaf – as the Cockney says – and consider what the guide has to say – for, in the end, what determines the validity of all of this research is whether the prophetic content of the messages can be checked for accuracy.

I would sooner accept advice from a manifesting entity who brought with him or her a feeling of presence completely different from that of the medium and an aura that inspired confidence – plus an evidential standard of communication that gave ample proof of precognition – than be impressed by some ham performance of a dodgy war dance straight out of a Western about the Apache raids.

Fortunately we had the experience of contacting a number of most impressive personalities through these

mediums who were only too happy to provide evidence of
their validity in order to get over to us some communication
that did indeed help our researches, or assist us in some
constructive way. It was these splendid exceptions which
made it all worthwhile, and through a number of these
extraordinary archetypal guides we received some remarkable information as to the future complexities of life, that
both helped us to meet and overcome the difficulties that
loomed ahead and enabled us to bring comfort and evidence
of survival to a number of grief-stricken people.

Having been through some exceedingly grim circumstances myself, I know how immensely valuable this kind of
guidance can be. So, whether the messages came through a
guide who was some facet of the personality of the medium
or via the manifestation of a discarnate entity who actually
had been a Red Indian, Zulu, Chinese or Arab or, for that
matter, Eskimo, Pigmy, Aborigine or other incarnate
human being at some previous time on earth, if what was
said was valid and genuinely helpful I, for one, was grateful
for the help and guidance.

More recently a favourite type of guide, manifesting, or
purporting to do so, through various circles and groups,
often claims to be Venusian or Martian. These two archetypal spacemen became less popular when Mars was found to
have no life on its surface and the atmosphere of Venus
hostile to any ordinary humanoid type of extraterrestial
life form. Nowadays archetypal guides often say that they
come from the stars – especially since the claims of Von
Daniken became so widespread and well publicized.

I'm not knocking them, nor their mediums' belief in them.
I only say that in our own case, we judged their presence by
the content of their messages. If they were valid, then we
accepted the validity of their communicators; and that, I
feel, is the only sane attitude to adopt.

Over the past forty or more years I have encountered a
number of guides whose personalities were outstanding
enough to register strongly with me and to remain in my

memory. Whether they were facets of their own mediums'
personalities or not, really doesn't matter very much. I
enjoyed meeting them, and they had some fascinating
things to say, all of which later proved to be true; and their
healing, if that was their forte, was invariably excellent. So,
from any point of view, they, whoever they were, were part of
a remarkable experience and one that I am grateful to have
known.

We had a fascinating encounter with an archetypal
entity just before the war through a young physician, who
was then setting up practice in Folkestone. Dr J. was, I
imagine, in his early thirties, when, with his young wife, he
moved into the town, having been in India for some time,
with either the Civil Service, or the Army. He met my
mother at the bridge club and, in the course of time, my
father and the young doctor discussed the 'paranormal', in
which area Dr J. was deeply interested.

Being a true researcher by nature, and having a first-class
brain as well, he had become greatly interested in the attitudes and beliefs of the different peoples of the sub-continent,
and inevitably this led to a scholarly study of the Indian
approach to the paranormal. He had been conducting a
number of experiments alone and, for this reason, had
become involved with a problem about which he was beginning to be worried.

During the initial phases of his researches he had followed the Indian approach to the Overmind by meditation
and concentration; and he had succeeded in contacting
what he believed to be a discarnate entity. While meditat-
ing, in a relaxed position, either sitting or lying down, Dr J.
held his hands together with the fingertips touching, the
idea being to allow this part of his body to be activated by
another intelligence. It is really the same as automatic
writing, or any other manifestation of 'bio-kinesis', i.e.
control of the medium's body by an external force.

Dr J. had worked out a simple code for communication by
rocking his hands back and forth – so many movements

indicated the five vowels and then the consonants in turn. One rock backwards was 'A', two 'E', three 'I', etc., for the vowels; the same sequential process worked forwards for the consonants – one for 'B', two for 'C', three for 'D', etc.

It was similar to table-turning, but because it was effortless to operate it could be performed at high speed – and, as with the glass, Ouija or planchette type of operation it had a built-in disadvantage. As I have already pointed out, the easier and more facile a method of contacting some other intelligence, the less effort or 'cockpit drill' is required to operate it, and therefore, the greater the margin for error and loss of control. I saw Dr J. demonstrate this method of communication to my father, and it really was startling to see the speed with which the 'answers' to Pop's questions came through his hands.

Being such a sensible and well-balanced person, Dr J. was completely open-minded as to whether this manifestation was a product of his own subconscious mind or was due to some contact with a discarnate entity. In order to pin down the phenomenon and define more precisely what was, in fact, causing its manifestation, Dr J. formulated a series of tests and specific questions which would depend for their valid outcome on their *total* accuracy as predictions.

One of these tests was most impressive. Dr J. had been given the information, via his hand code, that, if he went up to London by train on a certain day at a specific hour, and stood in the forecourt of Charing Cross Station, he would see walking, on the opposite side of the Strand, a young woman, who was minutely described, with a small dog.

Sounds ridiculous! But the description was so detailed, with times and date, etc. (I believe the time was set at midday) that, really, to *disprove* the information, Dr J. decided that he would indulge himself to the extent of carrying out the requirements set out so meticulously.

Feeling rather foolish, even in the cause of science, he set out on the specific date and by the train which had been selected by the entity. At a few minutes to noon by the Charing Cross clock he found himself waiting impatiently for the appearance, or non-appearance, of the lady in question.

To his amazement, as the clock struck the hour, there, on the pavement opposite the entrance to the station, the lady so minutely described walked into view, complete with the dog.

Anyone who knows London will realize that, even in the pre-war years, the Strand was hardly the ideal place to walk a dog, especially as there are other places quite near which would be far more suitable.

Dr J. was so astounded that he didn't attempt to contact the woman. He was in any case a shy man by nature, and so professionally inhibited that he would have been disinclined to go up to a stranger – a female one at that – and say: 'Good morning, madam. I am a doctor conducting an experiment in the paranormal. Can you tell me your name and explain to me what prompted you to walk your dog, today, at this precise hour?'

Those days were far more strictly governed by social and medical protocol, and Dr J. had too much respect for his profession to risk being had up before a magistrate for molesting. So he returned by the next train to Folkestone, firmly convinced that the predictive communication had been a valid one.

Of course he also considered self-hallucination but, in view of the minutely-detailed description of events and his own reluctance to carry out what he considered a rather foolish test, he had to admit to himself that this was a real puzzler.

Besides, a problem had arisen that he was much relieved to share with my father, eagerly seeking his advice. To put it bluntly, the whole operation was getting out of control and in this phase of the phenomenon the situation bore some resemblance to the case of L., the publican from Dover, except that Dr J., a highly intelligent and well-disciplined

person, recognized the dangers immediately and promptly
stopped the experiments. Or tried to - because he was
seriously alarmed to find himself waking up in the middle of
the night, with his hands, fingers touching in the communication mode, rocking rhythmically back and forth.

Once his alarm at waking in this way was over, Dr J., who
had a good working knowledge of psychology, thought that
his subconscious mind had become entrained; but when the
phenomenon was repeated and he found himself waking up
several times at night with his hands now 'flying back and
forth', he became seriously concerned.

Pop helped him to shut down the contact with whatever
was controlling him and suggested a sitting to try to obtain a
trance manifestation of the entity - if that was what was
causing the problem. This wasn't just a case of an
inquisitive amateur mind playing with the paranormal. Dr
J. was professional to his fingertips; yet even he had been
'hooked' with a problem which was basically a minor form
of possession.

By what? The question instantly springs to mind, just as it
did with my father in 1938, and obviously the first thing to
do was to pin down exactly what form of entity was
manifesting through the doctor's hands. The answer
seemed to be that here was a discarnate intelligence trying
urgently to take control.

Pop decided to hold a sitting. Both my brother Tony and I
were present and neither of us is ever likely to forget the
occasion. There was, however, never the slightest intention
of holding a Rescue Circle. Had this been the object of the
exercise, the sitters would not have included my mother,
brother and me, but would have incorporated Eddie
Partridge and other experienced stalwarts in that area of
the paranormal. This was intended to be a probe, if you like,
to determine what was the most likely cause of Dr J.'s
phenomenon - nothing more. Even so as Mrs J. was at that
time some months pregnant, my parents thought it unwise
that she should sit with us.

Dr J. had already sat with us at table sittings, at which an entity had manifested, identifying itself as an Indian. The Hindustani language was used – tapped out phonetically – and the fact that it *was* Hindustani was confirmed by another sitter who, like the doctor, had lived in India. But the bulk of the message was in English – of a sort – presumably because Hindi is not normally written in European lettering.

The use of Hindustani was not particularly convincing, because it could well have been the subconscious manifestation of Dr J.'s own knowledge of the language, and the predictive content of the message was not at that time verifiable. Therefore, the object of the second sitting was to try and get something more concrete in the way of evidence.

I remember that there was plenty of daylight left, so I presume we must have held the sitting in late summer, and I do recall that Pop drew the curtains of some of the windows to cut down the light. However, the drawing-room, where we were sitting instead of the little room which was reserved for more complex operations, was still provided with plenty of light, and none of us had any feeling of apprehension.

Surprisingly Dr J. almost immediately went into trance, which, up till then, he had given no indication of doing. He exhibited signs of distress and was obviously having some difficulty in adjusting to whatever entity was attempting to manifest through him. This wasn't too singular with a first-time trance experience and no one was unduly alarmed. My father helped Dr J. to calm down in order to 'bring through' the manifesting entity.

Seeing this sort of bald statement in black and white always gives me a jolt because it sounds so barbaric and primitive, but by this time my father, and the rest of the family had some six years of experience behind them, and this sort of manifestation was no more unusual to us than that of seeing a subject under deep hypnosis.

My mother, Tony and I were all yawning heavily; obviously considerable amounts of power were being drawn from us; and by now, Dr J. was breathing deeply, and guttural sounds began to issue from his lips. It was still not disturbing and in fact was quite in line with the normal threshold of trance when the manifesting entity is taking control of the medium's body.

The temperature had dropped significantly, and there was a feeling of power in the atmosphere of the drawing-room. Had my father picked up any indication of a negative force at work, he would have quickly brought the proceedings to a close. Then slowly, from the seemingly involuntary twitchings and uncoordinated body movements of Dr J., as he slipped through the portals of trance, a definite personality emerged and seemed to take over his body.

Communication with this entity, or whatever was manifesting through Dr J., was, of necessity, difficult, but this was not unexpected. We already had some experiences of foreign personalities manifesting through other mediums. We experienced the sort of communication difficulties I have met among tribes and individuals in Africa and S. America, when we used a combination of signs and acted-out demonstrations, backed up by a few words of English and the other language involved. On this occasion none of us spoke Hindi, except Dr J., and he was the channel, so that language could not be used at all. Of course, the entity spoke *some* language fluently, although with the usual difficulties experienced by a controlling personality in an 'alien' body. It was, presumably, Hindustani – but then Dr J. also spoke fluent Hindustani, so that could be accounted for quite naturally.

Always you have to rely on experience and intuition to distinguish between self-delusion, deliberate fraud or a genuinely different personality in the medium's body. This was obviously the last; Dr J. was far too intelligent for the first of these alternatives and too honest for the second.

In reply to questions like: 'What is your name?' 'Where do you come from?' 'What did you do in life?' 'How did you pass over?' – there were obvious difficulties in understanding, but no more than you would have between two living people of different races and languages.

The replies made sense. But the name sounded odd – something, I recall, like, Ay Ay Ay. One would have suspected something more like Abdul, Ali, Achmed or any name more usually associated with the sub-continent. The place was given as Lahore and, surprisingly, his job in life seemed to have been that of a professional wrestler. He conveyed this to us quite simply by standing up and using Dr J.'s body to act out the sort of stance and movements that a professional wrestler would make.

In writing, that sounds even weirder than usual but, strangely enough, *in situ*, in that warmly lit, bright drawing-room in Folkestone, acted out by the shy, quiet Dr J., whom we all knew and thought of as a friend – it didn't seem at all out of place. But then, if we had been asking a living Indian wrestler what he did for a living, and if he had little or no knowledge of English, he would have acted out his reply in precisely the same way.

I remember well how riveting that strange mime was, as Dr J., with his eyes shut, moved with grace, agility and obviously practised ease to demonstrate the wrestler's holds and throws against an invisible opponent. The feeling was so remarkably real that you could sense the tension of the wrestling bout and almost smell the sweat of fear – because we sensed that here was no amateur bout on friendly terms but a fight to win on *any* terms.

There was nothing evil or malevolent in that demonstration but there was a distinct sense that it was for real. Rather than play-acting it seemed that the entity was using Dr J.'s body to *re-live* an actual wrestling bout.

We all compared notes after the sitting, and I have exchanged viewpoints and memories of it, quite recently, with my brother. We are both agreed that what we saw tallied exactly with a re-enactment of an actual fight.

The last question: 'How did you pass over?' was answered for us in a most dramatic and, at the time, terrifying way.

It seems that the thoughts behind the questions communicate to a genuine manifestation of a mental entity in the same way that fear communicates itself to a dog or a sense of danger or threat is sensed by other animals or, for that matter, by a human being 'tuned' to receive such a contact.

The sense of the last question communicated itself to the entity in control of Dr J.'s body and he answered in mime. In other words: *he enacted his own death.*

The actual feeling of the reality of the wrestling match had so gripped us that my father sensed that the whole thing was approaching some sort of climax. He told me afterwards that he had been about to step in and stop the sitting when the controlling entity made the final moves in the strange dramatic charade which was being acted out before us.

Suddenly it seemed that the doctor's body was caught in a powerful lock followed by a heavy throw. There was no doubt about it, as we saw it. His whole body was lifted up and bent backwards, to crash down in such a terrifyingly unnatural position that it looked at though his back was broken or dislocated. At the same time a terrible scream shrieked out from his open mouth, as though he had uttered his death cry on the breaking of his vertebral column. It was so agonizingly real and unexpected that, with the exception of my father, we sat riveted with shock!

Pop had leapt forward and was kneeling beside the now unconscious doctor, tending to him as he wiped away the condition.

Immediately Dr J.'s contorted body relaxed into a normal posture and he sat up on the drawing-room carpet, obviously somewhat bewildered by being there.

We helped him up and he sat in his chair, apparently none the worse for an experience that had seemed to us, as we sat paralysed with horror, a terminal physical injury. He was neither aware of anything that had happened nor even sore, nor was he conscious of any injury or strain as a result of that terrifying contortion of his body. To him it was as if it had never happened.

The upshot of this extraordinary sitting was that Dr J. quite often sat with our family circle, and that any manifestation of the uncontrolled movements of his hands ceased forthwith.

He continued to be a family friend and a colleague in my father's researches, and his wife presented him, I seem to remember, with a fine baby. We only lost contact with them when, during the war, my father, as an alien, was forced to leave and sell up our home in Folkestone.

Recently, to my delight, he came up to me after a meeting at the Town Hall at Tunbridge Wells and stood shyly in front of me.

His first words were: 'Do you remember me, Michael?'

How could I ever forget him?

7 A Transfiguring Lady

From time to time, presumably to encourage us to absorb the difficult lessons we were being taught, we would receive some outstandingly different pieces of evidence. They reminded me of the old method of encouraging the donkey, by dangling a carrot in front of his nose.

Between 1932 and 1939 we had been through a seven-year course which, in other circumstances, would have earned us each a doctorate. Pop was, by now, a valid healer and a remarkable psychometrist. Ma had stilled her early doubts and fears and, with her natural skill at character reading, could distinguish the phoney from the genuine almost before they got through the front door. She had also been able to provide physical power for a number of sittings, in which evidence of this type of phenomenon was outstanding. There was now no doubt about it: Ma was herself, reluctantly or not, a strong physical medium.

My brother Tony had developed trance mediumship to an advanced degree and his healing had also become very effective. This left me way behind the others, albeit almost free of my stammer, since I had been trained at Eton by the skilful and imposingly large Dr Burgess, who had taught me to speak with 'a swing-and-a-rhythm-and-a-pause-and-a-run'. This odd form of speech gained me a certain fluency in communication, even if quite a few shopkeepers reacted nervously to this strange young man who spoke English like a visiting Martian.

Meanwhile the various nervous moments interspersed with experiences of sheer wonder and the occasional bout of extreme terror opened up my mind during those seven years to a world of imagery that has undoubtedly enabled me to make a living for myself and my family without hurting others. Had I followed my inclinations to be either a professional pilot or a scientist specializing in rockets and unrotated projectiles I would have been used as an instrument for destruction even more than I was used for that purpose during the war.

Those seven years of increasingly intensive study and observed experiences changed my whole life, and the coming war completed the process. In conversation with my father, who on different occasions alone with me was either lightly entranced or 'overshadowed' by another entity or personality, I gained a lot of insight into problems which had fascinated me.

The two personalities that apparently manifested through my father actually altered his whole physiognomy – his face becoming covered with a fine network of lines and somehow taking on a wizened appearance when the 'monk' manifested; and, conversely, rounding out into a plumper version of Pop but distinctly oriental in appearance when he was overshadowed by the 'Chinaman'. Whether or not these two personalities were projections of my father's complex psyche, they certainly changed his whole facial structure, and the message content was fascinating and, in the verifiable cases, proved one hundred per cent correct.

Discussing space-flight and its possibilities I got some answers which have proved to be totally accurate.

Like my contemporary and good friend, Patrick Moore, who is not only a fine astronomer and a riveting lecturer but has a wide-ranging mind which has been deeply into the study of the paranormal, I was totally absorbed in the thirties with the possibilities of space exploration.

Dr Goddard's famous paper, 'A method of Reaching Extreme Altitudes', had been published as early as 1929, but

I only became aware of its content through my father in the mid-thirties.

The questions I particularly wanted answered by the entities manifesting through my father were:

(1) Is there life on Mars or any other planet in the solar system?
(2) Will man reach the moon and other bodies in our system during my lifetime?
(3) Is the rocket the answer to space flight?
(4) Will man react favourably in space?

The answers, whether from my father's own psyche or through the medium of other entities, were enlightening.

1. No! There is no life on Mars because the atmosphere is not conducive to a humanoid form of life. However, there is a manifestation of apparent 'polar caps', giving the appearance of water vapour frozen into ice. This is actually carbon-dioxide. Furthermore, the 'canals' – the surface lines observed by Schiaparelli and later by Lowell and taken to be possible canals – are in fact natural features caused by the arid conditions and internal tectonic and seismic movement in the crust of the red planet.

2. Yes! Man will reach the Moon safely and find nothing living there – but he will make some interesting studies of the origin of the satellite. This will happen in your lifetime, but not for about forty years (spot on!).

Yes! It is possible for man to reach the planets, but, for practical reasons of the need for life-support systems (the actual term used was similar to this contemporary one) which would take up necessary weight and mass – both of which are critical – it is more likely that a probe (the actual term used was 'robot probe') will be used to explore space and that this will act as a near infinite extension of the astronaut (actual term used) and his senses while he will remain behind on earth guiding it by remote control.

3. The rocket is an intermediate method of space flight, but only as a means of projecting the instrumentation or space vehicle (term used) outside the earth's orbit and into outer space. The next stage of development will be a deep space machine utterly unlike a rocket's streamlined shape (for which, in near-vacuo, there is no need) taking its energy from the sun – (solar power). The final stage will be a combined bio-machine – man will explore the stars through an intricately complex space instrument without leaving the earth (while he is incarnate).

4. Yes! Man can survive in space in a pressurized artificial atmosphere and zero gravity. But for any length of time, without some sort of suspended animation immobilizing his body, the process is degenerative, and he will require a long time for readjustment to a life back on earth.

Periods of up to six months can be practical, but there seems to be little point in man being actually *physically* present in deep space when he can observe everything by either machine-linked remote control or by actual projection of his own Overmind.

Now all that information, as closely as I can recall it, was passed to me through my father in 1937 and 1938. Many predictions made by science-fiction writers of the thirties showed considerable foresight – but they weren't one hundred per cent accurate, as these statements proved to be.

As I discussed these predictions with my brother Tony from 1938 onwards, I do have one witness that Pop, or whatever manifested through him, was amazingly accurate in predicting those fields of human scientific attainment. This sort of information, and much more, was given to me in those last two years before the war. Most of it was verifiable – some of it only *years* later and some I am finding to be viable only *now,* in the last few years, when I have started to research dowsing with a team of able friends and colleagues.

Some of this information concerned the effects that form, shape and thus environment have on the human mind.

One of the concepts that I received was very like psychometry on a vast scale. I learnt that the deeds and actions of man affect and become a part of his environment – especially if he extensively remoulds or 'landscapes' his surroundings over the centuries – that he lives as a part of them. I had asked, for example, why some parts of the countryside around Folkestone gave me a great feeling of security and peace while others made me feel uncomfortable and nervous. The answer was:

> The part of the world that you live in has known the imprint of man for several thousand years. Many of these beings have left their mark on this landscape, and subsequent generations who have lived in the atmosphere and surroundings that you know and experience have been affected by these actions and, in their turn, have added to or subtracted from the landscape itself. Their personalities are imprinted on the organic substance of the line of chalk Downs that are the main part of the structure of this corner of Britain, and you are picking this up, as a sensitive.

Where generations of happy children have laughed and played among the Downs, behind this town, you feel secure and at peace with the world. Where people have huddled in fear of attack from the sea by raiding adventurers like the Vikings, or the invasions of the Romans, Angles, Saxons, Jutes, Danes and Normans you pick up terror and oppression.

It is like going to see a film, if you see a happy, funny comedy you come out of the cinema in a happy frame of mind. If it is a sad film, or a frightening one, you feel in turn sad or frightened. As a sensitive, you *replay*, like a gramophone record, everything that has been recorded on the chalk! Even the shape and form of the Downs – often moulded and cut by man – affects you. The nearest description we can give you is that you not only watch but become a part of a four-dimensional film of the past.

That is why you feel happy in some parts of the countryside and unhappy in others.

Whether it came from my father or from some other wise intelligence, that simple explanation of environmental conditioning is the most logical that I have come across.

For me this sort of knowledge was definitely a 'carrot', dangling in front of us to compensate for some of the long periods of patient waiting and slow conditioning required *safely* to wake the sleeping 'dragon power' within each one of us. Some of these carrots which so effectively drew us along the seemingly endless road of painstaking research were quite startling in their impact. I cite, as an example, the case of the transfiguring lady.

Mrs Balmer was a small, middle-aged woman of slight and rather frail build, with a gentle, lugubrious face which in no way made her conspicuous in a crowd of people.

What made her remarkable was her extraordinary ability to 'transfigure' as a medium. This meant that, through the manipulation of her ectoplasm by some means which we did not then and do not now understand, other entities could 'build' their faces and part of the upper half of their bodies over the medium's own. In other words, a transfiguration took place in which Mrs Balmer's face apparently dislimned to reassemble as a different face altogether.

When I first read about this type of mediumship it sounded just as impossible to me as I'm sure it must seem to you now. However, it worked, and I was present at the afternoon sitting when it happened in our house in Folkestone.

I had previously seen a transfiguration in which the phenomenon took place in very subdued light, only relieved by the occasional use of luminous reddish-coloured slates held close to the medium's face. The results weren't conclusive, to say the least, and most of the manifesting entities had to announce their names and origins in order to achieve any sort of recognition: 'I'm Fred - Fred Brown - don't you recognize me? I passed over in the war!'

This sort of transfiguration, which really looked as though the medium was pulling faces in the dim glow of the luminous slates, produced the same sort of embarrassed feeling that I used to get when watching a bad impressionist on the stage.

These sad performers - usually billed as 'The Man with a Thousand Voices' - literally had to announce who they were going to impersonate first and round it off with a: 'Well, thank you, W. C. Fields,' or whoever they were supposed to be.

Another transfiguration medium whom I saw at the time also used luminous slates and subdued lighting, but in his case the results were dramatic. The previous medium had contorted his features into archetypal shapes - blowing out lips for a Zulu, cheeks sucked in for a thin face or ballooned out for a fat one. This one, however, really did seem to achieve a complete change of face in what, of course, I imagined to be an optical illusion caused by the luminous slates held close to his strangely altered features.

This particular meeting had been held by spiritualists, which we never claimed to be and which I am still, mistakenly, identified with.

The seance was held in one of the upper floors of a tall house in Grimston Avenue in Folkestone, and the medium stood on a slightly raised part of the room that had probably originally been a large nursery on two levels. The lights had been lowered and the medium held his phosphorescent slates beside his face. They looked exactly like table tennis balls covered with luminous paint, which is probably precisely what they were.

None of my family present, including me, had been particularly impressed with the proceedings, feeling that we were watching a trick of the light, but quite a few of the sitters had enthusiastically greeted one or two of the transfigurations with cries of joy. Then, quite suddenly, for my mother at any rate, the aspect of the meeting changed dramatically.

The medium turned towards her general direction and his face seemed to dislimn and re-form into the features of a strong young person with a determined expression quite unlike his own. It wasn't just a contortion of the medium's own face, for years seemed to have fallen off this new face; and although the features had a rather waxen look when the eyes opened and the mouth moved to speak, it was obvious that, while being unearthly it certainly wasn't a mask but was undoubtedly *alive*.

The voice, also that of a much younger person, spoke only one short sentence. First came the word 'Floss'. Then a name that I can't remember and, finally, a number, made up of some eight digits – which were repeated.

My mother, to our amazement, gave a gasp of shocked surprise and then burst into floods of tears. This reaction was totally unlike my mother, who, though very affectionate, was not highly emotional. In fact she was so upset that Pop asked permission to leave the meeting and took her outside to comfort her.

Not long afterwards, the meeting closed. Naturally, my brother and I were, on the one hand, very concerned at Ma's sudden outburst and, on the other, intrigued to know what could have caused it. We had seen nothing in the phenomenon beyond the fact that it looked genuine and was a little eerie in its manifestation.

My mother had recovered her composure but we had to wait till we got home before she explained what had happened. The death of the young soldier from Westcliff who had been engaged to my mother before she met Pop had been a bitter blow to her, and the only information that she had received (passed on to her by his grieving family) had been the *number* of his grave.

The name Floss was interesting, in that, although my mother loathed the name Flo she accepted the nickname

Floss but *only* from her Westcliff family. Any friend outside
the Dawkins/Healey/Woodbridge families knew my
mother as Florence.

Ma had instantly recognized the face as it transfigured
and, combined with the nickname and confirmed by the
number of the Imperial War Graves Commission marker
stone, it had proved too much for her. I had seen my mother
under all sorts of emotional strain, including two occasions
when she helped people to pass over (one an old lady taken
fatally ill on a bus; the other a young man involved in a
motor accident) but I had never seen her so affected.

When Mrs Balmer came down to Folkestone to see us and
to preside at two meetings – one at the new spiritualist
church and the other at our home – we all expected the sitting
to take place in subdued light and with the aid of luminous
slates. To our surprise, Mrs Balmer preferred to sit in
ordinary afternoon light and, once again, the meeting, in
our drawing-room, was a late summer or early autumn one.
One of the drawing-room curtains, on the eastward facing
windows of that cheerful room, had been half-drawn to give
relief to the eyes of the sitters, who were lined up in a semi-
circle on rows of chairs facing the medium. Mrs Balmer's
slight figure was sitting, upright, on a high-backed,
Chippendale type of dining-room chair which was fitted
with arm rests and occupied the corner of the room.

The sunlight and the early afternoon timing of the sitting
would enable my father, assisted by Dr J. and Michael
Tomlinson, an interested young friend of my brother's, to
take photographs of the proceedings, with the permission of
the medium.

The Tomlinson family, including their son David – the
then-unknown actor – were friends of many years' standing
and lived a couple of houses up the road from us. Mrs
Tomlinson – a large motherly lady of great kindness – was
one of my mother's bridge partners, and Mr Tomlinson was
an astute London-based solicitor who was firmly convinced
that my father was quite mad. Michael, however, was

fascinated by it all and, being a keen photographer, had brought his camera to reinforce those being used by Dr J. and Pop.

My father's camera was a marvellous machine of ancient vintage and excellent pedigree, complete with a flip-up flexible black viewing-mask for focusing. It took quarter-plate negatives which were housed in metal and wooden plate carriers. I seem to remember that Dr J. had a Zeiss-Ikon camera of recent manufacture and Michael, I think, had a Voightlander. Anyway all three cameras were of a good semi-professional standard, and all of them were loaded with the new fast panchromatic film or plate. The sunlight outside was still strong enough to take a fairly short exposure – and, after all, none of the pictures was to be taken in colour, which was then still experimental.

The sitters, some sixteen or so in number, were all friends and colleagues, with a number of highly qualified people among them, some scientists and our magician friends from the Magic Circle of amateur conjurers. The wives of some of the sitters made our number up to around twenty-two all told, counting Dr J. and Michael – but excluding Pop, Ma and myself.

Tony, my brother, had been unable to make this sitting in time, but attended the next with Mrs Balmer, which took place at the little spiritualist church.

Mrs Balmer faced a highly critical but open-minded gathering of sensible and well-balanced sitters most of whom were there to assess what the medium could do in her unusual field of trance mediumship. Pop, Dr J. and Michael were stationed with the light on their left, at an angle, facing Mrs Balmer in her corner-sited chair and with the others to their right; so the medium was viewed from a different angle as well as being photographed.

Mrs Balmer said a short prayer and gave a simple explanation of what would happen – all of which took no more than a few minutes. Some suitable records of pleasantly relaxing music were played on our radio–gramophone, and we sat and waited.

The medium started to breathe deeply and, at a signal from my father the three cameras clicked. Then, just like an optical illusion, but this time in the good light of a late summer/early autumn weekend afternoon, Mrs Balmer's face seemed, to us, to go out of focus. I say, to us, because, comparing notes afterwards, that seemed to be the general view. Certainly to me, that appeared to be the effect of the transfiguration. Mrs Balmer's face blurred just like a picture going out of focus. At first I thought it was my eyes playing tricks, and blinked accordingly to clear my vision; but the illusion, if that is what it was, persisted.

The medium made no perceptible movements of her body other than occasionally turning her head slightly one way or another, to indicate, it seemed, the general location of the particular sitter whom the manifesting entity wished to contact through the medium.

Her whole head now appeared to be covered by a fine misty veil, which somehow seemed to be endowed with a form of life and movement of its own. This formed into features which suddenly sprang into abrupt focus and were clearly visible for some fifteen seconds or so. The impression given was quite startling and in no way suggested contortion of the medium's features.

The faces, as they manifested, were greeted by one or other of the sitters with a gasp of surprise as they recognized some dead member of their family. All I saw was a procession of completely different faces pass across Mrs Balmer's mist-covered features, as though they were being projected by some marvellous three-dimensional optical machine onto the foggy screen which Mrs Balmer seemed to generate around her head.

The nearest approach to this effect I have seen has been quite recently at a number of exhibitions, where an ingenious front-projected film is thrown onto a dummy's head which has been painted with some form of light-sensitive preparation. The effect is riveting and an excellent sales device to draw attention to the stand at the exhibition. But it requires quite a bulky piece of apparatus to perform the illusion. In no way could Mrs Balmer have had access to such a device, had it even existed forty-two years ago.

I can't recall the identities of the numerous faces which were now being greeted with amazement and delight by many of the sitters, but I do remember that their spectrum of characterization was very wide. It was far too wide to be either illusory – caused by auto-suggestion or hypnosis – or induced by a combination of self-delusion on the part of all those sitters and an amazing acting ability by the medium.

Indeed, the faces weren't, by any means, all of the transfiguration; for somehow the whole hair-style would change; hats would appear and dematerialize; and the faces ranged from those of young girls and women through boys and young men to old people of both sexes. Even clothes of a sort, such as the top half of a Victorian high-necked blouse or part of a uniform, would appear and then melt away: beards, moustaches and hair, changing from long lustrous coils of feminine locks to short curly hair and even complete baldness – all seemed to manifest in that strange swirling mist.

'My father!' 'Uncle Fred!' 'Mother!' 'Good Lord! It's Granny!' 'Oh! It's my sister!' This sort of spontaneous recognition of Mrs Balmer's transfigurations continued as a fascinating series of wondrous manifestations of the paranormal occurred and while the three cameras clicked away – the whole sitting lasting for about an hour.

I remember the lovely face of a young girl with long red hair; an admiral with a beard and a naval cap and, around his neck, a wing collar and dark tie in the style of the 1914–1918 wartime navy. There was no one that I actually recognized, but Ma gave a cry of joy as she saw her father manifest.

I was fascinated by the obvious excitement of the people

round me as they recognized some relative or close friend. Obviously, their reactions were genuine and spontaneous, and the whole sitting was an enormous success.

Being shy by nature, these larger sittings, of which we held a number at our house, were something of an ordeal to me, because if they turned out to be a 'bit of a frost' it naturally reflected back on my parents. Although I could shrug it all off, I intensely disliked having my mother and father dismissed as cranks – especially when I knew that their able and practised sincerity was the best yardstick by which to measure the results of their investigations.

In the case of the Mrs Balmer sitting there was little criticism, only an excited discussion and much speculation about what had actually taken place. The magicians were baffled and highly intrigued.

As our friend Major Webster put it: 'I understand Mrs Balmer got six guineas for the sitting, plus her fare from London and back. If she can reproduce the same effect in the Albert Hall, she could earn a thousand pounds a session.' That would have been a small fortune in those days (easily the equivalent of ten thousand pounds today).

Obviously the small, middle-aged, sad-faced Mrs Balmer wasn't a fake. That was instantly dismissed. So! Was it hypnosis, on a mass *and* individual scale? This seemed unlikely, as the medium had said little apart from a short prayer and two-minute explanation of what would happen – all delivered in a quiet voice almost without personality.

Self-delusion? Again unlikely, because most of those present were experienced sitters and, in some cases, researchers with excellent scientific disciplines.

Optical illusion? The light condition of afternoon sunlight in a brightly decorated drawing-room was a little unsuitable as an ideal environment for optical illusions.

Apparatus? How? What kind? That possibility was dismissed immediately. Feature manipulation by contorted facial expressions? Hardly – and it certainly wouldn't account for either the wide range of facial characteristics, from pretty girls to distinguished grandfathers, or for the apparent manifestation of different hair colours and styles and even uniforms and hats.

The final evidence should have rested with the three photographers, so busily clicking away at carefully timed intervals. This was one of the weirdest features of the whole business. When the plates and films were developed – Pop's and Dr J.'s by the local professional photographers, Hawkesworth Wheelers of Folkestone, and Michael's film by himself in his darkroom – the results were very strange indeed.

The first pictures on Dr J.'s and Michael's films, and Pop's initial quarter-plate were all quite normal, showing Mrs Balmer sitting in the chair occupying that corner of the drawing-room. So were the *last* pictures taken – once again showing the medium sitting upright in the chair. The rest – plates and films from all three cameras – were subject to fogging as though they had been exposed to some kind of radiation.

In those days we knew little about radiation, and Pop consulted Dr Rusack (my friend Kit's father), a golf partner and friend of my father's as well as being the foremost specialist in radiography in Folkestone.

I spent a lot of my boyhood with Kit and his family, and I remember the awe with which I followed Dr Rusack's description of his marvellous X-ray machinery which was built into his surgery. It was all pure Frankenstein, with large ebonite control panels and great lead screens, and I was duly impressed by these wonders of science.

This honest Scots doctor told Pop bluntly that what had happened was photographically impossible. 'If one of those plates had been fogged like that, obviously a high level of radiation was present at the time, and they must all have been fogged – unless they were protected in some drastic way. As for the films – if the beginning and end of the rolls were *unfogged*, there is no reason that we know of in radiography why the middle pictures on those rolls were fogged so badly.'

Of course I can't remember his exact words – but that is the burden of what he told us.

Michael's pictures were, I believe, the least affected; but his were developed an hour after they had been exposed. I don't know whether that might have had something to do with it.

What puzzled Dr Rusack, and Pop as well, was where such radiation had come from, and how had it lasted throughout the sitting of a full hour's duration? In any event, if such intense radiation had been present – what kind was it – Beta, Gamma, Alpha, X-ray, or what have you? And how was it that there had been no apparent effect on anything or anybody except those middle quarter-plates and the pictures from the two rolls of film.

All three cameras could not have malfunctioned at one and the same time and in the same way. That would stretch the mathematical laws of chance beyond the possible.

So what had happened? I can vouch for the plates of my father's that I personally inspected. The others I only heard about, although Dr J. and Michael both showed me the unaffected pictures, showing Mrs Balmer sitting in the chair.

For my father, my mother and my sixteen-year-old self, it was a remarkable and convincing demonstration of the paranormal.

What caused the phenomenon, how it was accomplished and what was the truth behind the extraordinary photographic results are matters for individual conjecture. I know what I think caused it all to happen.

8   A State of War Exists

At the outbreak of war I had already failed once to gain acceptance as a Royal Air Force air crew trainee, on the grounds of my father's nationality. However, the Honourable Artillery Company were not so choosy about my brother, who, within a few days of the declaration of war, was on his way to Loughton Camp in Essex to be trained as an anti-aircraft gunner and radar operator. (As the HAC still did pike drill on ceremonial occasions perhaps they didn't know that Peru had been liberated by Bolivar, and thought that it was still part of the Spanish Empire.)

I continued to volunteer for the RAF, and worked for the ARP (Air Raid Precautions) Civil Defence until, after a disastrous demonstration of First Aid during a mock air-raid drill when we nearly killed the volunteer patient, I decided to try my hand at the Local Defence Volunteer Force.

As France fell into the hands of the Nazis, I drove with my father down to the Town Hall, where we both offered our services. Pop was a first-class shot with rifle, shotgun and handgun, and had taught me to shoot nearly as well. We were told 'Thank you! But only pure-bred British are allowed to join the LDV.'

I had to go up to London for some exams at London University and, as Dunkirk fell and the exhausted British and Allied troops crept back across the Channel in a bullet-riddled fleet of small ships, I journeyed up by train – one of the only civilians in that crowded carriage-load of shocked

119

and beaten men. At Charing Cross, I watched in amazement
as a company of Guards got off the train and then actually
formed up under a spruce sergeant-major and marched
down the platform. I realized then that ritual, in the military
sense at least, was a powerful thing.

In London I stayed with my sister-in-law, Mona, a lovely
lady who, though a sincere pacifist herself, realized that
Tony had no alternative, and was keeping their home going
while doing voluntary work. There, in their flat in Ladbroke
Grove, I had a taste of fear as the heavy air-raids followed.

Between 1940 and my final ludicrous induction into the
RAF in 1942 I tried my hand as a Fleet Street photographic
journalist with Keystone Press, only to be literally bombed
out of that job, then as a repertory actor (for one week
only) and, eventually, as a Shakespearean actor with
that marvellous larger-than-life actor manager, Robert
Atkins.

I had also, to everyone's surprise, not least my own,
married a French girl, who was much too sophisticated for
my naïve but sincere devotion. Sadly, this union was an
unhappy experience for both of us – apart from the lovely gift
of a daughter who, I am delighted to say, has grown into a
charming woman, and seventeen years ago, presented us
with an equally lovely granddaughter.

Wartime marriages don't stand much of a chance, even if
the husband survives, and, with my wife working for the
Intelligence Section of the Free French and my own total
involvement with British Intelligence there wasn't too
much chance of our making our marriage a success.

In 1942, I found myself actually playing leading juvenile
roles, in such productions as *A Midsummer Night's Dream,
The Taming of the Shrew, Twelfth Night* and, at the
Westminster Theatre, *The Merchant of Venice*. My part as
Lorenzo had earned me a film contract, and I was learning
my part as Poins in *Henry the Fourth* when the ludicrous
incident occurred which finally led to my getting into the
RAF.

As I have stated earlier, despite a number of abortive attempts (in all some fourteen tries) I had never managed to persuade the RAF to accept me. Now I was suddenly confronted by two RAF policemen who, to my astonishment, arrested me as a *deserter*.

Robert Atkins was as outraged as I was, because he had kindly helped me during one of my attempts to join up! 'How the hell can he be a deserter? He's never been in the RAF!'

'He's sixty-five days AWOL,' insisted the self-important corporal. Then he turned to his assistant and said the unforgettable line. 'Take his sword, Fred – he might do himself a mischief.'

This of course made the whole situation even more absurd – for I was in full Shakespearean Tudor costume of doublet, hose, thigh boots, sword and cloak. Which is how I was hurried off to the HQ of the DAPM (Deputy Assistant Provost Marshal) in Exhibition Road, Kensington.

There I was put into a cell and in my despair at the insanity, I mentally asked for help. Instantly the idea sprang to mind: 'They have treated you like a criminal and insulted you as a foreigner – be one!' So I flatly refused to speak English until the Peruvian Ambassador was sent for.

By this time it was around midnight, and the RAF 'Fuzz' thought I was bluffing. When the corporal consulted my papers he turned grey with shock. For there was Pop's nationality, in black and white. 'Jesus Christ! Fred!' said that mental giant. 'He really is a wog!'

The DAPM himself arrived and, soon, the Peruvian Ambassador was contacted. He arrived in his Rolls-Royce and, I am delighted to recall, read them the Riot Act. He was quite magnificent and scared the hell out of them. I was duly escorted out with all the honours due to a neutral citizen who had been grossly insulted.

It sounds vindictive, doesn't it! But then I had had more than enough insults to my family to last me a lifetime.

A week later, at my request, I was interviewed by Group Captain A. H. Gilligan, the famous test cricketer and, at that time, the Station Commander at Air Crew Reception Centre, Regent's Park. He apologized handsomely and, as the RAF had now admitted that I was acceptable for air crew training, I settled my affairs and, two weeks later, was in uniform.

Shorn and in my ill-fitting blue-serge outfit complete with side cap and the white flash of an air crew cadet, I was sharply reprimanded by the same commanding officer for not saluting him as he passed by – but he grinned as he said it.

I would undoubtedly have qualified as a bomber pilot, and probably been slaughtered in the carnage of the 1943 night-bomber offensive, had not fate stepped in once again – this time in the middle of my training. The instrument of destiny was a hypodermic needle, wielded with callous indifference by a medical orderly. We had already had a number of jabs – inoculations – but this one was a booster, presumably administered to my batch of cadets prior to our going overseas.

As we had been told that we would be issued with tropical kit we were probably due to be shipped out to Canada. That was the type of brilliant ruse thought up at the Air Ministry.

I remember that inoculation with great clarity. It as near as damnit killed me. The orderly had just finished a batch of ATT/TAB (anti-tetanus/anti-typhoid) injections and had refilled his hypodermic from a new batch of the serum. There were only two or three cadets left. I got my jab and saw the next cadet, a youngster from Weymouth, get his. Then we were marched back to our barracks – a block of empty luxury flats facing Regent's Park where the Reception Centre was located and where, believe it or not, we ate in the zoo.

At the time, the fact that the air crew cadets' mess was next to the gibbons' cage didn't seem too strange and, viewed from a distance in time, it now seems appropriate. We were, after all, fit physical specimens of young manhood of supposedly fairly advanced intelligence, eager to fly and ripe for the slaughter. Why not feed us in the zoo?

Twelve hours after that fateful jab in my left arm, I was shivering and sweating alternately, and I tried to walk to the station medical officer to report sick. I got halfway down the road and passed out cold. My next memory is of intense pain as I writhed on a hospital bed at Abbey Lodge sick quarters, and I have a hazy and agonizing impression of being given a lumbar puncture.

I must have been running a high fever as I was delirious. My whole body seemed to be racked with convulsions and it was bent like a bow. Apparently, the medical staff didn't expect me to last the night and sent for my wife and my parents.

At a moment of nearly unbearable pain I felt myself suddenly released and outside my body. My anger and sadness at dying – for this is what I now knew was happening to me – faded into an awe-filled acceptance at the naturalness of the process as I gave up the struggle for survival.

This must, with variations, be the process of violent death – which this was, as far as I was concerned. When the struggle ceases an automatic process takes over; there is acceptance at the moment of release. I found myself standing in the presence of eternity. Infinitely small, surrounded by the infinitely vast. I felt no fear – only awe and an awareness that *this* was reality and all else an illusion. The scale of it was so immense that it passed all understanding. It was unrealizable, unknowable and absolute, and as natural as life itself.

This was the endless, boundless, infinite presence of God. I remember the sensation of standing in that presence, not kneeling or lying down but standing upright, with my arms outstretched in the form of the Cross.

Then came a transition. The universe seemed to recede, as though I was somehow being drawn back. I felt myself re-enter my body and the pain came back with my return, but bearably this time. My eyes fluttered open, and blearily I tried to focus on a small group around the bed.

A young nursing sister bent over me and smiled. 'You've been a long way,' she said gently.

I had! I wanted to tell her just how far, but I could only blink as I waited for my voice to come back. Then I saw two senior chaplains who were standing near the bed arguing in low tones.

'He's Catholic. His father's Peruvian or something. He must be Catholic.'

'C of E! It says so on his documents. He's mine!'

I groaned – a hollow dry-mouthed attempt to speak.

The chaplains bent over me, the RC one crossing himself. 'Yes, my son?' he said in a professionally sepulchral voice.

Not to be outdone the C of E padre smiled comfortingly. 'What is it, lad?'

My soul had experienced eternity and now I was back on pain-filled anti-Peruvian earth. I managed to get the words out as the two 'sky pilots' bent close to catch what might prove to be my last words.

'Piss off,' I croaked. 'I'm alive!'

The other cadet was wheeled in to see me about two weeks later. My eyes were extremely bad and both of us were physical wrecks (from the peak of fitness to just about as low as you can get). The RAF had done a great job. The cadet told me that he was to be invalided out.

At the time I was pretty low in spirits. I felt that if this was what the British forces could do, who needed the Nazis? However, I have a stubborn streak in my character – pig-headed if you like – and I was determined that, after all my efforts, I wasn't to be invalided out of the RAF.

Three months' devoted nursing by that marvellous staff at Abbey Lodge got me back on my wobbly, spindly legs; but my eyesight still troubled me. The condition that had so nearly killed me was put down as 'myositis' (which only means inflammation of the muscles). Obviously, what had happened was that the new batch of inoculations had not been serum but an untouched *culture*. Instead of being inoculated *against* tetanus and typhoid, we had been given both diseases at one and the same time. Nothing else, apparently, would have accounted for the rigors, convulsions, high fevers and other alarming symptoms.

The poisons slowly left my body, which now tipped the scales at around eight stone, and large abscesses formed painfully and left me exhausted and depressed. I prayed for help.

Something seemed to happen – and I felt a clear voice inside me say: 'You'll be all right. Stay in the Air Force.' Quite suddenly I felt the shadows lift from my mind.

As soon as I could walk, I asked for an interview with Group Captain Gilligan.

'I'm sorry, Bentin,' he said with sincerity. 'We're going to discharge you from the service.'

'Please give me another medical board! I've tried too long and too hard to be beaten now. Perhaps, sir, I could apply for the ATA?' (Air Transport Auxiliary, the ferry service that supplied planes from the factories to the squadrons.)

He smiled. 'All right, Bentin, I'll think about it. Get fit first and we'll talk again.' Maybe he felt he owed me something more than just the apology for that false arrest.

I worked at it with a will and, for some reason, now found myself posted to the International Squadron, which was also at Abbey Lodge. An even more unlikely cadet posted to the same squadron was Jack Watling, the actor, who was playing the part of a flight-lieutenant in Terence Rattigan's play *Flare Path* by night and was an air crew cadet by day.

I spent hours in the gym at Seymour Hall, and had various treatments. When finally I came before the medical board I was found to be A4B, i.e. medically fit but not as far as my eyes were concerned.

I went to see the 'Groupie' again. 'Flying is out, Bentin. I'm truly sorry.' He paused thoughtfully. 'What about remustering to another branch of the service?'

'Such as, sir?' I asked, without much enthusiasm. 'I only want to fly – to be with air crew. All my life I have lived with aeroplanes; my father designed them.'

'I was thinking of Intelligence,' he said slowly. 'You'd be helping air crew there.'

I laughed. It struck me as funny that first the RAF had me arrested as a deserter and now was inviting me to become a part of British Intelligence. It seemed insane, considering the treatment of my father as a foreigner and my own difficulties in trying to join the RAF.

'What's so funny, Bentin?' he asked sternly.

I told him and, to give him his due, he burst out laughing.

That seemed to settle it. Somewhere, someone or something manoeuvred my life path to yet another crossroads and I had been offered a choice. I accepted it and, once again, took off on another extraordinary course of events which changed my life.

Two months after the interview with the Station Commander, I was sent to Cosford to be turned from a remustered air crew cadet into an officer and gentleman. We were given lectures, vital to the war effort, on such subjects as the width of the braid on an RAF officer's sleeve, how to dig and site an Otway pit – for the hygiene of the airmen – the correct way to pass the port on dining-in night at the officers' mess, and endless drill. One-pause-two salute! One-pause-two! Left, right, left, right!

I don't think our instructors had ever been in an aeroplane. Only the small arms instructors knew what it was about – and here, at least, I wasn't bored! To their delight I shot the black out of everything they presented me with. My father had taught me well. I was young enough and raw enough to relish those hours on the range with rifle, revolver, sten gun and automatic. At last I felt I was preparing for something.

Four weeks later we were commissioned into His Majesty's company of Gentlemen Airmen. What a mixed bunch we were! Those who had been cooks were now catering officers; pay clerks were suddenly accountant officers; airmen clerks became adjutants; and fitters were transformed into engineering officers. All of us, by act of the Air

Council, who were next to God, were acting pilot officers. So now we could get on with the war.

Seven days' leave followed to enable us to get our uniforms, for which we had been fitted at Cosford. I learned that you can't fight a war properly without tailors. I then reported for the Intelligence course, which was held at the Towers, Highgate.

The main purpose of this introductory, wide-spectrum course in Intensive Intelligence was to familiarize the newcomers with an attitude of mind – security. At the Towers you could discuss the course and its implications freely with as many of your Allied colleagues as you could get to know. Outside it, you shut your mind off like a tap.

The officers who ran the show were themselves experienced professionals in subjects ranging from photographic interpretation to escape and evasion techniques. I never met an amateur there. Yet in a way we were all amateurs, for only one or two of us had experience of clandestine activities. Poles, Czechs, Americans, Free French, Belgians, Norwegians, Dutch, Canadians, Australians and even a Peruvian, we all had one thing in common – we hated the Nazis.

This was an all-service course – naval personnel, marines, army and airforce – and one of the most important subjects was evasion and escape. The MI9 section of British Intelligence only came into being as a result of the extraordinary escapes by Allied prisoners and evaders in the First World War. However, in the Second World War it didn't actually start operating till France collapsed.

The difference between evasion and escape is simple. An *evader* is making his way out of enemy territory before being caught, whereas an *escaper* has already been in enemy hands, usually in a prisoner of war camp.

One of the chiefs of MI9 at the time of my introduction to its techniques was that gallant man Airey Neave (at the time a captain). Many years later, I was to get to know him as a friend. His recent brutal murder by terrorists robbed

Britain of one of the most fair-minded and brilliant men the country has known.

His colleagues at the Towers were Squadron-Leader Evans and Flight-Lieutenant Durnsford Smith – both of whom had made daring and brilliantly conceived escapes in the First World War. I had read and re-read both their books before the war. Now I got to know them both, and they were kind enough to go deeply into their experiences with me. Both of them told me that they had relied heavily on their intuition, which their wartime experiences had sharpened for them. I told them about some of our own experiences with the paranormal and neither of them scoffed at the ideas.

I spent most of my time on that fascinating course listening to my wartime comrades from all over the world. All of them were older than I was, and many of them had escaped from the Germans' *Blitzkrieg* across Europe and had made their way, by a multiplicity of escape routes, to Britain. They had come through Germany, Sweden, Switzerland, Yugoslavia, Greece, France and Spain. Some had been wounded on their way to freedom. Many had killed to get through. All were determined to get back and destroy the Nazis.

One thing particularly fascinated me, and that was the respect many of them had for Freemasonry. This was because Hitler had sworn to control or wipe out all rival societies of a closed nature, and Freemasonry was a principal target as far as the Nazis were concerned.

All those members of the course who had either escaped from or evaded the Germans were aware that they had been aided or guided in some way during their adventures. The American airmen who had been shot down and evaded the Nazis called it 'playing their hunches'. The Poles, who were deeply religious, believed in guidance through prayer, and the spectrum of beliefs and opinions varied widely among the others. The sort of comments I heard were:

'Something told me what to do.'

'I felt that something was guiding me.'

'I just felt that was the right thing to do, at that moment.'

'I could feel that I was being followed.'

'I knew it was now or never.'

'I prayed and my prayers were answered.'

'I saw my mother clearly – she told me to get up immediately and leave that house. A few minutes later the Germans were there!'

I asked these men whether they had experienced precognition or prevision, and they told me that they had. Some admitted it reluctantly, while others felt a deep conviction that their experiences were influenced by the paranormal.

All of them said that under the stress of the absolute need for survival their senses were heightened, even when weak from hunger, thirst and lack of sleep. It was a revelation!

It is difficult to explain or even describe the feeling of comradeship that sprang up so quickly and readily in these circumstances, but anyone who has been part of a group or team of people under stress and who are working for the same cause will know what I mean.

The Poles, to whom I was posted as a Sprog IO (Trainee Intelligence Officer), taught me more about war and how to fight it than all the volumes of clever analysis ever written could do. It is simple really. *You fight it twenty-four hours a day.* You eat it, drink it, sleep it and devote your whole attention to it. Until it is over – and then you spend the rest of your life trying to make certain it doesn't happen again.

Of all our allies the Polish people suffered the worst betrayal. We went to war because of the invasion of Poland by the Nazis in alliance with Soviet Russia. At the end of the war we let the Soviets take Poland without a murmur. Whatever ingenious political back-somersault one performs, there can be no justification for that last action. The Poles fought valiantly and died in hundreds of thousands, and they deserved better, especially at the hands of Britain.

Before I left to join my Polish comrades I went to see my

mother and father. Pop told me that my cousin John was dead. We had been contemporaries and much as I loved all my British family it was to John that I was the most closely drawn.

The story of his passing and my father's awareness of it is remarkable. It starts in a small staff-room off a main road in a London hospital, about a week before I began my course at the Towers. My cousin Joan – John's younger sister – was on night duty with two other nurses when she noticed that both of them had dropped off to sleep. As all the hospitals in London were short-staffed and worked half to death, this wasn't too surprising. What was amazing was that opposite her appeared the fully three-dimensional figure of her brother John, from the waist up. (If there is only sufficient power for a partial materialization, obviously the top half of the entity will appear.)

Joan adored her brother, and was deeply shocked. She only had time to notice that her brother was wearing an RAF shirt and a Mae West life jacket, but not the usual sheepskin flying jacket.

She herself was wide awake, of that she was certain. Then she saw her brother run his fingers through his hair to show her that it was dripping wet, smile his devastating grin at her and dematerialize. Joan was terrified and gave a yell as the paralysis of shock left her. This woke the other nurses, who found her sobbing her heart out.

The next morning she rang Pop and told him what she had seen. 'I know John's dead, Uncle Adam!' her voice cried brokenly over the phone.

Pop tried to comfort her but knew instantly by the cold sensation of dread (which I also know only too well) that John had passed over.

When I got the opportunity to come and see Pop at the end of my course he told me an even more remarkable story. 'The same night Joan rang me I went to bed early and slept deeply. At first light I woke and, in that hypnagogic state between sleeping and waking, I saw how John died. I want you to remember this, Michael, because I feel that somehow this is very important evidence.

'I saw cliffs surrounding a bay which was covered with low cloud. The stones of the cliffs were nothing like the sort of rocky coastline that we have in this country. I felt that they were Mediterranean. I seemed to be viewing all this from above the sea, as though I was suspended below the cloud, facing the cliffs.

'Suddenly, out of the cloud, came a German fighter – a Messerschmitt, I think – pursued by a British plane, a Spitfire. The British plane fired at the German and sent his plane into the sea. Then it seemed that the British pilot circled the foam-covered spot where the German had disappeared, as though he was looking for signs of life. I felt that he would have sent a radio message for a rescue boat – somehow I felt that very strongly!

'While he was circling the area of the crash, a second German plane flew out of the low cloud and shot him down into the sea. The British plane sank immediately.

'Remember what I am telling you, Michael, because that is how John died.'

Shocked and sad at the passing of my close friend and cousin, I still wondered why it should be so important for me to remember details of his death when there was no chance of the evidence being substantiated. But I was wrong; this strange disturbing vision of my father's did prove to be a remarkable piece of evidence of communication from a paranormal source.

John was posted missing and the usual telegram arrived to a shocked Uncle Jim. Auntie Nellie had a stroke and never recovered, so John's passing became doubly tragic.

The scene moves to North Africa, where John's elder brother, Alan Dawkins, had been engaged on communication flying – transporting VIPs round the Mediterranean.

Sicily had fallen, and Alan had received word from the Imperial War Graves Commission that John's grave had been found near Catania. He was granted compassionate

leave and flew directly across the Med to Sicily. Several
hours later he arrived at a small cemetery, which lay on the
clifftop overlooking a bay on the Sicilian coast.

The War Graves official was a sympathetic human being
who had some strange information for Alan. The sexton
who looked after the small graveyard had actually seen
John shot down into the sea after shooting down the first
German plane. Through the interpreter, the man told Alan
how it had happened, exactly as my father had seen it
months before – but whereas Pop had seen the whole thing
from a position out over the bay the Sicilian had seen the
same thing from the clifftop above the beach.

Only when Alan came to see my father before returning,
after the war, to his work in East Africa, did he tell Pop what
the sexton had told him in the cemetery in Sicily. Alan had
no idea that Pop had seen it happen – but my mother was
there to confirm Pop's version as he had related it to me in
front of her.

Many years later, my cousin Alan, whom I hadn't met
since 1938, came to see me in South Africa where I was
performing. In front of my wife, Clementina, he confirmed
every detail of the extraordinary occurrence. He also
reminded me of something else that he had told my father
when he had visited him shortly after VE day. Apparently
the War Graves representative had pointed out that John's
body lay buried next to the German pilot whom he had shot
down shortly before his own death.

'Do you want your brother's body shipped back home?' he
was asked.

Alan thought for a moment. 'No, thank you,' he said. 'They
can lie here together – their war is long over.'

A week after seeing my parents in May 1943 I joined the
Poles at Hemswell, Lincolnshire. There were two Polish
Squadrons at this pre-war bomber station, which sprawled
on the top of the wolds near Lincoln. 300 and 305 Squadron
of Bomber Command were at the moment of separation, and

I arrived as the party was in full swing.

305 Polish Squadron was, like 300 Squadron, equipped with Vickers Wellingtons MK Xs, twin-engined bombers which had been, with the Whitley bomber and the Blenheim, the mainstay of the offensive on Europe until 1942-3.

By 1943, the four-engined Lancasters, Halifaxes and Stirlings had taken over the long-range heavy work of Bomber Command's night offensive.

The 'Wimpeys', as these sturdy aircraft were affectionately called, were the brainchild of Barnes Wallis, designer of Britain's most successful pre-war airship, the R100. They were of Duralumin construction, built of a web of interconnecting geodesics like a lattice and then covered with fabric. They were immensely strong. I have seen one flying with most of its 'skeleton' exposed – to land safely at its base with a third of its fabric burned off.

Barnes Wallis was also responsible for the 'Bouncing Bomb' that was used to breach the great dams of the Ruhr, flooding miles of the valleys beneath them. Many of the young crews on this raid, led by Wing-Commander Guy Gibson, VC, failed to return. One young pilot, Flight-Lieutenant Maudsley, was killed when his aircraft was blown up by its own bomb. He had been a highly-respected and much-admired contemporary of mine at Eton, and his passing was, like John's, an extraordinary example of the paranormal in action.

As near as I could make out from the information at the time, Maudsley's aircraft was diverted to attack the secondary dams after the Mohne Dam barrage wall was successfully breached. He attacked the second target, The Sorpe I think it was, rather than the Eder dam, and his bomb, which should have bounced like a thrown stone across the water, was late in its release and blew up under the Lancaster as he cleared the wall by a few feet. The pilots and crews who were watching the attack *all* said that his aircraft was blown apart in mid-air.

By sheer reflex action Wing-Commander Gibson 'called'

on the R/T, 'Henry! Are you all right?'

A faint voice was heard by him and also by the other crews orbiting the target area. The words, though they seemed far away, were quite clear. 'I think so - stand by.'

All the crews who heard it were agreed that, at that moment, such a radio message could not have been sent from his aircraft, which was literally in pieces, scattering their burning fragments along the valley below.

After the war I read an account of this phenomenon in Paul Brickhill's book, *The Dam Busters.*

300 Squadron numbered among its crews Catholics, Protestants, Jews and agnostics - and their ages ran from twenty to something like fifty, this last group being that of Squadron-Leader Kuzian, who (like Jack Benny) claimed to be thirty-nine, but as he had flown in the First World War and had thousands of hours in the air must have been fifty or more.

The intellectuals among the Poles discussed the Nazi hierarchy and their methods and were agreed that these perverted Germans were using rituals for their mass mind manipulation of the German people. The concept of the Parsifal legend, as glorified by W. von Eschenbach and later Wagner, was the key. They all agreed on this, and the belief was later confirmed for me not only by other Allied sources - mainly older men in the Intelligence services of many nations including members of the Resistance - but also in Germany itself.

One thing the Poles brought home to me and which was later confirmed by the appalled evidence of my own eyes was that the Nazis were criminally insane. 'They are mad dogs, Michael! You have to bleddy shoot them.'

Being a simple, earthly soul, despite all my instruction, I still think that they are right. So many Nazis got away with it. But then, 'It's all forgiven and forgotten,' a 'pragmatist' told me quite recently. He also said: 'What a berk you were to fight in the war. You didn't have to. Christ! They didn't even *want* you. You could have stayed out of it and ended up rich! Anyway, what was it all about? After all, they were only Jews.'

I couldn't believe what I was hearing, till I remembered those same words had been said to me before the war: 'All this talk of concentration camps. After all, they're only Jews.'

I served with my Polish friends for a few months before being posted (like a badly addressed letter, I got posted and reposted a lot) to Wickenby, a few miles away and part of the same (Number One) Group, Bomber Command.

Only a few years ago, my good friend Colin Morris, then a BBC producer of documentary films, persuaded me to let him do a TV portrait of part of my life. For some reason he had been keen to do this for five years, and I gave in when he said that he was retiring soon. It turned out to be a very odd programme, but the viewers seemed to be intrigued by it, especially by a short sequence where I went back to Hemswell.

It was autumn and the day was sunny and reasonably warm. As I stood on the long-disused runway, I heard quite clearly the heavy cough of the Wimpeys' big radial engines as they started up, and the muted roar of the propellers as the ungainly-looking machines waddled slowly towards the end of the concrete apron.

The caretaker of the airfield told us that the officers' mess was haunted and that his big Alsatian guard dogs wouldn't go near it at night. He was a retired long-distance lorry driver – not a breed renowned for nervous dispositions – and he freely admitted that he wouldn't willingly go there after dark.

Of course it was haunted! I felt them there, as I stood in that empty RAF mess, surrounded by friends – my 'bleddy' Poles. That day, once again, they opened for me the door marked summer – the summer of 1943.

9 *The Long Dark Night*

In the late autumn of 1943 I found myself at Wickenby
Airfield with 626 and 12 Squadrons, both equipped with
Lancasters MK III. I only had twenty-four hours' notice of
this posting, which was to help out as a spare IO during the
mounting intensity of the night bombing of Germany. It
was really a loan from Ingham Airfield, the satellite of
Hemswell, from which 300 Squadron had been operating.

I had briefed a number of their operations and was by now
familiar with the procedure involved. As I was a trained
draughtsman (mainly because of my brother), I could present
the details of the operations graphically during the briefing
and, being an actor, I had no difficulty with the presentation of the facts. I had, however, to gain the confidence of air crew, because I was a 'Penguin' (the RAF term
for non-flying personnel) and looked ridiculously young. (I
later found out I was the youngest IO in the RAF by a
number of years.)

With the Poles this had been no problem, because they
instinctively knew I wanted to fly and gave me unlimited
opportunities to do so. In M – for Mother – the dual control
Wimpey I amassed as many hours as I could while the Polish
crews went back and played 'Skat' and 'Brag' on the main-
spar out of sheer bravado. They also let me fly the big planes
while they each had a turn in the rear turret, firing the .303s
at drogues – great long sock-like targets towed by 'Miles
Master' aircraft.

Air Commodore Cozens had also kindly helped me to

apply for the ATA but, lensed goggles and all, sadly I had to face the facts. Dual-control OK! Solo - forget it! I just couldn't see well enough to be trusted with a valuable war plane. I contemplated training as a glider pilot, but this would have meant transferring to the Army and the RAF flatly refused my request.

Wickenby had a busy time that autumn and winter of '43, and needed every trained hand that they could muster. The crews were made up of all sorts of Allied Commonwealth (as they now are called) air crew - Australian, Canadian, East African, New Zealanders and others from most parts of the old British Empire and, because the Wing was so large, it took longer to get to know them. But they soon twigged that I knew nearly as much about their aircraft as they did, and the gunners got on well with me because I could shoot clay pigeons as efficiently as they could on the practice range. The word got about that the short-sighted Peruvian was a nut but an acceptable type, and nobody felt that they were being given the gen at a briefing by another bloody know-all Penguin.

Flying at Wickenby was much more difficult - mainly because, on one raid, the Group had just lost an Intelligence officer, a medical officer and a padre - none of whom was supposed to be on operations. Besides, we were so busy that time was at a premium; I don't ever remember being so tired as during that time.

If it was a strain for the Intelligence section, what must it have been like for the poor bloody frozen air crew? Let me try to tell you, as I gathered from my crews, what an average night-bombing operation was like. As this book is intended to be a simple recitation of my own and other people's first-hand experiences of the paranormal, I am including this as a broad example of the sort of ordeal these young men were called upon to endure. The fact that they did so, successfully, is to me in itself paranormal!

Take, for example, a raid on the Ruhr - the Happy Valley as the air crews euphemistically called it. The crew of a

Lancaster, in 1943, usually consisted of a pilot, navigator, bomb-aimer, flight engineer, wireless operator (with the 'S' for Signals badge) and three gunners – front, mid-upper and rear.

The aircraft was powered by four Packard Merlin engines, and these pulled it along at a service altitude of around 24,000 feet at speeds of from 240 mph to just over 300. It was armed with two Browning .303 machine-guns in the front turret, two in the mid-upper and four in the rear. The craft was unpressurized and cold (the average outside air temperature at that altitude, in winter, being around 20° *below* zero Fahrenheit).

The flight out and back, with a time over target of some ten minutes, would be somewhere of the order of six and a half hours – at least three-quarters of that time over enemy territory.

From approximately ten thousand feet upwards the crew would be on oxygen. They wore long-john underwear, shirts and white oiled-wool sweaters, with battle-dress tops and trousers and either 'sidcot' one-piece flying suits with electrically-heated inner suits for the gunners (who had to sit in their turrets for the whole trip) or heavy 'Irvine' jackets of lambswool and sometimes trousers of the same type.

Their sea-boot-stockinged legs were encased in fur-lined flying boots with tops that could be cut off to leave them lambswool-lined shoes to walk home in, which many of them did, assisted by MI9 and Resistance underground escape routes in Europe. With this in mind they were each issued with an escape kit, a plastic box containing Horlicks tablets, water purifiers, a rubber water bag, compasses, maps of Europe and the appropriate paper money.

Their aircraft were the best night-bombers of the war, but by today's standards primitive, noisy, draughty and heavy with vibration, especially when hit or damaged in any way.

Their contact with other aircraft was nil unless specifically called for as on the Dam Buster raid, and wireless contact with their home base or the radar watch was kept to a minimum. Their only contact within the plane over the noise of the engines was by R/T, and messages were kept as short as possible to avoid confusion.

In an aerial attack by a German night fighter the pilot was guided by his gunners, who shouted: 'Corkscrew port' or 'Corkscrew starboard', indicating the hair-raising rate-six-turn manoeuvre that saved many bombers from being shot down.

All through the long, exhausting, nerve-racking flight the whole crew wore Mae West flotation jackets with their Irvine parachute harness strapped tightly over everything else. Oxygen masks completed an outfit that was not the easiest to move about in.

The bomb-aimer, navigator, wireless operator and flight engineer only attached the parachute packs to their chest harness clips in an emergency. The pilot and gunners had seat-pack parachutes with dinghy packs attached to form a seat cushion.

All through the operation – even on take-off and landing – the gunners had to keep their eyes open for night fighters, who intruded right over Britain and infiltrated the landing pattern at their bases. Even the apparently friendly silhouette of a Lancaster could turn out to be a captured aircraft (the Germans were known to have used these in the bomber stream itself). This great line of four-engined aircraft would sometimes stretch eighty miles or more on its way into the target and on the return course.

From the enemy coast onwards the aircraft were under constant attack, from heavy flak and the ever-present menace of the enemy night fighters. The sexual reminiscences and fantasies so beloved by fiction writers, who never knew these young men or experienced even a fraction of what it was like to be on an operation, are a load of bullshit. If they had been indulged in to the extent that is suggested in books, the lack of concentration would have killed the crews in minutes. If your attention wandered for a few moments they could so easily be your last, as the·

cannons of the night fighter hit you. Even urinating wasn't easy. The main facilities consisted of an Elsan chemical toilet, firmly sited aft by the rear-gunner's turret, plus a long flexible tube for the pilot which was fitted with a funnel top and referred to as a 'desert lily'.

The target area and the run-in to it were the nearest things to hell, as seen from the air, that one could imagine. The fires surrounding the red and green TIs (target indicators) flamed and blossomed as the flaring bursts of the bombs exploded among them. The sky, lit by the blinding sweep of the searchlights seeking to 'cone' any unlucky aircraft in the focus of a dozen beams, was blasted by the concentrated explosions of the high-altitude heavy flak, while tracers from the light flak sought out the aircraft attacking from lower altitudes.

The pilot, holding his straight course for the bombing run, had to keep his eyes on the instruments to avoid being blinded by the glare of the searchlights and somehow avoid collision with other aircraft. Add to this the intense, mind-numbing cold and the nearly unbearable noise, and you have some vague idea of what it was like.

Through all this terrifying destruction the gunners searched endlessly for the night fighters, who often pressed home their attacks right into the flak zones over the target.

At the cry of 'bombs gone' the pilot closed the bomb doors and sped away from the target area on the long dangerous flight home, often barely making it back to base with one or even two engines gone, and often dead and wounded aboard. The last thing that many air crew knew was the blinding flash as they blew up in mid-air – or the long screaming fall to earth, in flames, unable to bail out because of the terrific 'G' (gravity) forces generated by a fatal spin.

Every trip was more or less the same for the crews, with obvious variations – sometimes a little better, sometimes much worse – but always dangerous, frightening and, in winter especially, bitterly, morale-sappingly, cold. The lucky ones survived thirty of these sorties for their first tour and twenty for their second - some of them actually completed third and even fourth tours. Group Captain Leonard Cheshire, VC, DSO, DFC, etc., was awarded his Victoria Cross not for one particular act of outstanding valour but for something like a hundred of these trips, often as Master Bomber. Some 90,000 of these young men died in Bomber Command alone, among them over 46,000 air-gunners. Remember that most of these youngsters were aged from eighteen to over thirty.

Many pilots died in their aircraft, which they kept flying, even in flames, until their crews had bailed out, and only then, often too low, attempted to get out themselves. They also died trying to bring badly-damaged aircraft home with seriously wounded aboard who could neither bail out themselves nor survive if they were pushed out (on static lines which would open their 'chutes' for them).

Someone recently said to me: 'Better to be Red than dead.'

Perhaps so if you feel like another person, who said to me, in 1940: 'I'd rather be a live Nazi than a dead hero!'

I have no choice in the matter: for I still have a debt to pay. I have to keep faith with my friends who died in that battle against the darkness, because, if I break faith, I have *nothing*!

During this winter of 1943-4 I found my clairvoyance channelling itself into an appalling rut. Now that I was accepted as a briefing officer and got to know my crews better the rapport between us became much stronger. This was a good thing for the work in hand, but it had a loathsome side-effect.

Every night that the Wickenby wing was operating I would make it my·business to drop into the mess - just to check that everyone had their escape kits and to chat to anyone who felt like it, about anything but the operation. Again and again, I would see the faces of one or other of these friends turn into a skull in front of my eyes, and I knew that he would die that night.

This was *objective* clairvoyance of a hideous sort, and although I had become used to *subjective* clairvoyance, and could control its manifestations – at least to the extent of stopping it if it became dominant – in this case the whole process was involuntary and I could *not* get rid of it.

Eventually, after trying every way of clearing the condition, I went to the chaplain for help. Our Padre, a wise First World War veteran, listened to what I had to say, and didn't call in the Senior Medical Officer to have me committed. Instead, we went to the small chapel, located in a temporary hut, and there knelt down and prayed together that the manifestations should cease – which, thank God, they did.

The worst part about it had been the frustration. Even if I could have warned them few of them would have believed me, and those that would could not have refused to go on the operation. The best I could do was to give them as strong a friendly 'take care' as possible, which wasn't much.

Any member of the air crews who refused to fly on an operation was branded 'LMF' on his documents. This appalling stigma, which was, I believe, inhuman, stood for 'Lack of Moral Fibre' and was a remnant of First World War military thinking.

If a member of air crew couldn't face the ordeals of operation any more, he should not have been allowed to go on flying, because, by doing so, he risked the lives of the whole crew. Many crew members did just that because they were more frightened of the LMF branding, which meant stripping off their rank badges (by 1943 *all* air crew were, at least, given the rank of sergeant), and disgrace.

The Brevet (the wings of a pilot, or the single wing and insignia of the navigators, bomb-aimers, signals, flight engineers and gunners) could *not* be taken from them and I saw ex-air crew NCOs reduced to the ranks, cleaning out latrines! (Officers could not be reduced to the ranks but could be cashiered.) It was disgusting and degrading and completely inexcusable. The air crews didn't need that threat to maintain their contact with the ethos!

The Americans were far more humane in their approach. If any member of air crew showed strong signs of battle fatigue they took him off operations immediately without shaming him. The bulk of our air crews operated at maximum stress, and even if temperamentally unsuited, made the best of it – to survive their tours or to meet their death or imprisonment with resolution. Even men like Leonard Cheshire admitted being afraid. Any member of air crew who said that he did not experience fear during operations must be either a thick-headed moron or a liar. Fear was part of the mechanism that super-adrenalated their bodies, to allow them to cope with the ordeals.

To label the victims of such fear as lacking moral fibre and punish them was the work of the same type of mind that strapped men, crucified, to the wheel of a gun carriage in the First World War. I cannot believe that it was necessary and in no way can I even condone it. It was pure *fascism*!

The constant turnover of crews, owing to replacements through battle casualties or the completion of operational tours, brought increasing numbers of young bomber crews who were painfully lacking in experience. The air crew of one replacement aircraft – all brand-new sergeants – looked as if they had come straight from school, which was probably true. These cheerful lads routinely reported to me, a grizzled twenty-one-year-old, on their first day with the Wing, got their escape kits and a briefing on how to use them, flew one night across-country the next evening, and got hopelessly lost, and were put straight onto a long-range operation on the following night.

This, despite the protestations of the Wing's Navigation Officer – a quiet-spoken, much experienced Australian, who made a strong recommendation for more training and a request for their temporary deferment from operations – and those of the Senior Intelligence Officer, a First World War pilot of great experience and courage. We were all over-ruled. The Commanding Officer wanted a maximum effort – and he got it.

They never returned. God knows where they bought it, but it is highly unlikely that they ever reached the target. It really was the Slaughter of the Innocents – that long, dark night of the winter of '43-4.

To be fair to the command planners, many of whom did come down to talk to the squadrons personally, most of the top commanders were First World War pilots themselves and still thought in those terms. One marvellous 'old' man – I think it was Air Commodore Broadbent-Cohen – often had to be physically restrained from flying on operations as a rear-gunner, which he frequently did.

To me, Air Marshal Lord Dowding had the closest mental rapport with his pilots, but then he was an exceptional man – and his team was much smaller and countable in hundreds. In Bomber Command there were thousands of air crew, and when you compare the casualty lists with those of other commands you get some idea of the dreadful price in human suffering paid by both sides in the bomber battle of Germany.

I lost one friend during my time at Wickenby, and saw him in clear moonlight within hours of his passing.

Flight-Lieutenant W. was referred to as 'Pop' because he was in his mid-thirties. A large, affable northerner with a sound, serious streak, he often dropped into our Intelligence operations room to discuss whatever 'gen' we could give him about the latest developments in the air war. We often chatted about the paranormal. He was sceptical but, being an open-minded and fair man, also interested in the subject.

My SIO, whom we all liked enormously, had told me to take a forty-eight hour pass, which he knew I needed to go down to London and see my small family. My marriage was going badly, and I wanted to see them, so I took his advice and, before I left, my navigator friend came over to say goodbye.

He had just finished his first tour of thirty operations and was off on leave to see his family, which, I believe, consisted of a wife and two children.

He told me how relieved he was to have made it through the tour, and that he felt that he was in for a cushy time training other navigators for the next six months.

I was glad that he had made it and wished him well.

'Hope to see you sometime, Mike,' he said, and I hurried off to get my transport to London.

It was midwinter, and the snow had fallen heavily enough to cover our dispersal quarters among the plantations of pine trees when I returned, at the usual 23.50 hours on the last night of my pass and, after reporting my return to the Guard Room, walked through the crunching layer of snow towards my hut. The moonlight was bright and near the full moon, so that when it came out from behind the scattered clouds the whole scene lit up in clear silvery light. As I approached the hut that I shared with air crew I saw the tall moustachioed figure of Flight-Lieutenant W. coming towards me.

I 'waved' a salute in greeting, and shouted out, 'Hi, Pop!'

He seemed to acknowledge my presence, but continued across my path about ten to fifteen yards away and disappeared in the direction of his own Nissen hut opposite.

Nothing seemed unusual, except that I felt a sudden chill which I put down to the clear, cold night. The moon passed behind another cloud and I gratefully crept into my own Nissen hut, as quietly as possible so as not to wake my sleeping friends; for they, of all of us, needed their rest. I undressed in the blacked-out hut by the subdued light of my torch and slipped into bed to fall asleep within minutes with the warmth of the pot-bellied stove which was still glowing dimly.

In the morning, at 6.30, I was awakened by our shared batman – a nice cheery, cockney LAC (Leading Aircraftman) who brought us our tea and shaving water.

'There's a flap on, sir,' he said. That meant the 'Y' form (the teleprinted secret plan for an operation) must have come in early. 'Have a nice forty-eight?'

'Not bad!' I said, sipping my 'Rosie Lee', which was so
strong that the spoon nearly stood up in it.

'Bloody shame about Mr W.,' he said, sadly. 'Nice bloke –
finished his tour and all. Bloody bad luck, sir!'

I sat bolt upright. 'What do you mean? I saw him last
night!'

'You couldn't have, sir,' my surprised batman insisted.
'He was dead long before then!'

'When? Where? How?' I was flustered, and showed it.

''Course, you wouldn't have known, sir,' he apologized.
'He bought it with a Sprog crew what came in the day you
left on your forty-eight.'

'Why?' I asked foolishly. 'He'd finished his tour. Why was
he flying with a new crew?'

'Volunteered, sir, so they say. The gen is that this crew was
a bit green and Mr W. agreed to show them the ropes on a
night cross-country. Dunno what happened but somefink
went wrong, and they pranged into the woods. Low cloud, I
fink they said it was. Bloody shame! You must have been
mistaken about seeing 'im, last night, sir!'

But I wasn't – I *had* seen W. within hours of his death – why
I don't know.

But I *do* remember Flight-Lieutenant W., and many more
like him, who had that extra something that makes all the
difference between the ones who feel that it is 'Better to be a
live Nazi than a dead hero' and those who, even when they
were safe, still cared enough about their comrades to give
them a hand.

But you could never explain that difference to those
who said about the concentration camps: 'After all they
were *only* Jews.'

10 The Grey Dawn of Freedom

The bomber offensive was now at its height. By day 400–600 US Eighth Army Air Force B17 Fortresses and B24 Liberators thundered over Europe escorted by the very successful long-range fighters, the P51D Mustangs. Their task was to destroy the industrial targets of Germany, the ball-bearing factories, aircraft plants and great tank and gun assembly complexes of the Ruhr.

By night, equally large masses of British and Allied four-engined 'heavies' crossed Germany and ranged down into France and even Italy, crossing the high Alps to bomb the great cities of the Third Reich and its Axis partner.

Berlin itself (code-named 'Whitebait': targets had the names of fish) was now constantly harried by Mosquitoes, the twin-engined wooden bomber that was almost as fast as a fighter and armed with cannon as well. These far-ranging aircraft also strafed German night-fighter airfields, and carried 4000-pound 'cookies' to drop on specific cities in the now all-out air war that brought such destruction to Germany. Leonard Cheshire used one of these wooden aircraft – made partly of Peruvian and Ecuadorian balsa wood, in a sandwich of spruce plywood, to mark the target area as a 'Master Bomber'. Once, when the target indicators burned out, he radioed: 'Bomb on the flash of my wings in the moonlight.'

I asked him about that extraordinary order, and he shyly remarked: 'It was perfectly safe – by the time the bombs got to where I had been, I was miles away.' He failed to point out that at the time he was orbiting the burning target area, which was heavily defended, at some two thousand feet.

As a matter of interest, on two separate raids on the Baltic Coast which I had briefed, my returning air crews reported having been pursued by lights which manoeuvred round their Lancasters at high speed without actually attacking them. Naturally we thought that these lights were probably airborne searchlights, carried by some new night-fighters in much the same way that our Coastal Command anti-submarine aircraft were equipped with powerful 'Leigh lights' to illuminate their U-boat targets at sea. The mystery was that the lights had shown no intention of attacking the bomber aircraft; that didn't make sense.

Someone suggested that the phenomenon was St Elmo's fire or some other manifestation of an electrical storm, but the crews were adamant. They were experienced air crews and had seen *that* type of electrical phenomenon before. They insisted that these lights were quite different. If they were airborne searchlights, why hadn't they opened fire with the cannon of their night-fighters? They couldn't *all* have jammed.

We reported it to Group, and a Group Intelligence Officer came down to check out the stories, telling us that the Americans had reported a similar phenomenon during a raid by day. The US Eighth Air Force called them 'foo fighters'. No one had an adequate explanation, and the whole matter was shelved.

I am an agnostic when it comes to 'flying saucers', but I have seen something that I can't explain, and I've talked to a number of experienced airmen, of whom these air crew of 12 and 626 Squadrons were the first, who told me about phenomena of this sort. There is no question in my mind that they saw something. Of that there is no doubt.

What it was – I don't know.

One day my SIO told me that I was posted to a Group at Preston. As this was a Fighter Command Group HQ and I was now a trained Bomber IO neither of us could figure out what the whole business was about.

I hurriedly said my goodbyes to the crews and got transport to Lancashire where the Group was located, hoping that at last my ATA application was bearing fruit. (I had acquired fresh hope of flying by meeting a pilot who wore the new contact lenses with great success – in those days they were made of glass and were the size of half ping-pong balls but were very effective). However, I found that I was posted to this Group to train as a Fighter Controller. This was absurd, because if my eyesight was dodgy enough to make flying too risky, how was I going to spend hours watching a radar screen and 'vectoring' (directing) fighters onto 'bandits' (German aircraft).

I made my usual mistake of being bluntly outspoken and immediately got the label 'mutinous'. The particular Captain Bligh of this outfit was an arrogant regular who was comfortably ensconced in his own little empire and had been there for a long time.

The raids on Liverpool and Manchester and the industrial North West had long since died down, and this Group was virtually non-operational, while I wanted to get on with the war in the manner for which I had been trained. In other words, I thought for myself. This didn't suit the bureaucracy.

With the exception of a good friend who later stood by me in need, I hated the whole place and showed it. The Group HQ responded predictably: I was made orderly officer for a full two weeks, presumably to 'teach the bloody Peruvian a lesson'. Among my duties every night I had to secure the headquarters, and I was horrified by the number of secret files left lying around the building. Every night I solemnly gathered these up and, with the orderly sergeant, returned them to the Central Registry, where they should have been kept under lock and key. Each night I also wrote a report, strongly protesting against this breach of even basic security and each time I was ignored.

One night I found a thick file marked 'Top Secret' and

labelled 'Overlord'. I checked its contents and to my horror
found it to be a master copy (they were all numbered, of
course) of the plan for the invasion of Europe. I put in a
'snorter' of a protest and obtained the usual receipt for the
document. Something told me (literally the still small voice-
but loud) to keep the receipt *personally* instead of filing it.

Forty-eight hours later I was put under close arrest.

My friend, Ray, couldn't believe it. 'What the hell for?' he
asked, bewildered.

I soon found out when I was wheeled into a solemn-faced
Court of Inquiry.

A large, well-nourished wing-commander who had probably never seen an aeroplane spoke in a doom-laden voice:
'You are to be charged with the loss of a secret document
through your neglect of duty.'

The small voice whispered to me: 'Tell them the name of
the document!'

'If you mean Overlord, I have the receipt for it.'

You could have heard the silence that greeted this
definitive statement.

In a voice choked with emotion, the fat wing-commander
ordered me to hand it over.

'With respect, sir,' I said firmly. 'Up yours.'

Had he been armed and able to use a gun, which I very
much doubt, he would have shot me there and then. The
board went into a huddle as I was wheeled out smartly by the
DAPM.

Back at my billet Ray got through to me. He was grinning
with delight. 'Jesus, mate! There's a hell of a flap on! What
gives? There's a rumour going round you're for a court
martial.'

I had an inspiration (still small voice again). 'Keep this for
me, Ray,' I said, handing him the receipt and my freedom at
one and the same time.

He didn't let me down, and when the service police
searched my room – what an incredible load of 'creeps' this
Group had gathered together – they found nothing.

Silence fell but I was out of close arrest. The next day passed playing chess with Ray and trying to figure out what it was all about.

The following morning a trim WAAF driver pulled up outside our billet with a car to take me to Blackpool, which was a centre for RAF training. The pretty girl knew nothing except that I was to report to some flight-lieutenant there right away.

On arrival I was conducted immediately into the presence of an RAF Medical Officer. He wasted little time on formalities, after ascertaining my identity.

'I understand that you are finding the RAF too much for you,' he started off confidently, in a somewhat aggressive tone.

'I don't follow you,' I said cautiously.

'I am led to understand that your attitude as an officer is not conducive to your retaining a position of privileged authority,' he went on smugly.

The light dawned! Somebody had been on the phone to this character.

'So?' I queried. 'What does that mean?'

'We feel,' I noted the royal 'we', 'that you would be better *out* of the Service.' The last line was delivered in an unctuous tone, as by one totally devoted to 'the Service'.

'What exactly are you?' I asked.

'I am a psychiatrist,' he said, with the sort of inflexion on the last word that implied that this statement alone would bring me into line.

'Some bastard has been on the blower to you!' I said flatly.

By his face it was obvious that I had scored a hit! I followed it up – guided by the SSV (still small voice): 'If you have any intention of recommending me for a discharge on psychiatric grounds – forget it, mate.'

'Are you implying—' he started, pompously.

'Yes! I *am* implying – that someone has been on to you with a load of bullshit and that you have already made up your mind to comply with orders.'

'How dare you!' he said loudly, but with a nervous tremor in his voice.

By this time, SSV or not, I was sensitive enough to detect any change in his manner. 'I'll tell you something, mate! If you want to practise medicine or whatever your speciality is called officially *after* this lot's over you'd better start to behave like a doctor. On what grounds are you going to make such a recommendation – without any form of examination?'

By this time the SSV was speaking directly through me: 'I demand a full medical board to look into my fitness to return to the duties for which I have been trained.'

The SSV played its Tarot trump – ''Or, as a *Peruvian citizen,* I shall make the same request through the Peruvian Ambassador.'

That did it! God bless Peru, not forgetting the SSV, whoever you were!

Back we drove to the Group and an excited Ray, to whom I revealed all. 'The bastards were trying to railroad you, mate,' he said, simply. 'They knew you actually had the receipt. They've been on to me to try to get co-operation – I told them to stuff it!'

Forty-eight hours later, I was on my way to London, where the Central Medical Board gave me a clean bill of health – other than my eyes: A4B – fit for all duties, but not operational flying.

A quick posting to Kirton-in-Lindsay, a Fighter OTU (Operational Training Unit), followed and then I was posted to 350 Squadron, 'Escadrille des Chasseurs' of the RAF/Belgian alliance at West Hampnett – the satellite of Tangmere on the South Coast. I was back in the war.

The Squadron was commanded by a stocky Belgian fighter pilot, Squadron Leader Michel Donnet, DFC, a friendly and clever young man who had made a daring escape with a colleague after the invasion of Belgium. He had purloined a TKI (a Belgian biplane similar to a Tiger Moth) and, after stealing sufficient petrol from German staff cars, had flown it to Britain. They were arrested when they arrived, but Michel Donnet had eventually become a most effective fighter leader in the RAF.

The day I arrived I was thrown in at the deep end once again – handed a CSC Computer (a navigator's aid for calculating courses) and told to work out a set of courses for the next fighter sweep, which was in an hour's time. There were no subtleties in these operations – any planning having been done on a higher level. The tactical attack plan was made then and there, as the Squadron got ready for take-off.

Soon the balloon went up in earnest. Constant fighter sweeps and 'Rhubarbs', 'Cab Ranks' and other code-named fighter operations were the key to Allied air supremacy over Europe – at least over France and Belgium. The whole success of the invasion of Europe depended on the complete reversal of the situation in 1940, when the Germans destroyed the Allied armies with their *Blitzkrieg* supported by the air superiority of the Luftwaffe. The invasion succeeded because any strong concentration of German air power was kept pinned down on the ground by the massive assault on European airspace.

The beaches would have been a shambles, as 'Omaha' nearly became, had not the fighters, fighter bombers, medium bombers and high altitude heavies, the whole might of the RAF and the US Eighth Army Air Force, been brought to bear on the beachheads and beyond their perimeters.

For a month, 350 Squadron's total effort was concentrated on the Normandy area and especially around Caen and eventually Falaise. Then suddenly we were pulled back and ordered to fly to Hawkinge, the airfield I had spent so much time watching as a boy on the Downs above Folkestone. The Squadron's role in the invasion was switched to a defensive one, against 'buzzbombs' which were being fired from the Pas de Calais area.

For those who don't know what a V1 (Vengeance Weapon No. 1) looked and sounded like, it was a stub-winged, streamlined cylinder with a pulse-jet engine mounted above the small fin and rudder. This robot bomb (which was what it was) was fired from a catapult mounted on a 'Ski-site' (Code-names 'Ski-Ball' and 'No Ball'), consisting of an inclined plane which held a track with a trolley running on it. This was, I think, propelled by a heavy discharge of hydrogen peroxide (the chemical that women used to bleach their hair) and launched the V1 on its way.

Anyone who was beneath those blood-chilling flying bombs will need no reminding – and will recall the heart-stopping moment when the engine, like a noisy motor cycle, suddenly fell silent, indicating the short steep dive to earth as the bomb lost its speed and climaxed by the shattering explosion of its warhead.

Over twenty feet long, with a sixteen foot wingspan, these deadly vengeance weapons poured over the channel and headed for London, first in dozens and then in hundreds. 350 Squadron was one of the experienced fighter units which were pulled back from the Normandy operations to fly the Spitfire Fourteens (with the Griffon-engine and multi-bladed propellors) that were fast enough to catch these V1s. The bombs belted along at over four hundred miles an hour, so our Spitfire IX Bs with their four-bladed propellers were too slow by some fifty miles an hour.

Within twenty-four hours of landing at Hawkinge in one type of plane, the Belgians 'converted', and within forty-eight hours they were fully operational in their new and unfamiliar machines. It was a feat of airmanship, and I was proud to be associated with such an operation.

Flying-Officer Van der Vecken flew me up in the Tiger Moth communications plane, and to our amazement we were fired on. How any anti-aircraft gun crew, however nervous, could mistake a *biplane* moving at eighty knots for a V1 robot bomb racing above them at over four hundred miles an hour is a mystery. We didn't feel like probing for an answer, and Van hugged the deck, hedge-hopping at full speed (i.e. 85 knots if you got out and pushed). We bucketed

over the trees with only feet to spare and contour-hugged the
Downs all the way – while surprised gun crews swung their
questing muzzles to follow us.

At Hawkinge we got out of the little Tiger Moth in
hysterics, overcome with schoolboy laughter, completing
the release of our adolescent emotions by having a
celebratory pee on the grass beside the plane. To have been
shot down by our own guns in a basic trainer would have
been too much to bear.

This was the grassy airfield I had haunted as a youth –
dreaming of one day flying from it in one of the beautiful
Hawker Fury biplane fighters with which we had so nearly
gone to war. It was also the airfield beside which Pop had
received that first extraordinary message in a bungalow
facing the north end of the perimeter track. I felt that I was
there for a reason, a feeling which became even stronger
when I found myself billeted at White Gates, a lovely small
country house a hundred yards down the road from Arthur
Condy's house. Arthur was no longer there, but his
bungalow Fairly Closeter (meaning 'fairly close to the
nearest pub') conjured up visions of my boyhood and that
jovial magician performing the Miser's Dream with
showers of coins pouring from his adroit hands into the
silver jug.

The crackling-engined flights of buzzbombs constantly
raced by low overhead; for Hawkinge was on top of the
Downs above Caesar's Camp, which, in turn, was six
hundred feet above the Folkestone cliffs. That meant we
were about half-way to the altitude at which the bombs
normally operated, and in fog, which we experienced a
number of times, the menacing sound of their pulsing jet
engines passed overhead invisible and untouchable.

One bomb, hit by the anti-aircraft gun belt which
stretched below the Downs, nearly put paid to me. I was in
White Gates having a quick shave just after dawn when I
heard the 'Diver' (code-name for a V1) approaching loudly.
Before I could do much about it, the engine cut out; and the

next thing I knew was that the blast had lifted me up and hurled me straight under one of the iron bedsteads in the room. When the plaster-dust cleared, and I recovered from my momentary blackout, I was only slightly cut by the glass from the windows, which had been open, and covered from head to foot in dust.

The V1 had exploded at the end of the orchard – and most of the blast had been taken by the line of well-foliaged trees, angling the blast wave above the house. Otherwise, a few yards further on and someone else would be writing this book.

An hour later, after a cold shower in the main Officers' Mess at Hawkinge, I was back on the 350 Squadron dispersal, briefing the next pilots to take off on the anti-buzzbomb patrol.

A week later I nearly bought it again. This time on the perimeter track of the airfield. A massive fighter sweep had been in operation, employing most of 11 Group's Squadrons of Spitfires and Tempests. One Spitfire, its overload belly tank still attached to its fuselage, had been badly shot up by flak and came juddering in for a shaky emergency landing. With his plane's hydraulic system shot out, the pilot had to make a belly landing and, because his flaps were inoperable, finally touched down in a spray of grass and dirt far beyond the safe limit of the airfield's turf landing surface.

I was standing in front of a brick and concrete revetment at our end of the airfield, riveted with growing anxiety for the pilot's safety as he screeched across the grass towards me. So far he hadn't exploded, so the buckled belly tank must have been empty and was now acting as a sort of sledge, which contributed to his rapid progress.

It all happened in less time than it takes to write, as he hurtled along, shedding both wings on the way, followed by his tail planes and – only a few yards from me – his massive Merlin engine. This, fortunately for us both, broke from its mounting and lurched sideways – red hot and menacing –

as his fuselage skidded straight towards me. Only then did I realize that, unless I moved quickly I should be 'creamed' against the revetment behind. My legs wouldn't obey me, because I was paralysed with fear. This had been brought on by my total anxiety for and concentration on the safety of the pilot. I couldn't summon up the extra adrenalin to hurl myself out of the way.

The racing remains of the fighter came to a smoking, slithering halt a few yards in front of me. Its pilot, with both legs raised in the air, was still securely strapped in his armoured seat. The paralysis left me and I got myself moving towards him, expecting to release a dead man from the wreckage. I suppose I took ten steps to reach him – my mind now clearing so that the urgent need to get him out of the steaming wreck became the dominating thought.

As I reached him he stared at me – not comprehending that he was alive. 'Jesus Christ,' he said hoarsely, and fainted, and I nearly followed his example.

In that detached timeless moment of shock I got him out of his Sutton Harness and, as I lugged him upright and attempted to lift him out of his seat, parachute pack and all, I felt strong hands helping me. Two of my Belgian pilots had seen it all happen and had raced across to assist. 'Bloody hell, spy,' said one. 'I thought you'd both bought it!'

So did I – and the miracle was that the young Spitfire pilot was, apart from shock, totally unscathed.

No more than a week later I was walking round the perimeter track on the southward side of the aerodrome, looking out over the view that spread below the top of the rise above Caesar's Camp and the whole panorama of Folkestone. As I stopped and gazed out, reminiscently, at the scene of my youth, the air was so still I could hear the droning of the bees and the call of birds.

I remember I was puzzled at how the scene had subtly changed since my boyhood, when I had laboriously bicycled up the hills to visit the airfield. Then I realized that a small copse of trees had been removed to give a better approach to the seaward side, and that this had opened up the view.

From a long way off I heard the sound of an express train racing towards where I was standing. My brain could only register surprise that the sound of a train, all that way beneath me in Folkestone, should carry so far, and so loudly - when, with a roar, the huge cross-Channel shell burst in the sloping field just below me. I remember the light, even brighter than the hazy sun, and then the blast wave threw me backwards, and I landed on my back in the long grass at the edge of the airfield. The rise of the ground had sheltered me, just as the thick foliage of the orchard's trees had diverted the explosion of the buzzbomb at White Gates.

The stink of picric acid and high-explosive predominated as I slowly sat up, feeling myself for injuries. Only then did I realize that I was stone deaf. Even that minor inconvenience passed in a couple of hours, but I did feel shaky for a few days.

I only mention these odd scuffles with the 'Fates' because they more than ever convinced me that there was something, or someone, keeping an eye on me. Had I walked over the rise, instead of just standing below it, trying to remember why it was that I could see the panoramic view which before the war had been hidden, I would have been much nearer the blast and undoubtedly would have been blown to pieces.

Shaken by three close brushes with death, I got a jeep and driver and went over to see if Eddie Partridge was still in Dover. When I arrived at his little corner shop, I couldn't believe my eyes. Everything behind it had been flattened into rubble and there were large gaps torn in the terraces alongside. As far as I could see Eddie's shop was untouched.

I opened the shop door - my mind racing back to the last time that I had done so, in that late summer before the war. I had been a boy then - now I was a man - yet somehow I felt just as shyly expectant, as if only a day had passed since I was last there.

Eddie was smiling at me: 'Hello, Michael! I was expecting you.'

There was no hesitation in his instant recognition of me, even though I was in RAF uniform.

I believed him and still do, because the next time I saw him was in 1953, when I went down to introduce him to my wife, Clementina. Eddie had retired by then, and lived out his days in a small cottage in a valley on the outskirts of Dover. His back was towards us as we trudged up the sloping garden where he was working on some plants.

As he turned, he spoke the same words that he had greeted me with in 1944: 'Hello, Michael! I was expecting you.'

On neither occasion did he pause before speaking, even though on this post-war visit I had a beard and moustache.

In that late summer of '44 I sat in Eddie's back room, and he and Biny told me the amazing story of their survival.

In 1940 a land mine had smashed the small house behind them, killing and wounding many people. Then a large bomb had tunnelled under their side road from the asphalt playground opposite and failed to go off. The bomb disposal squad had tried to evacuate them and Eddie had steadfastly refused. It was obviously not a DA (delayed action) bomb, or it would have exploded by the time the squad had located its final resting place. There seemed to be no point in digging it out at that juncture, and for all I know it is there still.

Other miraculous escapes had been from a number of huge trans-channel shells fired from the Pas de Calais – like the one that had nearly 'copped' me. The nearest had failed to explode and lay under the road beside them. The engineers had let that one lie there as well.

All in all, some ten high-explosive bombs or shells had surrounded that corner grocer's shop, and yet there wasn't one single pane of glass even cracked.

Eddie again told me I would survive the war, and that I would be in a great battle and see Germany beaten. 'But I've told you that before, Michael – you know it already!'

He was, of course, quite right, on both counts, he *had* told me before, and things came about just as he said.

He told me a lot more as well, but these things were of a
personal nature, and they, too, happened just as Eddie had
predicted.

I left the shop a couple of hours later and, on the way back,
I tried to explain to my bewildered driver what it was about
for the bombs' and shells' proximity to the undamaged shop
had nearly blown his mind. I didn't go into Eddie's strange
paranormal abilities too deeply – I don't think that my
driver could have handled that as well.

When I got back I wasn't too surprised to find a Lancaster
bomber – or rather the wreck of one – plastered against the
reinforced revetment that had nearly received our joint
remains when the damaged Spitfire had charged me a
couple of weeks before. The poor bomber air crew had been
shot up on a daylight attack on the defences in the Pas de
Calais and, with all their hydraulics destroyed, had tried a
landing at our small grassy airfield.

They had touched down too far along the aerodrome and
skidded straight into the revetment at the end. It had, at
least, stopped them smashing into the bungalows beyond
the field, but had cost the lives of the front gunner and bomb-
aimer. Two others had been badly wounded in the air, by
flak, which was why the pilot had brought his heavily
damaged plane back.

Forty-eight hours later, I was posted again, despite the
Belgians' protests – Michel Donnet being particularly upset
to see me go because we had all become close friends during
the Battle of the Buzzbomb.

However, 350 Squadron was to move to Lympne, and then
over to Brussels as soon as the Allies had captured it. For
this move it was thought politically expedient for them to
have a Belgian 'spy' in charge of their Intelligence. In fact he
was already on the way, straight from the Intelligence
course at Highgate.

I then had two quick postings – the first to another of those boring, nearly non-operational groups that the tide of war had left behind. This time near Bath – where I ran into the Wing Commander who had caused me a lot of grief at the group in Lancashire. He was subdued to say the least, though he was once more comfortably ensconced in his own safe little empire far from the battle area, and treated me with reserved courtesy, as one would an unexploded bomb.

I made my escape from that terrible atmosphere fairly sharpish, and a month later stepped ashore at Zeebrugge just as the troop transport behind ours blew up on a mine.

Tragically, with her sinking, a large number of ATS girls went to their deaths. There was nothing we could do. What little could be done the Royal Navy was already coping with.

As usual, there was a complete foul-up with transport, etc., but I managed to get a lift to Brussels, which was still *en fête* from its recent liberation. A few hours later I was back with my Belgians and we had a wild party. The next day I flew up, in style, to Helmond – the brick runway temporary airfield in Holland where a wing of Typhoon fighters was stationed. These machines, sturdy and tough gun-platforms, had originally been designed as fighters, but their final role was as fighter bombers and rocket-firing ground-attack aircraft. I joined them when the battle for the Rhine was about to go ahead.

We were billeted opposite the bare dusty little airfield, with its farm buildings converted into our control tower and Intelligence operations centre. Our billets were, somewhat surprisingly, in a monastery, which we shared with the monks, who seemed to accept us without a qualm, though the Abbot was a bit disturbed by our bar, not because of the liquor, which the brothers enjoyed from time to time – they were cheerful monks – but by the pictures of luscious 'Varga' girls which adorned it. He said, with good reason, that they disturbed the monks. They certainly disturbed us. Most of the local girls were built on the lines of a Dutch barge, so I can see his point.

Once again, I had to start winning over the air crews from scratch, and I was helped a lot by our gem of an Intelligence Corporal, Harold Taylor.

My first marriage had now foundered, and I had been posted so often, to so many different jobs and intensive courses, that I was becoming disorientated. I just wanted to get at the Germans, with as many weapons as I could lay my hands on, and get the whole bloody mess over and done with.

I know that many IOs who had been trained and operational, and *re*trained and operational again, and yet again, felt the same. It was never being able to discuss these techniques with another highly-trained walking encyclopaedia of Intelligence that was so frustrating. It wasn't like flying – that, and aeroplanes, you could talk about till the cows came home, even though 'talking shop' was supposed to be frowned on in the mess. Intelligence is *secret*, and that is drummed into you. 'Hele and conceal.'

I could never live that split-personality life again. It destroyed my first marriage and, had it not been for Harold Taylor and his quiet dry wit and kindness, I would have let it destroy me – because I drank far too much and (selfishly) didn't give a damn whether I survived, just so long as we had done with the killing. God knows, there was plenty of that!

With France and Belgium overrun by the Allies, much of the purpose of MI9 was over. As far as evaders were concerned, there was now only Holland, where British servicemen were being kept hidden from the Germans by devoted Dutch families.

There were, however, all the prisoners of war held in Germany, and we were very concerned that the Nazis might use them as a bargaining factor against their own lives, in the final dénouement. I talked with one or two specialists in this line of Intelligence, and I was briefed on the best course of action to pursue so far as air crew were concerned; and indeed several escapers made their perilous way across to us at this time. The fall of France released so many of our hidden evaders – some of whom had only recently been shot down, in the Beachhead and Falaise battles, that a wealth of new information had come flooding in.

I had already had news of two of my Polish friends, who had made a remarkable escape after being shot down in a raid on Posnán at the extreme range of their Wellington bombers. Eschewing conventional methods of evasion, these two intrepid Polish airmen had made their own way across Europe – passing through Germany, France and, eventually, the Spanish border by exploiting their remarkably virile charms among the man-hungry female populations of each country.

During the course of their outstanding evasion, they must have contacted, seduced and left a trail of willing women behind them. When they were finally debriefed, after M19 had picked them up from Portugal, via Spain where they had given themselves up, their story was at first disbelieved; but it was later confirmed by the fact that none of the usual escape routes or agents had been used. We called it 'Polish private enterprise'! The only thing paranormal about this evasion was the amazing sexual stamina of my two Polish friends.

Many evaders that were passed back to Britain on our way up through Belgium and Holland had remarkable escapes from the Abwehr (German counter-Intelligence under Admiral Canaris, a First World War spy) and the Gestapo. Talking to a number of them since the war, I have listened to incident after incident where 'sixth sense' gave warning of approaching danger. Time and again, I have heard the same story, with individual variations, of *precognitive awareness* in the worst moments of peril.

Such a warning came to a good friend whom I got to know well at Helmond, but in his case it came too late. Barry Gray, one of our ALOs (army personnel designated as Air Liaison Officers to co-operate with the RAF), was a cheerful fair-haired and moustached down-to-earth young man some four years older than I. He was the archetypal Briton – the result of a long line of genetic heredity from his Saxon ancestors.

Just before the Rhine crossing, in our final assault on Germany, Barry had a long talk with me. I knew that he was going in with the glider-borne attack, though of course we didn't discuss that for security reasons. We talked about survival and the paranormal, because Barry, who was happily married, knew that he wasn't going to make it. He was quite matter of fact about it, but I also knew that I would not see him again.

We talked far into the night, and he left the next day.

I heard what happened when another ALO attached to us learnt the details.

Barry's glider landed under heavy fire from an 88 mm dual-purpose gun, and was hit as it came to a halt. Barry got out, unscathed, and dived for cover, but his batman was hit and trapped in the glider. Typically, though he was comparatively safe, Barry crawled back to the machine to bring out his badly wounded comrade. The next shell from the 88 killed them both. I can see him in my mind quite clearly as I write these words.

That Rhine crossing cost us many fine lives, in the short bloody action on our narrow front. None finer than Barry Gray.

It was a high price to pay for the Grey Dawn of Freedom.

11 The Face of Evil

Germany stank of death. From the moment we lurched across the bridge we could smell it everywhere.

Goch, a small town saturated with high explosive from a massive air raid, lay stinking in the sun – the bomb craters interconnected like obscene lace. Someone had splashed the huge words 'This was Goch' in white, dripping paint on the one large wall standing upright in the rubble.

This part of Germany is full of history – and the atmosphere generated by the neat farms and orderly pine forests should have been one of purpose and balance, with the weight of its past giving it equilibrium.

The damage was minimal, except where pockets of resistance held out against the tanks, so the pattern of the countryside was almost unchanged. It was typically *Alles in Ordnung*, in the geometrically exact way of Teutonic thinking. But its infrastructure – its *ethos* was in chaos, and it reeked of evil.

By this time my senses were so sharp that a breaking twig had my gun out before it registered that I even had the weapon unholstered. It wasn't the 'twitch', as we called it, but something far more basic – the complete survival mechanism in operation. The whole line of advance was loaded with booby traps: grenades attached to doors of empty houses, trip wires leading to mines laid under piles of wood or even attached to dead bodies, and other delights thought up by the fertile minds of the SS men in the retreating German army.

At Achmer-Husted – a Luftwaffe base on the banks of the Dortmund-Ems canal – we lost some of our airmen. They were shot by small-calibre high-powered rifles fired from the wooded landscape across the canal.

I had only been with this Typhoon Wing for a few days – leaving my last one to replace an Intelligence officer who had been killed in action.

The CO was a South African – tough and resourceful and an experienced hunter. He called me over to where he was taking cover behind his jeep.

'Spy,' he said quietly, 'winkle the bastards out! Take the ferret.' (The ferret was a small armoured car.) He pointed towards the other bank of the Dortmund-Ems waterway, and I scuttled across to the small group of RAF regiment airmen who were trying to make out where the sniper fire was coming from. Their sergeant, a grey-haired, forty-year-old northerner, seemed surprised to see me.

'CO says to take them out – we'll use the AFV,' I said, and only then did I realize that their officer was one of those who had been hit, hence the CO's choice of me to do the job! As he had no idea of what my capabilities were in this line of work, I can only think that he was going by instinct, and, at the same time, trying me out.

We crossed the bridge – the fact that it was mined nagging at the lower half of my body, but 7th Armoured had raced across it hours earlier, and although pockets of determined resistance were still fighting in the woods, the chances were that there was no one left to blow it up.

As soon as we hit the shell-blasted road at the other end of the bridge bullets started to 'spang' off the sides of the tough little armoured fighting vehicle.

'Farmhouse left! One hundred yards.' I knew for certain, as I said the words, even though there were no gun-flashes visible. We swung round to face it, and the gunner chopped the top of the half-hidden building into splintered wood and plaster.

A thin cry of: *'Kamerad!'* sounded and, as we piled out to

crouch alongside the AFV, three small, emaciated figures stumbled out of the smoking farmhouse with their arms raised above their close-cropped heads.

'Christ,' grunted the sergeant, 'they're nowt but bloody kids.'

And so they were – thirteen-year-old Hitler Youth, their shocked gaunt faces running with tears.

One made a sudden move as he stumbled, and my reflexes nearly betrayed me; but in a flash the sergeant's hand fell on my gun arm.

'Nay, lad!' he said.

For a moment I didn't know what to do – but the sergeant did and, taking his army belt off, he bent each 'junior-superman' over his knees and whacked his backside till he howled. Their shocked faces dissolved into normal cries of any boy who had misbehaved being chastised by his father.

I don't approve of physical punishment, but the single basic action of that tough, honest Yorkshireman saved the sanity of those boys, who had been turned into murderers, or *heroes* (depending upon which side you were on) and who now realized that this whacking was the only punishment that they would get.

It saved our sanity too: we could so easily have shot them if they had tried to slug it out with us.

On the way back, the three young boys, for that is what they now were, excitedly discussed their first close-up views of a Typhoon.

I often wonder what would have been their fate if the positions had been reversed, if we had been *German* troops and these thirteen-year-olds British boys in an invaded England of 1940.

All this may seem irrelevant in a book about the paranormal, but I want to give some idea of the strange feeling of shock and detachment that so many of us felt at this time of kill or be killed.

This was the climax of nearly six long years of war. For

me, having been a part of it all, from amateur civilian ARP to professional trained operator, through the long pull of defeat right into the heart of the enemy, and then to find this personification of evil in the callous leaving of these petrified children to guard the retreat, it had all become a gothic nightmare.

Up till then, even under the tuition of the Poles, I had not considered my enemy as other than human. All the warnings that we had received in the thirties indicated to me that Germany was being led to war by a small number of evil men, practising rituals and perverting their country's ethos. This was the first time I had come face to face with the full realization of how brutally low a cultured and civilized people had been brought. Children had been left to die for the Führer who skulked in his underground bunker in Berlin. It was monstrous and twisted, like a painting by Hieronymus Bosch.

What happened next completed the horror picture of what National Socialism really meant.

Within a few kilometres of our advance airfield at Celle, set among orderly rows of pine trees, each equipped with a nesting box for the birds, was a wired-in compound surrounded by lines of temporary huts. At first glance it looked like a prisoner-of-war camp, with its watch towers and double barbed-wire fences, until the stench hit you and you realized that the long white mound of carcases piled ten feet high was an obscene pyramid of naked men, women and children – starved to skeletal death. Edgar Allan Poe, in his darkest nightmares, could never have imagined horror like that.

The smoke from the gas-fired incinerators was still hanging over the ghastly scene, for the inhuman monsters who had perpetrated this crime against humanity had been caught in the act of trying to destroy the evidence.

I am sure that clever psychologists and psychiatrists have neat labels and professionally acceptable explanations for the Nazi concentration camps and the mentalities

of those who were responsible for them. The ancients had far
better descriptions for the mental condition of men and
women who practised this sort of sub-bestial behaviour.
They called it demonic possession and, having seen it and
smelt it, and never being able to forget it, I agree with them.

How many of the scholarly and, no doubt, sincere
academics who have neatly categorized this behaviour of
the Nazis actually stood, stunned with horror, in the midst
of the hell of Belsen, Treblinka, Sachsen-Hausen, Dachau
and the other manifestations of the nether pit?

I am not going to describe it further – there are films – there
are photographs – there are whole television series devoted
to this subject. I can only tell you that none of them can
convey the full horror we experienced when we realized that
we hadn't been fighting Germany but naked evil itself.
Belsen hit us in the face with the foetid blast of Satanic
darkness. God knows what it did for the few survivors of that
unbelievable horror.

Many years later I did a tour of the RAF bases in Germany,
mainly to thank them for the help that they had so
generously given to the Peruvian earthquake relief operation in 1970-1. At one of the RAF bases at Rhine-Dahlen, an
army colonel had asked us if we would do a show at
Fellingbosch, in Westphalia.

Driving in this sparsely inhabited part of Germany, I got
hopelessly lost in the pitch blackness of a rainy night. Alfred
Ravel, the musical clown, and my manager at that time, was
as lost as I was.

'Don't know where we are, Michael,' he said, wrestling
with a damp map.

Then I felt it! That awful creeping sense of evil. 'We're near
Belsen!' I said, with horrified conviction, shivering in the
chill of realization.

'How can you possibly tell?' protested Alfie, who is a
practical soul.

'I know it – I can feel it!'

The car turned the corner at that point and, in the rain-lashed headlights, I could see the dim tunnel of the road ahead. A hundred or so metres further on we passed the entrance to that dark place. *It still smelt of death!*

The concert went well, and I was chatting to the chaplain, a man of my own age, with 1939–45 ribbons on his tunic.

Night firing from the tank range was in progress, and we could hear the loud whisper of the shells as they passed to the side of the camp.

'It's just like it was in '45,' I remarked.

'I was in that battle too,' said the padre. 'I took Holy Orders after the war and came back into the army. I was a subaltern then – Guards. Armoured.'

I told him about my experience at the entrance to Belsen.

'I'm not surprised,' he said grimly. 'It's a dreadful place, in the full sense of the word – the whole area of the compound reeks of evil. Do you know, no birds fly there – no bees either! No small animals ever seem to cross that awful space where the mass graves are. The helicopter pilots even say that there is a down draught over it. Nothing to do with the pine forests around it – but actually over the open compound itself. Like dead air. My dog won't go near it and neither will I. There is a *psychic barrier* around it.'

Then he paused and, suddenly, looked much older than he was. 'There are Germans who come there and picnic—' he said, at last.

They *must* have the same mentality as those people who 'feed' off a bad traffic accident and, ghoulishly, hang around the scene of an air crash. I met a number of their type during my investigation into my son's death only a couple of years later.

My friend Osmond Kelsick, a quiet West Indian fighter pilot, with whom I flew many hours in a captured ME 108 sports plane, summed it all up for me when we flew up to Kastrup airfield in Denmark just after VE day.

Our light plane tossed and bounced in the superheated air above Belsen as, below us, the flame-throwing tanks and Bren carriers moved in to burn out the centre of the concentration camp.

It was supposed to destroy the typhus, but we all knew that was only the *excuse*. The burning of Belsen was a symbolic cleansing of the soil and the appalling veil that hung over it like a shadow.

Osmond looked down at the rising flames and skidded the plane out of the turbulence. 'Thank Christ for that!' he breathed, and he did not intend it as a blasphemy.

To us both, the ultimate blasphemy was Belsen itself.

When the cease-fire came, it was like running at full speed into a barbed-wire fence.

I was in the operations caravan, which sat in the middle of Celle airfield, when the message came over the teleprinter. It was around one in the morning. The bomb line (beyond which we would attack each day) had not advanced since the last report, and the squadrons were readying for an all-out attack with their rockets on shipping in the Baltic. (A broadside of one Typhoon's eight 60-lb rockets was the same as that of a 6-inch-gunned cruiser.)

As the signals operator tore the message off the machine, I stared uncomprehendingly at it.

It was over! At last it was finished!

All day the German radio had played solemn music, from the *Götterdämmerung,* The Twilight of the Gods. Sobbing German announcers had informed the nation that the Führer was dying in his bunker at the head of the Third Reich – the *Herrenvolk*!

Beneath them, yes! At the head of them, no! That final battle was fought by fanatical SS, who had nothing to lose, and by ordinary Wehrmacht soldiers and anti-aircraft gunners of the Luftwaffe who turned their 88-mm guns against Soviet and Allied tanks, brave soldiers who fought till the last round and who had everything to lose.

Whatever their faults, the ordinary German soldiers fought the Battle of Germany with great courage and tenacity – only the fanatical Nazis remained unredeemed to

the end. Many of them skulked in civilian clothes. I flushed
out one – my batman! – an apparently reserved and polite
German private soldier who turned out to be an SS colonel.
After that I never allowed my gun far from my hand.

Another I caught with my dog, in a marshy piece of
underbrush not far from Schleswigland airfield, where we
had moved a week before. I disarmed him of a small
automatic pistol and marched him back to hand him over
to the service police.

Himmler was caught in much the same way, by someone
who 'felt' that he was not what he claimed to be. The instinct
is part of our survival mechanism. In my case, it was
subjective clairvoyance, the SS colonel just *smelt* wrong.

I was led to the other SS man, by angry shouts. He was
holding up a German farmer, to change clothes with him.
My dog brought him down when he turned to run. I'm glad
Sally, my Alsatian, an ex-German guard dog we had picked
up on the way through Europe, did the job for me, or I would
have been forced to shoot him as he ran off. Shooting people
in the back is not my line of work.

My poor 'bleddy' Poles! All the agony of Poland had been
in vain – even the last desperate uprising in Warsaw! The
Russians had waited across the Vistula till the ghetto and
the Polish Officer Corps – the two unlikely allies of the Battle
of Warsaw – were destroyed and only then crossed the river
and took the city for the Soviet.

One Polish air crew had been wiped out when their pilot,
unable to drop the desperately-needed supplies of guns and
ammunition to the Polish patriots, deliberately crashed his
four-engined Halifax bomber onto a German tank in the
main Square of Warsaw.

Now it was all over, and the Poles were the first to be
betrayed in the pragmatism of peace.

Czechoslovakia was soon to follow.

Berlin was divided, and the whole hollow sham was
declared to be VE Day. Victory in Europe! For whom?

As our RAF trucks had rumbled and juddered their way

up through Hamburg on the way to Schleswig near the Danish border I had seen the dull, hopeless hatred in the face of the great Hanseatic port. Hamburg was a nightmare, a lunar landscape of stinking death. One hundred thousand dead at least were buried deep in the ruins of the collapsed cellars. The survivors lived in holes.

Dresen was in ashes, the result of the firestorm that had killed another fifty thousand women and children.

As I pondered these things on long walks with my dog, I saw a test V2 rocket, fired from Husum, wing its way upwards at the head of a great plume of steam till it vanished into the high cirrus cloud of the summer sky. VE Day? Or the start of World War Three?

I got a jeep, and a driver, and went down to BAFO HQ at Bad Oeynhausen – I needed something to do, rather than just sit there, disarming the northern forces of the Luftwaffe. I suggested that I could be more usefully employed collecting pieces of German research aircraft, about which I knew quite a bit. But their decision was typical. I was with the wrong section. I was not an engineering officer. Therefore, etc.

I explained that my father had designed aeroplanes, and that as he had taught me a lot, I also understood the principles of rocket flight.

No dice! So back to sitting around, twiddling my thumbs, till my demobilization came through.

A wasted journey, but for one thing – an experience that I had while lying on my back on the slopes of the Minden Hills. It was a beautiful day and, as I lay on the grass, my mind went back to my childhood in Folkestone. How many times as a lonely boy walking my dogs along the Downs, had I lain back on the long stalks of waving grass and felt my hands dig into the chalk beneath me?

The sky was clouded and I felt my breathing slowing down until I was taking deep lungfuls of that pure pine-tree scented air. Then I noticed a small cloud rising in the distance and the thought came into my mind. 'A cloud, like a man's hand.'

It grew rapidly in size as it approached me, until it became a great swirling spiral of white vapour; and I seemed to see that it was made up of hundreds of thousands of souls – in a huge flying cloud.

I lay, spellbound by the subjective clairvoyant notion, and my mind felt the contact and the release as I heard the sky ring with their silent shout: 'It's over! It's over!'

Thirty years later I read some notes written by Nicola Tesla in which he described a similar sort of subjective vision concerning his dying mother. His had been inspired by a picture of angels and cherubim that he had retained in his subconscious mind from his youth. Mine I recognized as a mental projection of a picture that I had admired among Gustave Doré's illustrations to Dante's *Inferno*.

It was a classical case of an archetypal manifestation of my own Overmind (or supra-conscious). In the first peaceful and utterly tranquil surroundings that I had found since the war had ended, I released my vision of the dead who had been sacrificed in the long struggle against evil.

I went back to my jeep, which I had left a mile away, my mind full of peace – and walked safely through a *minefield* without even realizing it.

When I got back to Schleswigland my SIO had received a new instruction from BAFO, via Group. We were to help RAF engineering officers to locate any German research aircraft that were left scattered in the area between Schleswig and the new Russian border. What an original idea! It hadn't been a wasted journey after all.

There were plenty of these science-fiction-like machines hidden away in various workshops on airfields all over Northern Germany. V1s with cockpits and extended wings had been hurriedly converted for use by half-trained young Nazi fanatics. They were equipped with jettisonable undercarriages and were about as stable as a flying cow. Those poor deluded youths would have been lucky to have got them airborne, let alone fly them.

Hanna Reiche, the phenomenal woman pilot who had tried to rescue the Führer from Berlin in a Fiesler Storch monoplane, had actually flown one of these V1 people's fighter which was a sort of crazy 'Volkswagen of the air.'

The Nazis were mad! Of that there was no doubt – a raving mad fanatical bureaucracy which had lost all touch with reality. Many of these weird 'research' aircraft proved the point that, technologically, they had gone berserk.

The 'Natter', a tiny rocket-propelled fighter armed with an explosive warhead or rocket shells, was designed to be launched vertically from a tower and piloted by a German kamikaze pilot, who, just before he rammed the bomber formation which was his target, was given a slim chance of blowing himself free with an explosive charge. Only a raving lunatic could have designed such an aerial abortion, and the one brave but insane pilot to attempt to fly it performed a four-hundred-mile-an-hour loop on take off and rammed himself and the Natter into a crater many feet deep. The Research Section of the German Ministry of Aircraft Production was still trying to get another simple-minded pilot to fly Natter Mark II when the war ended.

At BAFO and in discussion with the various individual IOs from Allied teams of specialists investigating the Nazi infrastructure, I learned how right our pre-war messages had been regarding the Nazis and their use of ritual practices of the most perverted kind.

I was told about large quantities of Nazi files, and shown some of the evidence relating to SS rituals and their detailed organization. Both the SS and the Himmler empire of perverted fanatics reeked of twisted magical rituals and unbridled megalomania. Take, for example, the dressing up in the black sombre garb of death, the runic insignias and banners, so reminiscent of those of the 'Golden Dawn' and other magical societies, the grisly paraphernalia of the Nazis with their glorification of the 'Heroes' death', the Valhalla image of the fallen warrior – these are all soaked in magical symbolism.

Now it was coming out into the light of day, and reason totally rejected it. As far as the Allies and the free world press were concerned, there was nothing other than political significance in this insane mumbo jumbo. It was described as Nazi propaganda and hurriedly shoved under the official carpet of pragmatism.

Already, the defeat of Nazi Germany was being ascribed solely to better Allied war production, better quartermastering, better organization, a better political system, better training, better bureaucracy, better leadership – in fact to anything but the supreme effort made by the ordinary people: not by the professionals who had been so soundly and completely whipped at the start of the war but by the everyday men and women who had made that tremendous six-year effort that finally led to the complete reversal of their earlier defeat.

The ineptitude and inefficiency of their so-called leaders had brought them and their countries close to the brink of disaster and near-slavery. It was the people, believing in their ethos, who had freed Europe from the obscene bondage of the Nazis, not the politicians, pragmatists, media manipulators and safely protected bureaucrats. It had been a Peoples' War and they had won it.

Now, despite all that sacrifice and suffering by the ordinary folk who had brought victory, the bureaucrats claimed the credit and were already busily engaged in forging their own private empires in post-war Europe.

The industrialists moved in to resuscitate the near-dying German production machine and to stake their claim in it. The financiers assembled to divide up the spoils and to inject new life into the bankrupt financial system of Germany, which they would now control. The politicians argued and bargained with the Soviet – using as currency the freedom of millions of innocent people.

VE Day in Europe? In God's name – in what context? Within weeks our disillusionment was complete. It was obvious to the thinking men and women who had fought the war that the Allies were going to lose the peace.

In despair at the extraordinary inertia that seemed to
have gripped everything, I took to going for long walks with
my dog Sally, who seemed to be the sanest individual that I
knew amid the chaos of those early days of pretended peace.

Sally saved my life.

I had been culling the overpopulated deer of the
Schleswig-Holstein forests and had wounded one. I hate
killing but when I have to, I kill clean.

I followed the wounded deer until I managed to despatch it
– and then started back through the marshy country into
which the poor beast had led me.

I felt light-headed and feverish and very unsteady on my
feet. At this time I only weighed around nine stone eight
pounds which, for my height of five feet nine inches and
bone structure, was far too light. I must have had little
resistance left, because I had, in Kipling's words, 'Strained
nerve and brain and sinew' in those past three years since I
had been brought back from the dead at Abbey Lodge.

I don't remember much more, except coughing up a lot of
blood and a violent pain in my chest. Sally kept me going as I
stumbled along – and got me near to the airfield. Then she
brought me help! I woke up in my bed in the mess – drifted off
again and woke again in Schleswig hospital.

For a time I hovered between life and death, because I
wasn't particularly interested in either – then I remember
Osmond Kelsick standing beside my bed.

'Come on, you stupid bastard! Where have you been?' he
asked, his familiar grin shining at me. 'Come on, Michael!
Don't just lie there. Remember, we've got a lot to do! You're
coming to the West Indies! We're going to smuggle rum to
Key West.'

This was a private joke that we shared as part of our post-
war plan. Pity we never did it!

The medical staff put up quite a battle for my tired life –
and won it! I don't think I did much to help them – being quite
resigned to drifting in and out of consciousness. I just didn't

care, which was very selfish of me, as one of the sisters pointed out forcefully: 'There are a lot of people doing their best for you. Don't you dare let them down!' Of course she was right.

When I finally came out of it my nerves had taken rather a pounding and now showed it. I was as jumpy as a cat and my eyes kept watering.

One day they started crying in earnest – even though I didn't feel particularly depressed. It wasn't a question of sobbing or tearful sadness – just endless tears which poured out of me – necessitating my drinking quarts of water to replace the fluid and taking bottles of salt tablets and potassium to counteract the cramping.

From Schleswig I was taken down to 8th Base general hospital near Bad Oeynhausen – at Bad Salzuflen I think it was – and put in a ward with other exhausted flotsam and jetsam of the tide of war.

These were all air crew who, for some reason, had 'gone round the bend'. None of them bore that filthy stigma of LMF on their documents; one had been awarded the Conspicuous Gallantry Medal, four had received DFCs – and all of them had had too much.

One, a commissioned air-gunner – and the one with the Conspicuous Gallantry Medal – had been forced to bail out of burning bombers once too often. Now he 'bailed out' of bed about three times a night. Two of us would climb out of ours and put him back, shivering with shock.

Another sat there, glowering at any female who came into the small ward. He was a pilot with two tours of operations, and he had gone round the twist when his pretty young wife wrote him a 'Dear John' letter to tell him that she was pregnant by a Yank. It had taken six friends to hold him down, till the MO could get a hypodermic into his arm. His peculiarity manifested itself in throwing full urine bottles at any nurse who unknowingly supplied him with an empty one. Except for this dangerous habit he was a nice person.

Feeling a fraud because, apart from my skeletally thin

body and constantly leaking tear ducts, I felt OK, I was flown back to Britain that autumn in a DC3 (Dakota) filled with badly-injured airmen. Many of them had been smashed up in car wrecks when they were deliberately run off the roads by German truck drivers supposedly working for the Allies. A German had tried this on my jeep, until I fired a burst of 9 mm alongside his driver's cabin, when he had quickly pulled over to let us pass. Other men were broken or burnt in air crashes – most were badly injured and many were in pain.

The weather clamped 'solid' over the North Sea, and I went up front with the air crew. If I was going to 'buy it' now, I wanted to be where I belonged – with the airmen flying the plane.

We landed at Manston, which is perched on the cliffs above Ramsgate, in minimal visibility, and without FIDO but guided down to safety by a new technique called GCA – Ground Controlled Approach – by which radar operators 'talked' the pilot down to the end of the runway, where he made his visual contact at the last minute. (FIDO was a huge wall of flame which literally burned up the fog to clear the flare path for landing.)

Nowadays every plane landing in low visibility uses GCA, plus all the other electronic marvels. In the autumn of 1945 it was a miracle! Without it a planeload of badly injured men would have gone into the sea, or head-on into the cliffs, attempting to land in that foul weather.

At Wroughton General Hospital I had time to think what I would do now that I was on the way to demobilization, or a medical discharge – whichever came first. I had no doubt that I had been guided by some power that had steered my headlong rush from one hazard to another. Whether that guiding influence was a manifestation of my own supra-conscious, a relic of the survival mechanism of my early ancestors or the work of a discarnate entity assisting me in moments of peril I didn't really know. But since 1942 'it' had brought me back from death itself, saved me in two bombing incidents, in London and from a V1 at Hawkinge, warded off

a trans-Channel shell with a few feet of high ground and
stopped a charging Spitfire only yards away. Counting the
number of things that had been fired at or around me – from
88 mm high velocity shells to the odd bullet from sniper fire –
'it' had done well to keep me alive. Even my reason, though a
bit shaken, was still in one piece.

I was extremely grateful, and could only ponder on what
might be the purpose of my survival. In effect, I wondered
what I was supposed to do next, to justify these odd escapes.
My brother sent me a beautiful cartoon of two angel
stretcher-bearers carrying off an exhausted guide with his
eyes crossed and a bent halo twisted round his head. 'Poor
bastard!' said one of them. 'He's been in charge of young
Bentin.'

In my section of the ward at Wroughton was a Spitfire
pilot with a broken back, which he had sustained when a
'Sprog' pilot flying a similar machine had climbed into him.
The other machine spun in with its pilot dead inside his
flattened cockpit cover, but my chum – broken back and all,
had managed to bail out. He was encased in plaster from his
hips to his neck, and he concealed this heavy cast with a
high-neck pullover – which he wore with his hospital blues.
These dreadful garments, of bright ultramarine, made one
look like a symbol of wounded poverty. What their purpose
was I shall never know. To preserve our worn-out uniforms,
perhaps? Or was it to elicit sympathy from the rest of the
world?

In these sad but colourful outfits my broken-backed
Spitfire chum, accompanied by my cheerfully weeping self,
would amble down to the local pub for a leisurely beer. I had
been told to drink as much *water* as I could, and this is what
the local beer largely consisted of.

The regulars at the pub, mainly farmers, were fascinated
by my chum's drinking technique. As he couldn't bend back
his head, he hung onto the bar with his left hand, with both
feet firmly against the bottom rail, and bent back his upper
half so that he looked as though he was performing a slow

motion back flip. He then poured the beer from the tipped glass in his right hand into his backward slanting mouth. It was really spectacular to watch, as I stood behind ready to 'field' him if his left hand lost its grip.

Bets were also laid as to whether I should actually 'weep' beer. Free beer was provided to test the theory, but the results were inconclusive. At least, thank God, I hadn't lost my sense of humour.

The same could hardly be said for the psychiatrist to whom I was sent for examination. He was only the second psychiatrist that I had encountered in the RAF, the first one being the nasty piece of work at Blackpool.

I wasn't too impressed with this one either. Firstly he had a bad twitch, which didn't give the patient much confidence. Secondly he was humourless and totally literal. I'm sure he was completely credulous and would accept anything the patient said as gospel.

He asked me some extraordinarily impertinent questions about my sex life, and my relations with my parents and, being bored, I thought up some quite impossible answers. This seemed to brighten him up no end and he started to make copious notes. He even brought out a Rorschach test pad and we made ink-blot butterflies. These were supposed to convey something highly significant to me, and I didn't want to disappoint him, so I conjured up some way-out associations for him to play with.

He was delighted, and his pen fairly flew across the paper. Reluctantly, he let me go, urging me to come and see him again soon. I went to my Senior Medical Officer and asked if I could see someone else in that line of work, as I felt that he might keep me there just to write a thesis about my peculiarities.

The SMO made an appointment for me with another psychiatrist and, when I went to see him, my previous psychiatrist was there already – the first patient.

In February 1946, I went to the Olympia Exhibition Centre in London and walked out, an hour later, dressed in a grey pin-striped suit, a white riding mac, a brown trilby hat – and carrying shirts, underwear, socks and a tie in a paper parcel under my arm.

By an Act of the Air Council, I was once again a civilian. I had been officially demobilized. I also carried, in my pocket, £55 sterling, the war gratuity for over four years of my life that a grateful, if somewhat parsimonious, country had awarded me.

I felt that it was cheap at the price.

12 Goon Magic and the Bug-eyed Monster

After those long years of war, suddenly becoming a civilian again was quite difficult to get used to. I had no marriage left, and no other home to go to, and so my parents suggested that I come to live, temporarily, with them. I didn't like to impose on them, but I was a shadow of my former self and I could see the kind wisdom of their offer. Their financial circumstances, which had taken a heavy blow when they were forced to leave Folkestone, had reduced their standard of living considerably. My mother no longer played bridge, but devoted her whole time to looking after my father, and now me as well!

I had rather grudgingly been offered a pension by the RAF, and I had turned it down. It was a half-disability (whatever that meant) pension and would have amounted to £3 a week - on account of the after-effects of the faulty ATT/TAB injection, administered back in 1942. I told the pension board that I felt I could make my own way in life without their limited assistance, and they insisted that I should immediately sign a document waiving any future claim. I signed it and washed my hands of the whole sorry business.

Furthermore, I was told that, because I was a volunteer and of dual nationality, I had no right to the free university grant which was being handed out to young people who had served in the Forces under compulsion - often only for a matter of a few months. It was this blow to any chance I would have had of completing my education, which had

been so brusquely interrupted by the war, that finally
decided me on my next course of action. I determined to by-
pass a university education and concentrate on making a
living. However, my choice of a career seemed to have
narrowed down to going into the chocolate trade or
becoming a comedian. My chances of making it as an actor
on the legitimate stage were now low, as my stammer had
returned and was a definite handicap outside the declama-
tory type of stage roles which were the province of
Shakespeare, and I had an introduction to a well-known
firm of chocolate makers, given to me by an old RAF
colleague.

Then the choice was made for me when my old friend Tony
Sherwood turned up and we had a joyful reunion. I hadn't
seen him since 1941, when we had met in a night club where I
had a temporary engagement as a drummer and our
friendship had been instantaneous and lasting. Tony had
been trained in Canada, on a pilot's course, and had flown
Oxfords (twin-engined training planes) during the war. As
he had been an apprentice draughtsman at Hawker's just
prior to the war this talented amateur jazz pianist had been
reserved for training air crew rather than risked on
operational flying (in spite of his many protests).

Together we made a good team, and seemed to have a
natural rapport – both playing jazz or just being good
friends. We laughed a lot – and Tony (my brother) gave us an
idea for a double act. It was to recite a Russian fairy story, of
great grimness, and to accompany it with a sort of demented
mime. It was really Goonery, long before either of us had
thought about comedy on those lines.

We rehearsed the act for two months and then tried it out
at an audition at Collins Music Hall in Islington. It was
received in deathly silence. Nothing daunted, we had
another bash, this time at an audition for Vivian Van
Damm, the owner of the Windmill Theatre.

This tiny showplace, in London's West End, had the
motto: 'We never closed.' Meaning, of course, during the

whole war - including the two blitzes of 1940 and 1944. It also featured stationary nudes who, for some reason, were allowed to appear naked on the minute stage only so long as they didn't move!

Van Damm liked the audition and hired us for a six-week season of six shows a day. We had got the act off the ground.

Those 216 shows broke us into what an audience can be like! When you consider that some of the stalwarts in that small audience stayed in the theatre for all the day's shows - starting at 10 o'clock in the morning and finishing at 10.20 at night, you can see that the comedians had a tough job - because not one word could be changed after the act had been approved by the Lord Chamberlain.

After the short run we were both out of work again. We played a couple of dates for Butlin's Holiday Camps and did a BBC broadcast on *Variety Bandbox* on radio and two television shows on Christmas Day 1946.

Then Tony Sherwood was offered a scholarship and a grant to study piano at the Guildhall School of Music. We talked it over, and I told him that he couldn't turn down a chance like that. So we parted professional company and I went solo.

While I was at the Windmill I had met Harry Secombe at an audition, and we instantly found ourselves on the same wavelength. Harry played that theatre in the show before our Russian Act moved in, and we often used to meet at Allen's Club across the street - a tiny private club where you could get a drink out of hours and where Pop Allen would often mark it up on the slate as we were all so broke.

Harry introduced me to an emaciated and wildly articulate Irishman called 'Spike' Milligan who was playing guitar with the Bill Hall Trio, a hilarious mime act of considerable musical skill. They had been gunners together in the Royal Artillery in Italy, and had both finished up in CSE (the Army Entertainment Section), giving shows by soldiers to soldiers.

I had been writing radio scripts with Harry for that

marvellous good-natured and brightly intelligent Welsh-
man to perform, and one of these had clashed with another
star comedian's script. So we were both invited to meet the
other, rival scriptwriter, who turned out to be an ex-major
from First Airborne, now a post-war publican in his family-
owned pub, the Grafton Arms near Victoria. Two pints of
good English ale each later, we were all happily discussing
comedy and the madder side of war as though we had known
each other for years. A few days later we brought Spike down
to the pub and had a wild evening of ad-lib comedy.

Jimmy Grafton was clever enough to see that here was the
nucleus of a brand-new type of comedy team, and when,
shortly afterwards, our small group of iconoclasts was
joined by Peter Sellers, whom we had also met through the
Windmill and Allen's Club the Fates decreed that the four of
us would be the cause of a comedy revolution on radio.

Meanwhile I had been working intermittently as both a
writer and a comedian, mainly the latter because so few
other established comedians would employ me as the
former! I was still living with my parents, who never ceased
to help and encourage my effors to break into the music-hall
side of show business.

Pop had made a number of friends in this medium when
he had successfully healed Adelaide Hall, the talented black
singer who was one of Britain's favourite music-hall and
musical comedy stars. She, in turn, had recommended Pop
to a highly successful comedian called Jack Warner.

Their first meeting was over the telephone, when Jack
rang up my father, at Adelaide's insistence, to tell him that
he was in bad trouble with his ankle and in great pain. Pop
·picked up his exact condition and precisely where the pain
was located over the telephone, and told Jack that he would
be healed during the night.

Around three in the morning, Jack woke up with the
sensation of great heat in his ankle – as though very hot
hands were manipulating it. After that, he fell asleep,
considerably relieved from the pain, which had been almost

unbearable. The next morning he woke up with the pain gone, and well able to do his shows that evening – something that, the previous night, he had thought would be impossible!

Jack is one of those straight-from-the-shoulder Englishmen, a Londoner of great charm and wit, and he became a very close friend of my family. He also helped me with advice and encouragement and, to this day, is a valued source of friendly advice on performance and material. He is a real professional and, as he trained as a motor engineer in France, speaks fluent French. He is also a fine actor, as well as an entertainer, and it was in this role that Pop saw him clairvoyantly. One day, after the war, when Jack had come over to our family's flat in Barnes, Pop told him that he would become famous as a policeman. Soon afterwards Jack got the part of a copper in a film written by Ted Willis, *The Blue Lamp*.

Jack rang up to tell Pop the news: 'It's not the longest part I've ever had, Adam! I get shot in the first twenty minutes, by Dirk Bogarde.'

Nevertheless, Pop picked up that it would be a milestone in Jack's career, and, in fact, he stole most of the Press notices when the film was premièred.

Often Jack would come over to discuss his career, because Pop, since 1942 or so, had been accurately predicting its course.

Once again Pop told him: 'You're going to be famous, as a policeman.'

'Do you mean as a detective, Adam?' asked the puzzled Jack, because after playing PC Dixon, the policeman who had been shot, he had gone on to play one or two detective roles in other films.

'No!' said Pop, determinedly. 'It's as an ordinary copper – the policeman on the beat – that you will be most famous!'

I remember another occasion when Pop told me, in Jack's presence, that he could see him, in a copper's uniform.

Not too long afterwards Jack rang Pop and told him:

'Funny thing, Adam, they've asked me to play a policeman. It's for the BBC – a television series about a police station. It's written by Ted Willis, who liked my performance in *The Blue Lamp* so much that he's resuscitated PC Dixon.'

'That's it!' Pop almost shouted out the words. 'That's the part to take! You'll never regret it.'

My father told me about a visit from Jack after that phone call, when apparently he had been in two minds whether to take the TV part or to make another film which had been offered to him at the same time. Finally he accepted the role of PC Dixon, and the TV Series *Dixon of Dock Green* ran on BBC television for over twenty years.

Abruptly my own career, an erratic hotchpotch of 'extra' work in films, the odd cabaret engagement and bits and pieces of television, took an unexpected turn for the better. I had been staying for the weekend with my brother and sister-in-law, two of my favourite people, and we had enjoyed a wildcat session of imaginative comedy and a lot of laughs. Suddenly, the old chair that I was standing on to illustrate some comedy point broke off at the back – leaving me with the fractured piece in my hands.

'Blimey! I'm sorry, Bro!' I said, knowing how broke we all were and wondering how much a new chair would cost.

'Not to worry!' said my brother. Then, grinning broadly, he took the chairback from me and held it like a submachine gun. 'You'll be shot at dawn, of course,' he chuckled.

Then and there, using the oddly effective shape that the broken back of the chair made, Tony, Mona and I took hysterical turns to mime all the different articles that its silhouette suggested.

When we finished, weak with laughter, Tony said: 'You'd better keep it as a souvenir, Michael! I'll turn the bottom half into a stool.'

It was a calm, clear, winter's night, and I walked back to Barnes in the bright moonlight – a distance of a few miles from Tony's small flat in Mortlake. All the way I kept playing with that intriguingly shaped chairback that I had accidentally broken.

I really only took it with me to show Pop and Ma, as a joke. I had no money so the only way I could repay all their kindness was to make them laugh, and the chairback looked like doing just that.

About half-way along that lonely walk back to my parents' flat, I suddenly realized what I *really* held in my hands – a comedy routine of complete originality. In the morning when I showed them a rough routine – which I performed like a politician's speech – Ma said: 'That's it, Michael!'

'I know!' I said. 'Now, all I have to do is to work out and rehearse a nice tight comedy routine!'

It actually took three months of rehearsal before I got it right. Sounds ridiculous, doesn't it – but that is how long it took me to turn a rough, halting series of visual pictures into a smooth, rapidly-flowing, fast moving and totally natural sequence of visual 'gags' that fitted the high standard of professionalism required by a music-hall performance.

I don't believe that the 'accidental' breaking of that chairback when three visual minds were present was purely by chance. Certainly the flash of realization on that long walk home was pure, subjective clairvoyance. Of that I am sure. Someone told me, and showed me, what to do with the broken remains of a Victorian wooden dining-room chair!

People who saw me perform my broken chairback routine still remember it because it was so completely original; and one part of that strange, oddly effective mime was when I turned the chairback like a giant key opening a door! It proved to be another key to my door marked summer.

Armed with that broken chairback I walked onto the small stage at the Nuffield Centre and, four minutes later, received a standing ovation. No one was more surprised than I. In that four-minute flow of near-breathless visual comedy I had come to another crossroads which would change my life once again.

As I stumbled off the platform, literally wringing wet with nervous perspiration from the sheer physical and mental effort, I was confronted by two smiling men.

The older one, a small, quiet-spoken Jewish man, said simply: 'That is the funniest and most original thing that I have seen in years! My name is Monty Lyon – I'm an agent and I'd like to talk to you about showing that act of yours to Val Parnell.'

Had this cheerful man, with the laughing eyes and hawk-like nose, told me that I would be having an audition with God himself the shock could not have been greater.

His young companion broke into my amazed silence. 'I'm Dennis Sellinger,' he said, grinning impishly. 'He's my uncle – and he means what he says! Don't faint!'

I suppose I must have looked about all-in, as I hadn't been eating regularly because of nervous tension as well as acute poverty.

These two straight, honest and highly intelligent angels of the Annunciation, as they seemed to me then, have been my good friends for nearly thirty-five years. Was their presence at the Nuffield Centre, which they visited once in a blue moon, just a chance coincidence? Four minutes later and they would have missed my act altogether! They told me that they had only popped into the Nuffield to catch another comedy act, and that it was by pure accident that they had seen mine.

Three weeks later Monty and Dennis were as good as their word and, one morning on the stage of the Prince of Wales Theatre, the 'iron curtain' rose to reveal an auditorium empty apart from five men sitting in the middle of the stalls. They were Val Parnell, then the head of Moss Empires and the London Palladium – the most powerful man in British show business – 'Charlie' Henry, his production manager who had helped Parnell to create the Crazy Gang, Robert Nesbitt, his top director of spectacular musical variety, and Monty and Dennis.

'All right, son,' came Val Parnell's voice from the

auditorium. 'Let's see you!'

I took a deep breath – clutched my broken chairback like a life preserver/talisman, muttered a short: 'Please help me, Lord!' and plunged straight into my act. I was so intent on the performance that I didn't realize that the odd sound coming from the yawning dimness of the theatre was laughter. Good old honest belly laughter!

As I finished, streaming with sweat, the iron curtain clanked down in front of my shaking body and Monty and Dennis came round to tell me the news. 'Michael, you open in two months time in Val Parnell's new show at the London Hippodrome. It's to be called *Starlight Roof*.'

Vic Oliver, Pat Kirkwood and Fred Emney starred in Eric Maschwitz's 'musical extravaganza' and, tucked away in the billing, were the names of three unknowns – Jean Carson, Julie Andrews and Michael Bentine. We ran for thirteen months and played to capacity houses for most of them. I got £30 a week, which to me was a fortune. It started Jean Carson on her career, which culminated in *Jeannie*, her successful American TV series, after which she settled down to being a happy housewife. Julie Andrews used to stand shivering with nervous tension alongside me in the wings while we gave each other moral support. What an odd pair we made, a twenty-five-year-old man and a twelve-year-old child, appreciating each other's fears of failure and cheering each other up.

That bond between us has lasted through thirty-three years and Julie is the godmother of my younger son, Richard. She was a lovely child then, and she is a lovely woman now.

There was, in that talented company of fine singers and dancers, a young and stunningly pretty ballet dancer called Clementina Stuart. She told me that she thought I was quite mad when she saw me for the first time – rehearsing my broken chairback in the wings. Over thirty-two years of marriage to me hasn't, I suspect, changed her views. She has just got used to me – that's all!

Pat Kirkwood, a lovely, lively Lancashire lass, had her dressing-room at the top of the flight of stairs on the OP (opposite prompt) side of the stage, and it became the social centre of the show. 'Pat's Parlour' we called it. Her natural and captivating ebullience drew you to her like a magnet and her outgoing hospitality welcomed me to her dressing-room, which was presided over by her mother Norah and kept supplied with endless cups of tea and biscuits by her formidably Junoesque dresser Bessie.

I used to visit her every show – twice a night – and marvelled at the flow of interesting folk who passed through that room: Baron the photographer, then the top man in his profession, with Tony Armstrong-Jones as his bright young assistant; Lieutenant Philip Mountbatten of the Royal Navy – soon to be engaged to HRH Princess Elizabeth – and many others, among them a well-known physiotherapist of great manipulative skill called Stephen Ward.

All sorts of subjects were discussed in that lively atmosphere of Pat's dressing-room at the old Hippodrome. Inevitably, among them was 'the occult' – as it was then called. Stephen Ward was particularly interested in this subject, and the charming, good-looking Irishman became especially intrigued by some of the experiences that Pat asked me to relate.

He himself was a fanatical Marxist and, at his treatment rooms near Harley Street, he apparently proudly preserved letters from top Soviet leaders such as Khrushchev. We discussed Marxism and South America and, as Britain had become Socialist almost overnight in the post-war era of Russian goodwill and United Nations concepts, we found we had much the same outlook, especially in our mutual hatred of Fascism and the Nazis.

When Stephen realized that I knew what I was talking about regarding paranormal experiences, he told me that he was fascinated by the subject and was himself investigating ritual magic. He asked me to join his circle. On subsequent occasions, when I met him at charity shows and big social functions at which I was appearing, he continued to invite me to join in his magical activities, but by this time I was happily married and already had two young children, and was far too busy surviving in show business.

I said that I would be delighted to come to one of his seances if it took place in *daylight* and if I could safely bring my children. His reaction confirmed what I had long suspected – that Stephen Ward was engaged in ritual practices of a sexual/magical nature – and that the natural course of such rituals would lead him, and his group, into Black Magic and possibly Satanism.

He changed a lot over the years, his youthful charm and his undoubted skills as a physiotherapist were dissipating. His pasty complexion and an odd air of seedy conspiracy showed that he spent too much of his time plotting and conniving indoors. I 'picked up' this degeneration in the way that any sensitive would, and what I saw I liked less and less – so much so that when he confronted me with an open invitation, almost in the form of a challenge, to come to his cottage at Cliveden on the Astor estate I equally bluntly refused.

'Why, Michael? We both have the same interests! If you really are a psychic why not show *us* what you can do?'

'Sorry, Stephen!' I countered. 'I pick up that you are on a different path from mine – and, if my family can't participate in your rituals, you must be following another way altogether.'

I had no doubt about Stephen's original sincerity as a Marxist – but I asked him, point blank, why, if like myself he was a dedicated anti-Fascist, he hadn't fought against the Nazis?

'I'm Irish,' he said, evading my question, 'a neutral!'

'So were a lot of my comrades in the RAF. Are you a conscientious objector? I fully respect *that* viewpoint – because it takes a lot of guts, in wartime, to stand by your beliefs.'

'No, Michael! Let's just say that I helped in my own way

during the war. I can't say more!'

So that was why he so carefully and proudly guarded his letters from Soviet leaders, I thought to myself. Well, what of it? We weren't at war with Russia – but the incident left a nagging doubt in my mind. And when I saw how well in he was with many leading socialites of the day (something that I shrank from) I became alarmed to think that Stephen Ward could well be a Soviet Agent.

I dismissed the thought as fanciful, but, being a trained Intelligence operative and having had the added advantage of service with the Poles and other Allied organizations, I continued to wonder.

In 1963-4 Stephen Ward became the instrument which destroyed the Tory Government, and afterwards apparently committed suicide. The final word on him I heard from the lips of the Anglican exorcist, Dom Robert Petitpierre, whom I have already mentioned.

As far as I recall, in reply to my question, 'What is it like to carry out a really difficult exorcism? One where there is strong resistance?' his answer was: 'One of the hardest struggles that I had against the forces of darkness was at a cottage at Cliveden, on Lord Astor's Estate. It belonged to Stephen Ward.'

'Good heavens, Dom Robert! You don't mean *the* Stephen Ward?'

'Indeed I do. He was a black magician, you know, a Satanist! He held his meetings with a coven in the cottage, unknown to the Astors, of course. It reeked of evil, and it took me a long time to free it entirely from the horrible aura that pervaded it: I was called in as an exorcist when the place became so disturbed after his death as to be untenable! Did you know him?'

I am grateful that I wasn't involved, in all innocence, with that coven of which, presumably, Stephen was the head. But then, I had been definitely warned off: *'This man is engaged in dangerous ritual practices – stand well clear.'*

In complete contrast to this unpleasant interlude another 'magical ritual' of a quite different type had taken a hold on the young and not-quite-so young of the nation. It was called *The Goon Show*, and over its long life on radio it became a weekly *ritual* enjoyment for millions of listeners, from the Royal Family to schoolchildren, university professors, miners, soldiers, sailors and airmen – and show business folk in their entirety. Here was a simple example of *visual* evocation of archetypal imagery by sound alone!

The whole procession of surrealistic nutters were joyfully and devotedly followed through the marvellous barmy convolutions of their gloriously insane adventures. The climate of post-war Britain was ideal for this mad land of violent and funny imagery, a world of distorting mirrors where anything could happen and usually did. Comedy catharsis isn't a bad description and, throughout, good-humoured idiocy and lack of malicious satire were the keynotes. Burlesque without brutality. Iconoclasm without hatred! A zany Golden Dawn to unwind the tensions of war.

How it came into being is a fascinating story. Both when *Starlight Roof* opened and during its run in the West End of London I got a number of good Press notices and write-ups and, as I was the first of our group of young comedians to make it in the West End, I used this excellent publicity to push the Goon angle to the BBC. With the help of Pat Macneile Dixon – a splendid eccentric and scholar who was the senior producer for light entertainment with BBC Radio, I was able to get the BBC hierarchy interested in the idea of the Goons, who would consist of Harry Secombe, myself, Peter Sellers (who was then a comedy impressionist) and Spike Milligan, then almost unknown.

Spike would write the radio show, with Larry Stephens (an ex-paratrooper), and we would all 'kick in' ideas. Spike often dropped round to my home, or to the Hippodrome where I was appearing, and we would toss ideas back and forth.

Slowly, with the invaluable aid of Jimmy Grafton who

was now Harry's agent, the BBC Light Entertainment hierarchy (pushed ever harder by Pat Dixon) came round to our way of thinking, and eventually allowed us to do a pilot show. To our horror, they called us the 'Junior Crazy Gang' and the show 'Crazy People'. It took all Pat's efforts to persuade them to change it to *The Goon Show*.

Volumes have been written about the Goons by worthy and erudite people, analysing and dissecting the reasons for its strange, magical effect on the listening public. All of them, except Jimmy Grafton's latest *Goon Show Companion*, miss the essence of the show, the *Leitmotif* if you like. It was essentially the humour of ex-servicemen who loathed bureaucracy; and so the target areas were clearly defined – pomposity, bureaucratic imbecility and establishment futility and absurdity. We were all fans of Beachcomber (the *Daily Express* column of inspired nonsense – written mainly by H. B. Morton), and our comedy was iconoclastic but never vicious; and it derived also, of course, from our mutual love of cartoon films and Stephen Leacock's glorious nonsense novels.

All of it was performed with professional skill (not the least being provided by the BBC's marvellous sound-effects department) and was backed by the brilliant orchestrations of Stanley Black and, later, Wally Stott, and the direction and production of stalwarts like Peter Eton, Denis Main-Wilson and others – above all, by our pioneering mentor Pat Dixon, for whom we all had profound respect and great affection. Pat put the show on the radio map, and but for him it would have soon sunk without trace – because the BBC hierarchy did not like it, or approve of it, at first.

I stayed with it from the beginning (two years before it went on the air) and for a further two years of its pioneering run. Then I left to produce *The Bumblies*, a TV children's show, and later to work in Australia (where I had been given a one-year contract which I could not refuse).

The BBC hierarchy responded in its usual way, by severely reprimanding me for daring to leave the show.

Unfortunately some of the Press took this attitude as well, and the whole thing became sadly unpleasant. But luckily, it did not affect my friendship with the Goons, nor with Pat Dixon and Jimmy, and that is really what counted for me.

How many people have said to me: 'Oh! We never missed a *Goon Show*. It was a regular ritual with us.' Or, 'We always hurried home to catch the *Goon Show*. No one was allowed to speak while it was on. It was a real ritual.' And they meant it!

Of course it was - a gloriously barmy ritual which was pure magic! They were all archetypes: Bloodnok, the cowardly military brass hat; Harry, who played the sincere simpleton enmeshed in the endless madness of the marvellous surrealist world of Goonery; Osric Pureheart, the mad inventor of the early shows; Bluebottle, the definitive imbecilic adolescent; Eccles, the original idiot (derived from Walt Disney's wonderful character, Goofy, created and drawn by Ralph Wright); and the nineteenth-century world of Minnie and Henry Crun, those superbly geriatric embodiments of fossilized Imperialist thinking.

It was all projected into the evocative medium of radio and brought to marvellous life and visual reality by the character voices and the power of the magical sound effects - those superbly devised and executed surrealistic audio images that transcended time and space and stimulated each individual listener to enter the Goons' wonderful world. Pure Kabbalism if you really think about it!

People often ask me why I never featured in the many repeats of the show even though I had been an original Goon and very much a part of those early years. Quite simply someone in the BBC hierarchy wiped *all* the tapes to which I had contributed; over two years' worth of *Goon Shows* ceased to exist. Nevertheless I am glad that all that early work and effort I put into the pioneering years of *The Goon Show* is, at the least, partly responsible for its magical appeal. To me, it is fascinating that there, for anyone to listen to and think about, is a definitive example of the effect of the simple magical principles of repeated ritualization and its proven ability to evoke instant and potent archetypal images in the minds of the participants in its rites.

The Golden Dawn, Stella Matutina (another significant magical group), Royal-Arch Freemasonry, the dark rituals of the Nazis or, for that matter, the beautiful rites of the Tridentine Mass – *all* of them use the same basic principles of mind entrainment by ritualized symbols and deliberately evoked imagery by sound that we (unconsciously) used in the construction of *The Goon Show*.

It sounds far-fetched – until you really think about it. Then it becomes self-evident! How interesting it was that *The Telegoons* did *not* have the same amazing impact on the viewing public that *The Goon Show* had on the minds of the listening public with exactly the same vocal performances by the same cast.

The reason is, once again, simple. As a radio show in the true medium of mind communication by sound alone *The Goon Show* evoked definite individual images in each listener's mind. Eccles was short or tall, stocky or thin and emaciated, fat or what-have-you in each entirely different incarnation in the mind of every individual listener. His puppet image could never agree with *all* the preconceived diverse images created by Spike's voice in all those different listeners' imaginations. Therefore, although Harry Secombe's puppet image looked vaguely like a caricature of his already famous, chunky, good-natured self, none of the other puppets could possibly look like the individual images that had been so intensely evoked in the minds of each listener. Only those young viewers who hadn't been *Goon Show* fans were satisfied by the visual version of those gloriously funny scripts.

With my own children's TV series *The Bumblies* and *Potty Time* there were no previous radio versions, and they had a very strong impact and a lasting effect on their young and not-so-young viewers.

Listeners in English-speaking parts of the world such as

Britain, Australia, New Zealand and other parts of the Commonwealth still affectionately enjoy the old recordings of the magical *Goon Show*.

Long may they do so! Not just because they are old friends of mine but because good valid magic like that of the Goons is all too rare in our troubled world.

I often wish that their inheritors and copyists were as good-natured in their comedy as those original pioneers of the magically ridiculous!

Sadly Peter passed over, suddenly and painlessly, after collapsing at his suite in the Dorchester. At the cremation the music of Glen Miller's 'In the Mood' was played at his express request. It was a typical Peter touch. He knew that Harry, Spike and I would appreciate the wry humour of it, which we did, and it cheered us up no end. We knew that Peter heartily disliked 'In the Mood' and frequently made fun of it.

A few days later, Lynne, his young widow, came to see my family at home and to meet Doris Collins who was an old friend of Peter's but whom Lynne had never met. Lynne arrived in a depressed and nervous state and she and Doris sat together alone in our drawing-room. An hour later a relaxed and smiling Lynne joined us for lunch.

None of us would pry into what passed between Doris, Lynne and, presumably, Peter, but from that moment on Lynne has been much happier and that, after all, was the object of the exercise.

Typically the Press got hold of the story and over-dramatized the whole thing. The simple fact was that Peter apparently manifested in some way and provided his widow with convincing personal evidence of his survival. The good news was that Lynne felt much better about the whole situation and has now been able to come to terms with her tragedy.

If radio can condition the minds of the listeners to accept

carefully evoked images over quite a short period of time –
pause and think what Adolf Hitler's propaganda machine
could have accomplished with the global satellite-relayed
coverage of television.

When my other country – Peru – was taken over in a near-
bloodless coup in 1969, the primary targets for the pre-dawn
coup-de-main were the television and radio stations in
Lima. Profiting by the fatal mistake of the German generals
in their abortive attempt to oust Hitler, which had been in
their failure to realize that they had to take over the radio
stations at the same time, the Peruvian generals, and
subsequently the leaders of many other military coups in
South America, aimed their shock-troops at the media –
concurrently with their take-over of all strategic centres.

At six o'clock in the morning, when the cleaners came into
the studios, to open them up for the day's work, the special
troops, in civilian clothes, entered the buildings with them.
When the broadcasting staff arrived an hour or so later, the
studios and transmission equipment were in the hands of the
army. So, when the public switched on their sets for the
'breakfast shows', everything appeared to be normal. Then
the newsreaders and programme presenters told them that
the take-over by the military was a *fait accompli*.
Resistance was, at a stroke, reduced to the minimum – so
well conditioned were the minds of the great mass of the
viewing public.

Let me explain why – because this will lead us, once more,
into the realms of ritual magic and its effect on the mass
mind. Cast your mind back to the days of the early movies,
'The Golden Silents' as we called them, when I presented and
co-authored a major twenty-six-part series of half-hour
films about them for the BBC. When the early black and
white silent movies were made and distributed during the
first quarter of the twentieth century they made a terrific
impact on countless millions of people, who flocked to see
them first as a nickelodeon novelty and then as part of a
weekly *ritual*.

What then was the real reason for their remarkably rapid grasp on the minds of their audience? The answer lies in the word popularly used in English-speaking countries to describe this new form of entertainment. It was 'the flickers', or the 'flicks' as they came to be called.

The flickering effect of these early films was caused by passing in front of the carbon arcs of the projectors a series of photographs to give the effect of movement. The speed of this cyclic effect varied between 16 and 20 cycles a second. In other words, a light source was 'strobing' the eyes and minds of the viewers.

If a light is regularly flashed into the eyes of a person, at certain frequencies, an entrainment of the human mind occurs. To put the principle quite simply: if Charles Chaplin – an excellent and talented music-hall comedian – had been able, by some miracle, to perform 'live' before the millions of people whom he reached through his early films, he would *not* have produced the same instant effect that was achieved by appearing through the medium of flickering films.

Would he have had an effect? Yes, of course, because he was an exceptional artist; but *not* the same effect which the entraining medium gave him. This added ingredient virtually turned him from an unknown into an international film star in two years.

The attention-riveting flickering of the black and white image, many times life size, was the missing ingredient between his live and talented presentation on the stage and the concentrated essence of his art on the screen.

I was a cinema addict from the age of four, when I was taken by my big brother, aged ten, to see the flicks. Such was the power of entrainment of these flickering images on my young mind that I can *still*, over fifty years later, recall whole sequences from the films that I saw then.

In the small Folkestone cinemas of the twenties, the Central, The Playhouse and the Savoy, with their primitive, hard tip-up seats, there was no fascination to entrain my mind – until the lights dimmed. As soon as the projectors started to whirr and the first flickering images appeared on the screen – the *magic* started and, in a matter of seconds, my mind was released from those grubby surroundings and I became the riveted witness of the action that followed.

The same effects were noticeably absent when the 'slides', usually of advertisements or announcements, were projected in front of me. Only when the flicker effect started did the mind-entrainment occur, and usually I would leave the cinema reluctantly, with the atmosphere generated by those images still filling my thoughts.

Lenin said: 'Of all the arts, the *cinema* is the most important for us.'

Why? When the talkies arrived, the projection speeds were altered, to synchronize with the audio/visual requirement of sound films, to a projection speed of 24.9 frames a second (i.e. 24.9 Hertz). Jean Luc Godard (the French film director and an expert on the medium) described the cinema as: 'Truth being projected, at 24.9 frames a second.'

That this entrainment of the mind of the film viewer is an undeniable fact is borne out by the tremendous revenues which poured into the Hollywood studios that produced the bulk of the talkies of the thirties. These colossal sums from all over the world were simple proof of the universal efficacy of the medium of the cinema. In the space of a few years, a whole giant industry was formed, which not only produced a mind-manipulating medium of entertainment but even created a star system of archetypal gods and goddesses – who were even more fervently worshipped than those which had previously been created by the great religions of the earth.

Why then, could not the same effect have been created by the theatre? The answer is simple! The live theatre does not have a flashing light projected onto a screen and reflected into the eyes of its entranced audience.

If you doubt these simple statements, cast your mind back to your first experience of live entertainment, in a theatre.

Can you remember, without an enormous effort, who you saw? What they did, said, wore, etc. in that first theatrical experience? It is very difficult to recall. That seems to be the general reaction when I ask people to carry out this simple experiment.

Now, do the *same* memory test – but this time try to remember the first time that you went to the 'flicks'. You will find a surprising difference. Whereas with your attempts to recall the faces and identities of the actors and actresses in your first theatrical experience, you will have found only hazy memory patterns, when remembering the screen images of your first film you will suddenly get clear flashes of memory of whole scenes.

I remember Buster Keaton's film *The General* with great clarity and, when some forty-five years later, I saw it for the second time, whole scenes sprang back into my mind.

How? Because the *flickering* effect, even of the later 24.9 frames a second, strobed my vision, entrained my mind and left an indelible impression on my subconscious. Had they been live performances on the stage of a theatre, I would have had enormous difficulty in recalling them.

If you are still in doubt, think how many impressionists, such as Mike Yarwood in Britain and Rich Little in America, give impersonations of film or television personalities rather than stage stars. They also impersonate politicians and sports commentators, but *their* individual characteristics are only familiar to viewers through the media of the television and movie screens.

In other words, they instantly spring to recognizable form, with the minimum of effort, *because* they are originally associated, in our mind's eye and ear, with their television image. For the 'Box', the 'Bug-eyed Monster' in millions of living-rooms strobes the viewers' senses at precisely 24.9 frames per second. The viewers of films or TV are being constantly exposed to a visual entrainment which then has a deep subliminal effect on the mind and memory.

It is sheer hypocrisy when the various television

companies and authorities declare that they will not use subliminal advertising in their transmissions. Quite rightly the insertion of individual frames or sets of frames bearing definite written messages or images of a commercial or political nature has been loudly condemned. But in reality it makes no difference. The whole medium has an enormous effect on the suggestible level of the mind.

How effective then is this entrainment? The proof of the pudding is in the eating. A multi-billion-dollar global industry has grown up since the first post-war TV transmissions came into operation. *Any* company, with *any* product, properly presented and regularly exposed on the television screen, can guarantee to recover the necessary large investment in TV commercials and then show a profit over the cost of the product and its marketing budget. For example, in Britain it will cost approximately half a million pounds to ensure that a television commercial lasting some thirty seconds is shown at peak exposure times and is viewed by a large proportion of the public, say, thirty exposures in the spring and another thirty in the autumn. This is a total of only thirty minutes' exposure time in a year!

That investment will be returned in the stores, in direct proportion to the skilled marketing of the product, *within the same period*! The mind entrainment of those viewers who saw a significant proportion of the commercials is that effective.

Some commercials, such as the one for Murray Mints in the early days of commercial television in Britain, or the Martini jet-set type of advertisement, have boosted the sales of their products by enormous amounts, and advertisers queue up to have their products shown – even at today's prices. The Campari commercial with the beautiful 'Cockney' Lorraine Chase rocketed sales up by more than 36 per cent. While it was being shown Lorraine became a household name, the Eliza Doolittle of the box. To produce a television commercial lasting thirty seconds to one minute can cost almost as much as a feature film. That is an indication of its value.

Another interesting experiment that you can try for yourselves, I think you will find bears out my observations. Walk into your living-room or wherever your family are viewing a television set and, while standing to one side, try to hold a conversation with them. You will find that their attention is divided by the TV screen and that the process is difficult.

The next time, switch off the sound of the TV set but leave the picture on and once more try to hold a conversation from the same position. Again, it is very difficult, because even the mute picture will hold the attention of the viewer.

The third time, switch off the picture but keep the sound on, and the whole process becomes much easier. In other words – while the 'scan' effect of the frames is manifested to the viewer, he or she will be partially entrained by the flickering strobing light source.

Alarming, isn't it? Because it means that *whatever* is being pumped out by these means will be impressed on the subconscious memory-patterns of the viewers. It is, quite simply, a perfect application of mind-manipulation by the methods and techniques used originally in ritual magic.

To give you some idea of what I have learned during my thirty-four years' experience of the 'Bug-eyed Monster', let me hypothesize the production of a political debate on television.

This, of course, could only happen if the producer was politically biased and wished to use that bias for his own purposes.

The producer/director has total autonomy if the programme is going out live and, depending on the degree of top management back-up, complete control of editing if it has been videotaped. He can instruct the interviewer, or allow him, to favour one or other of the 'victims' in this 'Trial by Television' and, by giving the favoured one prior notice of the questions or line of attack, bestow an enormous and unfair advantage.

By placing sympathetic audience members at strategic points in the studio and by cutting away from the person that he wishes to disfavour while he is talking to shots of these audience plants, the director can virtually control the flow and effectiveness of the argument.

I have seen these techniques in use all over the world – especially in countries where one political party has control of TV or has a big say in the running of a particular channel. I have seen people 'crucified' on television, their reputations tarnished in a few minutes. I am not going to say that this sort of thing happens here in Britain but, human nature being what it is, it is unlikely that it hasn't.

There are so many tricks, such as editing-out on video tape, over-emphasis on certain wording (something that Lord Reith would never allow in news reading), sympathetic or hard lighting and proportions of head size to lens to give a dominant effect on the screen, favouring one or other of the participants, cutting in on an argument if it is going against your side, etc. The list is long, and during my long involvement with the media, I have seen them all used.

I have never been politically active, and I do not use my TV work as a platform, but in 1963 I was approached by a senior official at the BBC and plainly told that it would be a fine thing if I used my programme *It's a Square World* for bashing the Establishment (then the Macmillan Government).

I was told that I would be backed up to the hilt by the hierarchy if I complied – a result which to this particular VIP was a foregone conclusion.

My unexpected refusal made me most unpopular and my BBC career came to an abrupt halt.

I once saw a young man – for whom I have considerable respect – show a petulant disapproval of the last election results on live television. It was, I think, obvious to viewers, whether they were professional television experts or not. This sort of display of political bias is unwise in a television presenter of professional polish and experience and, because the medium is so sensitive to atmosphere, it can have a profound suggestibility effect on the mass viewing public.

I believe that it is important that the viewers become aware of these facts. The psychologists, psychiatrists and media analysts who put their skills into the scripts and visual imagery are all paid highly for their expertise. Political control or biasing in documentary-type programmes, and *even* in light entertainment, can have enormously far-reaching effects. Therefore, it becomes of supreme importance to the viewer, whose whole life can be altered by the short- and long-term effects of such mind-manipulation, that everyone is made aware of what films and TV can do to their lives.

I was recently hauled over the coals for mentioning the name of a firm whose product I was demonstrating at an exhibition. The reference was probably two seconds long in screen duration.

I pointed out that shortly before, a replay of a *Match of the Day* had screened, for a total of *minutes*, poster-banners for insurance, banks, building societies, motor cars, cigarettes (which are banned from TV advertising) and various other specially-produced high-visibility layouts – plastered round the perimeter of the field.

All the principles of ritual magic are incorporated in television production, of both commercials and the carefully orchestrated programmes. These are, simply stated, a combination of logos and slogans, light and colour, form and shape and, above all, the driving force of a dominant personality on which to hang the message.

Couple the audio side to the visual presentation and you have two magical principles at work at one and the same time. The driving beat and brilliantly orchestrated and manipulated recordings, their multi-tracks, have a tremendous instant effect – especially on young minds.

Sport – particularly football – has grown exponentially in direct proportion to the enormous all-year-round coverage, until today footballers change clubs for transfer fees which are well into the million pound figure – while gangs of fanatical supporters weep and rage, cheer and scream for their heroes, and violence is rife in the stands, resulting in injury and even death. For millions football has become a substitute for religion and politics – entirely because of that unremitting and seemingly endless coverage.

Match of the Day and its replays, *Match of the Week* with its analyses and post-mortem arguments – this immense coverage has changed football into a giant ritual which sways the lives of millions of people.

Football, soap, drink, breakfast foods – whatever you are subjected to in the form of a hard or soft sell – the very fact of the media's operations makes you the target of a huge mind-manipulating industry. Its techniques open doors, almost instantly, to the sub-conscious; and in this case you must, for your own mental stability, learn to be your own door keeper. For your children, that door opens even more quickly, and remains wide open whenever the flickering light is operating. It is up to you to see that the view beyond the portal is one of spring and summer, not an endless procession of violence and fear, greed and envy. You have the key to that door within your reach – it is a button marked 'on/off'.

Of all the media used to disseminate propaganda the Bug-eyed Monster is the most effective. Yet it is also totally *neutral*. It can teach and it can condition, bias or truly inform; it can bring a feeling of relaxed pleasure or great unease; it can terrify or pacify.

Parents of young children often come up to me and give me enormous pleasure by recalling the Bumblies that they enjoyed as children twenty-five years before. I hope the Potties have the same effect, and I am delighted to say that they seem to be well on the way to that result. Yet recently, in all innocence, I had a 'Potty' show banned. Made almost a year before, this little programme showed a battle between two London embassies – side by side, with even the worms in the embassy window boxes fighting each other.

Outside the police waited to nab them for double parking (the only charge they could make). The programme was scheduled to be transmitted (nearly a year after it had been made) on the very afternoon that the terrorists took over the Iranian embassy.

On the credit side of television the marvellous Muppets have shown what television can do for family enjoyment. They are the products of a dedicated team of artists and performers/writers and, during my short personal acquaintance with them, in 1964, I saw the essence of their art. For me this is the epitome of the Bug-eyed Monster's ability to open the door marked summer.

Remember! You hold the key to its complete control: public opinion and the viewing figures!

If you don't like something – *switch it off,* and complain loudly and often, by phone, by letter, by telegram and by lobbying your Member of Parliament.

That way you can make television your servant and not let it become your subliminal master.

13 Some Close Encounters –and Gus

By 1952 my marriage to Clementina had brought us two
children - Marylla (Fusty) and Stuart (Gus) and the
friendship and invaluable help of 'Nursie'.

Frances Forbes, one of the last of the Great British
Nannies, had come to us in order to 'bury' Gus, who, in the
first six weeks of his life, two specialists had prognosticated
would die.

'Nursie' refused to confirm their prognosis. 'There's
nothing wrong with this child,' she said , in her firmest
voice, and gave our son some brew of her own concoction
which did the trick.

Gus lived for twenty-one happy years, until his death in a
light-plane crash, and I can never thank Nursie enough for
each one of them.

She also disagreed with another specialist that Fusty
would never walk properly after an infant bout of polio.
Once again she was right, and Fusty is the living proof of it.

Nursie is very sensitive, and is a joy to watch with babies
and children, who flock to her as to the Pied Piper of Hamlyn.
Friends still ring us up from all over the world to ask Nursie's
advice about their offspring and nowadays their grand-
children.

In her retirement with us Nursie enjoys gardening and
gives the same marvellous love and care to her flowers -
chatting them up as though they were children, and it works
too!

When she was with her first family, looking after a baby

girl called Patricia, the elder brother of the family was in the RAF as a very young pilot officer. One sunny morning Nursie and her charge were walking in the garden when she heard a voice call: 'Truki!' (This was the elder brother David's nickname for little Patricia.)

Nursie looked round, startled, to see the life-size form of the young pilot manifesting, in full light!

Only the top half of the body was fully materialized – a fact that registered on her with a chilling shock.

'He was smiling and his face was radiant,' she told me.

Before his small sister could turn round he was gone.

Compare this with my cousin Joan's experience, when John, her brother, materialized in the staff room in a London hospital in 1943. This experience of Nursie's occurred in the summer of 1940 and was also a half-materialization, but this time in *full* summer sunlight. Once again the ectoplasm seems to have been used to its full effect, i.e. to form a *life-size* manifestation of half the body rather than to appear as a scaled-down materialization of the whole figure.

Since then Nursie has seen other manifestations (including, recently, my son Gus). All our children – Fusty, Gus, Peski and Suki (Richard and Serena) – know how much they owe her in sheer love and happiness, because Nursie has that marvellous ability to open any child's door marked summer.

When I brought my family home from a two-year tour of Australia I found that things had changed a lot.

Commercial television had arrived, at last, and the BBC's monopoly was broken. Within a few months I was deeply into writing and performing for ABC Television; my director/producer was a young and then relatively unknown American called Richard Lester.

In all we did some thirty-nine television shows together, starting in Birmingham – live – and eventually videotaping these successful half-hour shows at the Teddington Studios near London. The format has become the accepted one for action-cum-chat shows, and many talented performers gave of their best to make the series a hit.

Among the people I chatted up was Jayne Mansfield, the shapely and beautiful film star, who was on a promotional trip to Britain. With her the gimmick that I used was to superimpose – without her knowledge – a little submarine with a cartoon figure in the conning tower which viewed her outstanding figure through the periscope. What the U-boat captain sees turns the sea into steam and, with his legs through the bottom of the little submarine, he runs off the screen. It worked beautifully, and Jayne Mansfield joined in the laughter when we showed it to her on the videotape afterwards.

She struck me as essentially an uncomplicated person, and her sense of humour was quite spontaneous and genuine; but while we were chatting I had an overwhelming sense of tragedy looming over her, and brushed it aside. I couldn't think why, because the atmosphere was so light and cheerful in those shows.

Not too long afterwards, I was shocked to hear that she had been decapitated in a car crash. In order to make our harmless little cartoon work, Dick had brought the camera in close, virtually 'cutting off her head' so that the only part of her to be seen, dominating the screen, was her splendid bosom. When I read about the horrible facts of the crash, I suddenly saw the mid-shot of that lovely woman and the ridiculous little cartoon on her Junoesque chest.

Soon afterwards I was in the middle of a disastrous run of the stage version of our television show, which Dick Lester had produced and directed for us, when I pushed myself too far and came down with a virus pneumonia. The show folded and I, still being the dedicated professional, carried on immediately with a small part in a film with Ernie Kovacs.

He was concerned about the high fever that I was running, and that nice, talented man told me that I was mad to carry on.

The same night I passed out and very nearly bought it, as we used to say in the RAF. But thanks to Dr Ralph Scrivener, my family doctor at that time, and the devoted nursing staff at Bolingbroke Hospital I made it back through the veil.

Three days after I returned to 'battleground earth' I was hit by massive thromboses in both legs. The bright mind of a little Lebanese nurse saved my life. She saw what had happened and, as I writhed in pain on the bed, rushed off and seized an equally bright young house surgeon.

Immediately he injected me with a heavy dose of Heparin (the anti-coagulent in use at the time), and the 'Battle for Bentine' went into phase two.

As near as damnit I 'died' once again, slipping out of my body and hovering in that strange limbo between life and death.

I also nearly lost my left leg. My specialist told me bluntly that if the gangrene which was developing spread any further it would have to come off.

That was quite a weekend! Harry and Peter sent messages of cheerful encouragement, and I really found out who my friends were. All sorts of unlikely people came to visit me during that 'rough go', while others whom I would have expected to at least phone didn't bother. Such is life!

Florrie Dott, my father's housekeeper after Ma had passed over in 1952, came to give me healing that weekend as Pop was far too ill to leave his flat. Pop concentrated on me at the same time (pre-arranged), and I felt the warmth of Florrie's hands as she held them over my gangrenous and now revolting-looking left leg. The pain, which even under the heavy sedation was excruciating, left that blackened and grossly swollen limb and I fell into a long and blissful sleep.

When my specialist arrived early on the Monday morning all ready to perform the amputation, he couldn't believe the difference in my condition.

'What happened?' he asked simply.

'A healer had a go at it,' I replied.

'Doesn't surprise me, Michael! I've seen this sort of thing before – spontaneous remission, we call it, and it doesn't really describe it! I just call it a plain old-fashioned *miracle*!'

So I kept my leg and, even though it doesn't work too well it has seen me through a further very active twenty years of demanding use.

Thank you, Florrie! Thank you, Pop! And thank you *all*, whoever you are, for the gift of a whole body!

I apologize for boring you with the grisly details of my body's malfunctions, but I have written about this sort of thing deliberately to show you that, apart from the pain involved (something that drugs can alleviate considerably), there is really very little in the death change.

With many people the whole process is so quick that they are completely unaware it is happening. Of course, none of us 'enjoy' it. To think about it too much is unhealthy and unnatural. But when it happens and the struggle is over there is a sense of the natural order of things.

Harry Secombe has experienced the near-presence of the death change and feels the same way about it. None of us relish the thought and, quite naturally, we fear the mechanism because that is part of our survival system.

Harry nearly 'bought the farm' on a flight from Australia to San Francisco. The crew wanted to rush him to hospital in Hawaii, on the way, but Harry held out for Barbados. He felt strongly that he *had* to get there. This did not make sense – the facilities, both surgical and medical must be more extensive in Hawaii than in Barbados!

He was right, however, because, arriving on the West Indian island almost dead, his life was saved by a young and brilliant local doctor who had been trained in Edinburgh.

Happily, Harry is still very much with us, marvellously good-natured and as lovingly outgoing as ever.

The first time Peter Sellers nearly 'crossed the bridge' was when he was seized by a series of massive coronaries in Los Angeles. His heart actually stopped and was restarted a number of times in intensive care.

Having a special relationship, we Goons sent him unconventional telegrams like:

HARRY: 'I thought it would be me first!'
SPIKE: 'Wait for the laugh!'
SELF: 'Your best dramatic performance so far!'

Callous? No! We are all ex-servicemen and have great affection for one another. We went through a lot of good, healthy laughter-filled experiences together. That makes a bond way outside the area covered by conventional platitudes.

When Gus passed through the portals of his door marked summer, Harry and Peter sent their love and immediate offers of help, and their positive thoughts helped a lot. That's really what it is all about.

According to Peter, his mother, Peg Ray, an indomitable little lady of immensely strong willpower, influenced his life in many ways long after she passed over. She and I got on very well. Peg knew that I was a friend and that I admired Peter's talent enormously and wanted nothing from him.

After Peter's massive coronaries he completed many films and, through movies like the Inspector Clouseau series, gave great pleasure to millions of people. The constant threat of a recurrence of that near-fatal condition did not keep him inactive for, as he once told me: 'When you've been half-way through the door – you never feel the same fear of it as you did before!'

One of the young mediums tested and found to be completely genuine by Pop was Joseph Benjamin, an East-Ender from London, and this remarkable clairvoyant and psycho-metrist is an old friend of mine of over forty years' standing.

Joe had enormous respect and affection for my father and, though I hadn't seen him for some thirty-five years since we last met during the war, he gave me some remarkable evidence from both my father and my son Gus. It confirmed

all the confidential findings that I had uncovered in my
investigations into Gus's and his close friend Andy's passing in that dreadful light-plane crash. Joe has also confirmed many of the conclusions that I have come to during
the course of my researches into the paranormal.

This down-to-earth Cockney, with his sharp, shrewd
intelligence and brimming reservoir of wit, has comforted
and helped thousands of people. He agrees with me that the
death change can often be largely what you yourself choose
to make it.

A fine, sensitive and sensible man, Joe has suffered
persecution and savage antagonism from some so-called
investigators during his long life as a psychic. Yet his life's
work bears him out.

'The Power is not there *all* the time, Michael,' he once told
me, gently. 'Sometimes you have to whistle for it! Whistling
in the dark I think is the expression, but, when you finally
feel the contact, you *know*!'

Amen, Joseph Benjamin!

A recent example of fine clairvoyance, and fine healing as
well, was through another close friend, Doris Collins, whom
I mentioned earlier. This occurred at our home, where old
friends from the United States had come to dinner.

Micky and Irene are two special people. Micky is an ex-
Eighth-Army-Air-Force wartime pilot, who flew B17 Fortresses from these islands, and Irene is an attractive and
witty red-head of great charm. Tremendously successful in
television, Micky had come over for a short holiday and,
within minutes of his arrival in London, phoned me.

By a strange mix up they came over to dinner at the same
time as Doris and her husband Phillip. I didn't know
whether Micky and Irene were interested in the paranormal,
and felt some slight apprehension that they might not hit it
off with Doris. But Doris had no such qualms, and described
Micky's father to him with such accuracy as to leave this
shrewd and contained Hollywood producer stunned with
surprise.

Irene was, of course, eager to hear something equally convincing about herself, but oddly enough Doris could get nothing for her or, at least, appeared not to.

In fact, as she told me on leaving: 'I'm very concerned about your friends; I pick up a terrible head pain. Please tell them to be extra careful.'

Earlier, Doris had told Micky: 'You are planning a trip up north - I pick up Scotland.'

'Correct,' said Micky, smiling.

'It will be changed. Your plans will be changed.'

'Impossible. I've arranged everything - car, chauffeur, everything, including hotel bookings.'

'Nevertheless it *will* be changed. I'm sorry,' replied Doris, and changed the subject.

The next evening the four of us had dinner with Muir Sutherland, the head of Thames International Television, which sells TV programmes, including mine, all over the world.

Irene didn't seem to be her usual ebullient self.

I was worried about what Doris had said, and warned Micky to take special care. Naturally I had interpreted the violent head pains to be the result of a possible car accident. We saw them back to their hotel and, the next day, they set off for their trip north.

At two o'clock the next morning, Micky rang me from Llandudno in North Wales.

He apologized, and then quietly said: 'It's an emergency, Michael. Irene has been taken seriously ill, with violent head pains. The doctors here think it is an aneurysm. What do you know about the London Hospital? We are coming straight down to London. I'll ring you as soon as I get in to a hotel.'

By eight thirty I had details of that splendid hospital from Dr Michael Dixon, our present family physician and, when Micky rang me at nine o'clock that morning, was able to reassure him that the neurological unit there was one of the finest in the world.

'Where are you?' I asked.

'We've managed to book into the Intercontinental, but they can only keep us here for one or two nights. Everywhere is full as it is the height of the season.'

'I'll be with you in an hour, Micky. You won't believe this, but I am doing a show there for ITT, the radio and TV electronics firm, at the same hotel!'

I arrived by mid-morning to find my producer, Bernard Braden, already rehearsing the show. I explained it all to Bernard (another old friend), and he arranged for Micky to stay as long as he liked at the hotel.

We then dashed off to visit Irene, who was already in bed at the London Hospital.

'It looks like some place straight out of Charles Dickens,' she quipped wanly.

'Nevertheless, love, it's a great hospital.' I grinned back at her.

Micky then told me that Irene had not got an aneurysm, but a tumour was suspected. He asked me, point-blank: 'We can fly back to LA, Michael – what do you think?'

'Micky, I *feel* strongly that Irene is in splendid hands. Why risk the long flight to California? I'm no physician, as you know, but I do know enough to feel convinced that you won't get any better treatment in LA than you will here.'

Meanwhile, Clementina had been talking to Doris, who was about to fly to Switzerland on a lecture and paranormal demonstration tour.

'Irene will be all right,' she said. 'But there will be complications after the operation. Don't tell them. They've got enough to worry about. I pick up that she will recover and will return home soon. This is just for evidence.'

The operation was brilliantly carried out, and the tumour (fortunately benign) was removed. Micky met me for dinner and told me so. I did my show but I don't remember it too clearly except that it was a success.

Later Micky telephoned me at home. 'There are complications. Haematoma. They must operate again.'

I gave him Doris's message in full. The second operation relieved the cranial pressure and Irene was safe.

A month later we all met up at Micky's home in LA. (He calls it the 'Kibbutz'.) Irene was exhausted, but had stood up well to the long flight.

This experience of accurate precognitive evidence has impressed both Micky and Irene. (It also got the hospital considerable help, through our contacts with the Variety Club.)

Is it then *all* coincidence? Think about it!

My friends came to dinner on the *wrong* (or was it the right?) day, which meant that they met Doris and Phillip. Then Doris gave Micky some remarkable evidence about his father and a warning that was clear and definitive – an interrupted journey and the violent head pains (which Doris told *me* about).

A house surgeon in Llandudno diagnosed Irene's condition as serious, and a bed was made available immediately, at a time when it was almost impossible to get one right away, especially in London.

The problem with the hotel accommodation was solved by my being at the same hotel at the same time (a chance in a million).

Doris's second message was, once again, totally correct (the complications and recovery).

A month later they were back home in LA and the hospital is now considerably better-off through help from the Variety Club.

Coincidence? I don't really think so and, I suspect, neither do you!

One sunny afternoon my eldest son Gus, Clementina and myself were sitting in the nursery/cum TV viewing room at home – laughing at some ridiculous story that our twenty-one-year-old offspring was joyfully relating.

As he lay back on the much-worn carpet, his cheerful grinning face suddenly changed in front of my eyes into that of a corpse. A cold feeling of dread seized hold of me as I once again felt that awful precognitive horror that I knew so well from my wartime experiences.

I gave an involuntary cry of fear, and Gus sat up with a startled: 'What's wrong, Daddy?'

Clementina was looking at me with shocked surprise. Before I could stop myself I choked out: 'I've just seen you as a dead man, Gus!'

At the same time, with total clarity, I *saw* a light training monoplane with a 'parasol' wing (high wing) flying erratically under low cloud as though it was in trouble. It stalled and immediately nose-dived, to crash out of sight without catching fire. This was a clear subjective clairvoyant experience.

Clementina and Gus were so distressed that, after attempting to comfort my wife, I took him aside into the drawing room.

As soon as we were alone I told him simply what I had seen. 'Now listen carefully, Gus. I seldom, thank God, ever see such a definite warning as this. So pay attention to it. I am absolutely serious. The impression I get is that if you fly with Andy (a close friend of the whole family) you will both die. Do you understand me?'

'What on earth have you got against Andy?' queried my shaken son.

'Nothing at all. He's a hell of a nice lad and, I'm sure, absolutely reliable. What I *am* saying is that if you two fly *together* you will *both* die.'

'But he's a very safe pilot, Daddy,' insisted my son.

'Gus! Try to understand what I have seen. Someone has warned me of a probability pattern, which *can* happen. I don't object to you flying, and I'm sure that what you say about Andy is true. He's a very nice person and completely trustworthy. You do sub-aqua diving together, and I am inclined to think of that as far more risky than flying, which, after all, I was brought up with. I'm just telling you straight. I have no objection whatsoever to you diving with Andy.

Just don't fly together. That is what I have been told! Please for *all* our sakes, tell Andy.'

'But he's a good pilot – never takes risks. He's well-trained and he's got quite a few hours logged. He's been flying since he was an air-cadet at Marlborough.'

'I don't care if he's another Richthofen! The simple facts that I have been given are that *if the two of you are together*, in a light aeroplane, that plane, for some reason, will crash and you will *both* be killed. I'm sorry, Gus, but I have to tell you.'

It was the first time I had ever definitively warned any of my children about a specific danger.

Like all fathers, I had said things like: 'Take it easy in the car!' and, 'Watch it, son, it's Bank Holiday weekend!' That sort of thing, but nothing like this blunt warning of impending death.

What made it even weirder and more horrifying to me was that I happened to like and trust Andy in every way. If ever a young man, a couple of years older than my eldest son, epitomized reliability, self-assurance and a balanced logical and rational mind it was Andrew, who was a successful young accountant and a keen sportsman. As a weekend glider and light-plane pilot he flew for 'flight and reward' (that is he would pilot the tug planes which towed the gliders into the air in return for an hour's free flying at the end of the day's work). I trusted Andy and it went completely against the grain to say what I had to say.

The weeks passed and I said no more on the subject – explaining to Clementina that I had been shown a definite warning and that the lads should heed it. It was important.

That the warning was dreadfully accurate became a ghastly fact some three months afterwards. I had been filming a part in a Ned Sherrin film near Hatfield, and, as I was told that I was required the next day and that my old friend Spike Milligan would be there filming as well, I phoned Clementina at around eight thirty that evening and told her I thought it would be a bit pointless to drive back to

Esher that night (some thirty-five miles), only to leave at about seven o'clock the following morning to drive straight back to Hatfield. My wife agreed and as I couldn't get into my usual hotel, I found a room for the night in a motel just next to the Hawker Siddeley aircraft plant at Hatfield. Strangely, I was the only guest in the entire motel, and I hardly slept at all – tossing and turning restlessly all night.

In the morning I felt completely exhausted. I got up and showered and, after breakfast alone in the dining-room, made my way to the location which was a small disused wartime airfield where we were shooting some scenes involving an old Bristol Wayfarer transport plane. There I found that I was not required after all until Monday or Tuesday. But as Spike was coming I hung on for an hour or so, just to say 'hello', and then drove home. I felt tired and ruffled, because of the unnecessary discomfort of a disturbed night, but I put it down to 'show business'.

When I got home the August Bank Holiday weekend was in full swing. Gus had left early with Andy, either to go sailing on the Solent or, if their friends had other plans he had said that he might pop over to Lasham to do a bit of gliding. As he was a reliable and considerate son, Clementina and I felt no sense of dread.

That Saturday, we had our very close friends the Kershens over for the day. This was always a delight, and Sam and Marty Kershen were as happy as ever that we were all together. Our relationship was one of long and laughter-filled standing and I am very grateful to them for that friendship, particularly for the marvellous support they gave us, as a family, when the blow fell that weekend.

I started to feel restless and disturbed when we all went for a walk, but I put it down to my bad night at Hatfield. Nursie, on the other hand, had sensed the tragedy the night before, when Gus hadn't telephoned.

'He usually phones to say where he is,' she said, really upset.

'Don't worry! I'm sure it's just that Gus can't get to a

phone, especially if they're out sailing. He'll phone soon.' I comforted her, explaining that Gus was probably at sea in a small yacht. But a nagging doubt was creeping into my mind; I deliberately put it aside.

Anyway, it was already too late. As we found out later, Gus and Andy died instantly when their Piper Cub towing plane nosedived into a wood within a mile and a half of a busy main road, at approximately 12.15 in the afternoon of that fateful Saturday. The mystery of the whole dreadful business was that the aero club to which the plane belonged didn't check on the whereabouts of their plane (one of two similar light planes) during the rest of the day or night.

By the afternoon of the Sunday my heart was beginning to ache with that dreadful doubt, and eventually I phoned Lasham airfield to ask them if, by any chance, my son was there.

Their answer was no.

Had he been there? It was possible – but they couldn't check up – the airfield was too busy.

I told Clementina and Nursie not to worry – the boys must have gone sailing – probably to watch the round-the-islands race. But the cold fingers of fear clutched my soul.

By the evening my conversation with my good friends was a hollow sham.

Marty said: 'You're really worried, aren't you, Michael?'

'Yes I am, love. I'm going to phone again.'

This time, as I got through to Lasham, I *knew* that Gus was over on the other side.

Once again I got the same answer. All their aircraft were accounted for.

God! I thought. Could Gus be dead in the car somewhere? Why did I only get a blank?

I told Clementina that everything was OK and Sam tried his hardest to cheer us up and even gave good reasons why everything was OK.

I excused myself, deliberately took a sleeping tablet and went to bed because I knew that it was of paramount impor-

tance that I should get a few hours' sleep. Tomorrow all hell
would break loose!

It may sound callous of me not to have spent that night
comforting Clementina - but then I *knew* what had
happened! Quite suddenly and dreadfully I *saw it*, with
complete clarity - as my mind shot back to that summer
afternoon twelve weeks before and the warning.

Clementina just couldn't accept the possibility of the
worst happening and, as she restlessly fell asleep beside me
and I slipped into merciful oblivion, I prayed for help. Please
Lord, help us! The night passed without incident, and in a
deep dreamless sleep for me.

The morning dawned as a hollow nightmare and we all
walked around like zombies. By this time Nursie was as
certain as I was that it was all over and that Gus had passed
from our midst - but, human nature being what it is, *still*
none of us would admit it to ourselves or to each other.

By noon, the airfield at Lasham admitted that one of their
aircraft was missing.

As I stood in the garden of our home, I prayed to the forces
of light to guide me and - suddenly, my door marked summer
swung open.

There beside me was Gus. I felt his touch on my shoulder
and heard his anxious voice in my ear: 'Daddy! I'm terribly
sorry - so sorry!'

Then the words came clearly: 'It wasn't Andy's fault!'
They were the last words I would have expected to hear, in
view of that dreadful warning.

'The bloody machine went wrong in the air.' Those were
his final words.

Like a breath of summer breeze he was gone, but I felt him
close - my son - for those few short moments, and his words
stayed with me.

I told Clementina, and we both clung together till the
shock passed its peak. Then I set about finding out what had
truly happened.

It was a long and grim quest - not helped by some of the

Press, who gave us no peace. They even found us in Paris two months later - when news of the aircraft having been located came to us through Fusty, our eldest daughter.

It had been broken to her at home, in this fashion: 'The *badly-decomposed* body of your brother has been found.'

I would have given a year of my life for five minutes alone with whoever, in Britain's Press, gave that unfeeling message to my daughter - to haunt her for a long time.

Two Pressmen had already come to our front door a few hours after the news of the plane's going missing and *demanded* pictures of Gus. 'You'd better co-operate with the Press,' one arrogant young swine had said, 'if you want to find your son.'

I told him to get out or face the consequences. They knew I meant it and left.

Twenty minutes later their editor, a large overblown bully, arrived and started berating me. I was accompanied by Gus's close friend, from his schooldays, Chris. He is built like a battleship; we both told the big so-called Pressman to go away and leave us alone or else! I said, quite simply, that I had shot better men than him. He left, breathing threats.

A few minutes later the local police rang me. Was I having trouble with the Press? they asked.

I explained that with some of them, yes. With others no.

The desk sergeant then told me that the large bully had angrily denounced me for threatening him.

'What did you tell him?' I asked. The voice lightened in tone over the wire. 'I told him that I didn't think you made idle threats,' he said.

I am deliberately making these points to convey to you some of the horror that accompanied the death of those two young men. For they show how far down the road this country had gone by 1971.

Had one of our aircraft - service or civilian - gone missing in 1945 for even a quarter-of-an-hour after its tanks were dry, a whole 'search and find' operation would have gone into operation.

But I am referring to wartime aviation, or even to private aviation a few years after the war. Then it was compulsory to book out and to state your intent or expected destination before taking off in a light civilian plane. By 1971 the permissive attitude rejoiced in by so many had destroyed even those simple safety rules.

Within hours after I started my investigation, a good friend of many years' association in gliding phoned me with an offer to help. Dick's splendid efforts were far more fruitful than mine. I began to lean harder and pushed my investigations to the limit.

A threatening phone call, made to my *unlisted* number, led me to contact Special Branch. Within twenty minutes a splendid young SB sergeant called. I can never thank that tireless organization enough for their help and sympathy.

There were others, too – some who helped and some who, misguidedly, hindered our efforts to improve the appalling lack of safety conditions in private flying. One of those who, surprisingly, made my efforts that much harder, was a nice young man whose honesty and straightforwardness blinded him to what was going on. His name was Prince William of Gloucester and, as an official of the British light-plane association, which was so outspoken against my accusations of permissive safety conditions, he went on record as saying that I was hysterical over the loss of my son and therefore was not thinking clearly. Anyone who knew me at that time would refute that. I was thinking very clearly indeed.

Tragically this fine young man died when the plane that he was piloting in an air race crashed after hitting trees on take-off. With him died a very experienced pilot with over five thousand hours' flying. They met their quite unnecessary end when one of them attempted to make a steep turn *directly* after take-off, without sufficient speed or height, an incredible mistake. My family, and I'm sure the whole country, were shocked and appalled by their deaths. What was strange was that it happened exactly 365 days, *to the hour*, after the death of my son and his friend. That is the price of permissive safety conditions.

The Air Accident Investigation Branch is another organization for which I have unbounded admiration. The team who investigated the crash of the Piper Cub in which our son died laid out the whole wreckage (surprisingly intact) at Farnborough. Their report is published and is there for anyone to read. Their conclusion was that 'the pilot, flying low in turbulent conditions and poor visibility, was forced to enter cloud to avoid overhead power cables and that he became unable to control the aircraft in cloud because it lacked blind flying instruments.' They also noted that 'Technical examination of the wreckage revealed a fatigue crack in the cabin heat exchanger but the evidence was insufficient to indicate whether or not toxic fumes were present in the aircraft cabin.'

A disturbing factor that emerged from the investigation that I was engaged in (aiding the Special Branch and with further help proffered by one or two old professional friends) was the strong evidence of widespread illicit activities involving private light aircraft in Britain.

I am obviously not permitted, nor would I wish, to go into details regarding what we uncovered; but within a few weeks I was forced to approach my local MP, an honest and brave man who had served with distinction in the 1939–45 war while seconded to the SAS. The result was an in-depth investigation into private flying activities involving smuggling by air. It has no place in this book. Its findings are for the private security records of the country.

One thing I know for certain, and I hope it is of some comfort to our good friends, Andy's parents. Their son was doing *everything* that he possibly could to keep that light aeroplane flying, up to the moment he died. Even the ignition was switched off. No blame, in my view, attaches to him, in that needless and futile accident. The Air Accident Investigation Branch, and the words that seemed to come to me from Gus, in my own garden, so soon after his passing bear this out.

I should like to add in the interests of research into the paranormal that both my daughters, my other son Richard and Nursie have all seen Gus since. So have I.

That is why I can still open my door marked summer.

14 The Foci

In the last few years I have attempted to assess the small amount of knowledge that I have gained by personal experience of paranormal research. I use the word paranormal because it gives some sort of definition to the hazy frontiers of human experiences and differentiates them from the gross materialism into which we have allowed ourselves to be manipulated.

The great monolithic capitalist states or the vast monopolies of corporate industrial giants would be happiest if man didn't think at all, apart from the technology or skills required to further their relentless pursuit of power. Therefore the foci which release the mind from the bondage of mass mind-manipulation become of great importance to the individual. All of them are paths to Samadhi – the state of awareness of the Overmind and the essence of Man. Through that state of open-mindedness is the contact with all nature and all consciousness.

An overstatement? I don't think so, because from personal experience, utilizing a number of different foci, I have been able to experience that extraordinary and rewarding contact on many occasions. During these moments of rapport it has become obvious to me that such an 'opening' must only be of short duration (certainly at first experience) and should only be sought when the pressures of the material world become insufferable. One could liken the intensest of these contacts to sexual orgasm, and to attempt to prolong the experience by the use of drugs is far more

dangerous than the use of such chemicals as methyl nitrate
to arrest the moment of orgasm. Anyone who doubts the
perils of the misuse of hallucinogenic drugs and other
methods of inducing states of altered consciousness should
visit a terminal addiction ward.

The foci are, quite simply, 'doors' – some practising
magicians call them 'portals'. Through them it is possible to
experience contacts which can be variously described – as
the universal Overmind, collective unconscious, astral
plane, astral light, Akashic record – and many other
definitions of the indefinable.

As an artist I have experienced this contact in the sudden
realization of the living beauty of a sunset, a sunrise, dawn
over misty mountain peaks, beams of light through clouds,
shafts of grey-green radiance in the Rain Forest, swirling
vapour over the boiling entrance to the rapids of the
Marañón, the forms and shapes of great trees, the
Pyramids, a child asleep and a thousand other things that, if
my state of receptivity had been less attuned at that moment
of opportunity, I would not have particularly noticed.

'Day dreaming', listening to inspiring music, the moment
of capture on paper or canvas of one fragment of visual
truth, are all fleeting contacts with the universal Overmind
of nature – the true *collective unconscious*. To have tried to
hold on to the moment of ecstacy would have been, at the
very least, a fading disappointment and, at the most, an
artificial overkill of what should have its own natural
duration and no more.

To survive on the surface of 'space-ship Earth', with all its
natural hazards, is difficult enough, and to further increase
the hazard factor beyond reason is imbecilic. We are already
surrounded by an over-abundance of material dangers,
such as our erratic methods of transportation, junk foods, a
dangerous level of air, water and earth pollution, and now,
as I hope to have brought to your notice, mental pollution on
a massive scale. Misuse of the foci will only increase the
hazard factor, while to enhance the probability of the

destruction of mind and body by the use of such hallucinogenic drugs or other preparations known to heighten out-of-
the-body experiences is plain madness. I know, from
personal experience. I suffered withdrawal symptoms, of an
acute nature, from pethidine and omnipon. They had been
medically prescribed and professionally administered for
the extreme pain that accompanied the near-loss of my left
leg. I deliberately requested a total withdrawal from these
drugs, as opposed to a tailing off, as I wished to experience
something about which I had warned young people but had
never experienced myself.

I would not attempt to repeat the appalling forty-eight
hours which I then went through – and I understand from
specialists in these fields that I suffered the effects of only a
comparatively minor withdrawal, compared to those
experienced by an addicted person. Since then, only when
pain is so acute as to be nearly unbearable will I take an
analgesic – nor will I use either sleeping pills or tranquil-
lizers unless I have no alternative. Being a sensitive – by
chance and training – I am more sensible to pain than is
usual, because of my heightened sensitivity.

I can fully understand those unfortunate people who,
through pain, have become addicted to soporific or
analgesic drugs. But I can find little sympathy for those
who, despite warnings, have caused their own addiction in
the pursuit of enhanced sensations of pleasure. The pseudo-
mystical experience of self-hallucination can be quite easily
achieved, and is completely different and alien to an actual
contact with the Overmind and, through that channel, with
the infinitely wider reach of the universal collective
unconscious.

You can, after all, go on a simple and safely enjoyable
'trip' with music alone. Light, shape, form, etc., can also
induce a light entrainment of the mind, and each experience
should add to your accumulation of knowledge and
awareness of the need for control.

Day dreaming, light entrainment and simple relaxation

techniques are, of course, highly beneficial if carried out sensibly. They are excellent ways to renew the drained energies of the body and mind – but even these can have dangers – the most obvious being that of unconscious mind-entrainment while driving a car, flying an aeroplane or being involved in any other similar highly-concentrated activity which demands quick and skilled reactions.

Self-evident? One would have thought so but the numbers of accidents induced by the mixture of concentrated physical activity and uncontrolled mental release are amazingly high. The appalling figures for motorcycle accidents, where speed and emotional stimulation combine so readily, are an indication of this sort of simple entrainment. Where pillion riders are involved the natural excitement of two young people in close proximity responding to the stimulus of riding a fast-moving machine can easily affect judgement and reaction time.

The foci, such as the Tarot and I-Ching, although they can be used with discretion and care as portals through which the consciousness can pass into contact with the universal Overmind, still hold a great deal of danger for the irrational and impetuous, who would be far better advised to leave well alone until they can learn to control their character weaknesses.

A 'focus', inducing a deeper state of mind-entrainment or a trance state of some depth, should never be attempted without the presence of a knowledgeable colleague, preferably medically qualified, who is capable of monitoring the whole process and providing a safe return for the researcher.

There are a number of books on the Tarot, of which the most coherent classical work is that of A. E. Waite, an accomplished scholar and magician and a one-time member of the Golden Dawn. His book is as much a critique as a definitive revelation and is the one that I would recommend to a researcher who wishes to investigate the validity of Tarot predictions.

Unless one realizes that the real interpretation can only

be in accordance with the stage of development reached by the operator, Tarot reading is worthless. I have conducted a strictly rationed and reasonably comprehensive series of Tarot readings for my own interest, and found the results to be extraordinary – but then I could have used other channels and achieved the same results. For me, the Tarot is a valid focus and one of which I can say, yes, it works – but proceed with caution. Where a mixture of chance and manipulated telekinesis is in control of an operation of this type the motive for the use of the focus is of paramount importance. As with the Ouija board, the planchette or automatic writing – or, for that matter, table-turning, the Tarot is a *physically*-based operation and, therefore, close to the *earth plane* i.e. *material frequencies*. By this very nature, the portals will be the focus of forces which approximate to the same frequencies, and these can be best described as low-frequency elemental forces. It is unlikely that the results will be of a highly spiritual nature, but rather more in line with a simple pattern of predictive or precognitive projections of the material and mental life of the investigator.

I do not believe that the Tarot would be the ideal channel to achieve a more elevated contact with a highly-advanced aspect of the universal Overmind. For that, meditation, controlled fasting and abstinence from the materialistic side of life would be the best focus with which to open the contact.

You play with the Tarot pack at your peril. The same principles apply to the use of the I-Ching – a system of divination and life-guidance which was developed by the Chinese and which has been in general use in China for hundreds of years and throughout the rest of the world since the opening of that country to Western civilization.

Originally the readings were the result of the study of the various forms and shapes found on the shell of a tortoise, which was probably first developed by King Wan in the twelfth century BC into a system of permutations based on combinations of broken and whole straight lines to form trigrams and hexagrams. There is also a belief that the Emperor Fu Hsi (2953-2838BC) was responsible for the original Yi-King or Canon.

The method is, like the Tarot, partly telekinetic and partly divinatory in its interpretation, which, of course, depends largely on the degree of the operator's clairvoyant ability and partly on a book of classical interpretations. The best one that I have found is called *The I-Ching: The Book of Changes*, published by Dover Publications, edited by Max Muller and translated by J. Legge.

Once again the focus opens the portals, to bring into play the contact with the universal Overmind, and the combination of telekinetic manipulation and intuitive interpretation does the rest. But with all these methods reason must be the controlling factor; if you throw that away you face the appalling situation of the possessed publican of Dover.

Aleister Crowley, who was drug-addicted in addition to his other disadvantages, became equally addicted to both the Tarot and the I-Ching and never made any significant move without consulting them. His fine brain finished up totally confused and ineffectual, which was the ultimate tragedy for such a scholarly academic.

Few people would believe the extent of the use of I-Ching and Tarot today throughout the world – and among highly-intelligent practitioners – but the centre of I-Ching is still the Far East, where the hexagrams have as much to say as the radio and television news broadcasts. In both cases it is how you interpret them that counts (and, as I have pointed out, that applies to radio and television as well).

I think every one of these telekinetic/clairvoyant methods should carry a warning on them, like cigarette packets: 'These methods *can* be dangerous to mental health.'

Reading the tealeaves, the interpretation of shapes in sand, reading symbols into the moving shapes of clouds or the leaping flames of a fire, the lines of the hand, random words taken from the pages of a book and many other methods of focusing the contact with the universal Overmind – all are valid *if* the operator is well developed in clairvoyance or psychometry. All act as a portal, if the operator allows them to, and the extent of their efficacy is, likewise, controllable, or should be so.

I have no personal experience of numerology and astrology and so I cannot vouch for them, other than by describing them as further foci to entrain the paranormal faculties of the mind. Yet I know many practised and skilled astrologers, such as my life-long close friend Hans Holzer, and I fully accept their validity as interpreters of the heavens.

Patrick Moore, whom I have also counted for years as a friend, and who has often played Devil's advocate for me in discussions of this kind, finds no valid grounds for the astrologers' claims that their methods are scientific. But he is the first to agree that the skilled interpreters seem to be practising an *art* and that their system contains a focus for their intuitive faculties; and, as a practising astronomer, Patrick knows that certain forces in the cosmos have decided effects on our planet and the people who live on it.

In France, Michel Gauquelin has come up with some interesting results when examining astrology's principles, in character traits and birth signs. So has Professor Eysenck, another scholar of proven academic ability who is not afraid to stand against the Establishment.

In the nineteenth century, Helena Petrovna Blavatsky, the Russian medium and authoress, founded, with Colonel Olcott, the Theosophical Society, which provided a magical basis for the more modern version of Theosophy today.

My father often spoke of her life, and considered her to have been a genuine psychic and a remarkable woman – driven involuntarily to the practice of, or involvement with, some fraudulent aspects of her work as a medium.

A splendid book by Symonds – the biographer of Aleister Crowley – gives a fair picture of this extraordinarily gifted woman, and though, as a boy, I met a number of elderly people who had known her in their youth, I never remember anything of a disparaging nature being said of her. She undoubtedly, as her disciples told me, employed a number of foci and had genuine clairvoyance of a highly developed order. She also used the Tarot and I-Ching. Sadly, financial worries and the breakdown of her health robbed her of a large proportion of her abilities before her death in 1891.

To use the foci at all effectively requires the expenditure of considerable amounts of mental and physical energy and, where ectoplasm is generated, the lowering of body resources is inevitable. Therefore, the resulting depletion in nervous and physical energy levels must present a further hazard if disproportionate over-indulgence in these activities is unwisely undertaken. Once again, it is the question of balance, of maintaining an equilibrium without over-dependence on the foci, over-indulgence in their use and over-straining of the researcher's natural resources in nervous and physical energies.

I have made a reasonable study of the lives and fortunes of a number of magicians of the ritual schools of magic, that is to say, practitioners of magical systems in which repeated ritualized acts and ceremonies have produced mental attitudes leading to the opening of contacts in the Overmind of the magician. (This is often referred to as 'Passing through the Pillars', i.e., to enter an altered state of consciousness.) In every case in which there has been deep involvement *without* the requisite control of the brake of reason, a rapid rise to a position of temporal power – or the *illusion* of it – has been followed by a disastrous fall into mental disorientation and subsequent ruin.

The methods used by the Golden Dawn magicians – some of whom approached the whole operation with great arrogance – led to egos inflated to the point of belief in God-like qualities. This resulted in disastrous individual tragedies, such as that of Liddell Mathers, one of the order's founders. The passing of this scholarly and self-deluded man took place in Paris, in very sad circumstances, and was partly due to the machinations of the equally arrogant Aleister Crowley when the Golden Dawn became divided and eventually collapsed.

Today, its rituals, mainly preserved by Dr Israel Regardie and originally published in a limited edition of four-volume sets, forms the basis for a number of practising magical ritual groups in the UK, Germany, the United States and Australia. I have studied the remarkable scholarship involved in compiling these rituals, and I am amazed at the extraordinary imagination shown by Mathers in formulating most of them.

It is fascinating to consider the lives and careers of men like Nietzsche, Rasputin, Crowley, Rudolf Hess, Karl Haushofer, Lanz von Lebenfels, von Sebottendorf or, for that matter, Idi Amin – *all* of whom were deeply involved in the study of the occult and its manipulative powers upon the human mind. The *pattern* of their lives has a remarkable stamp of similarity.

All of them rose meteorically on the strength of their fanatical beliefs, though the matter of degree is vastly different. They then enjoyed a vogue, which encompassed, in the case of Rasputin, Hess, Haushofer and Amin, a temporal power that few men apart from Napoleon, Hitler, Mussolini and the Soviet leaders have wielded. This was followed by a sudden fall – and ended, for most of them, in a dreadful fate.

Rasputin was pushed under the ice after being poisoned, clubbed and shot. Hess sits alone, except for his multinational guards, in Spandau fortress (a nightmare situation accepted by the world). Haushofer died, as a suicide, by the traditional method of seppuku (death by self-disembowelling). Amin's final fate remains uncertain, except that it seems likely to be grisly.

Von Lebenfels and Sebottendorf, whose individual work in the establishment of the mythology of the hyperborean religion and its relationship to the *Thule Gesellschaft* and the *Germanen Orden* was so effective, can claim notoriety, if not infamy, from the results that their efforts had on a great part of the emergent Nazi party dogma.

Nietzsche died insane; and his theories were also used as the basis for much of the madness of the National Socialist Party. Except for him, all these men tried to acquire power by fanatically exploiting their contacts with the Overmind in its universal context. All of them, including Nietzsche, showed evidence of unnaturally inflated egos, and all of them became megalomaniac, leading to their disorientation from reality and their consequent fall into chaos and disaster.

Each had his individual foci: Hess and Haushofer both used astrological methods, Tarot and, especially in the case of Haushofer, the I-Ching; here again we see the vital importance of motive and rational restraint. Their motive was to gain and manipulate unlimited power, and it led to disaster for both.

For Rasputin, the door to power came through the focus of healing, which one would have thought as a far safer route to the contact with the universal Overmind. But yet again the appeal to vanity brought about megalomania.

Crowley died, a pathetic drug addict, in Hove, in 1947 – a very different figure from the 'Great Beast' of the twenties and thirties, when my father classified him as a powerful practising black magician.

Amin's involvement with the foci is well documented and, as with Hitler, syphilis contributed its deadly destruction of the brain cells. He used ritual voodoo – the perverted version of the earth magic and fertility rites which are the ethnic and perfectly respectable religions of the African peoples.

This perversion of the earth religions of these natural people was also used, most effectively, in the ghastly initiation ceremonies of the Mau-Mau in Kenya.

Kabbalism – the study of the Kabbala, Cabala or Qabalah, the Judaic system of mind-training and manipulative techniques – is another prime focus for those interested in opening their contacts. But with it goes a stern warning. Its study is not encouraged, even in the most liberal of Rabbinical circles. But, to make an academic study or research of Kabbalism is safe *provided* one accepts informed guidance, preferably from a scholar of the Jewish faith. To launch oneself into Kabbalism according to the haphazard do-it-yourself methods offered by a number of uninformed authors in paperback, quasi-scientific publications is extremely dangerous.

I have had to deal with the results of such 'dabbling' in the Kabbala by one or two misguided enthusiastic young people, and I know, from first-hand knowledge, the mental pain and anguish caused to these tragic young folk and their families. Once again drugs were part of the combination of mind-blowing factors which resulted in these disasters.

The Kabbala itself has had many translators and, in its pure form, is really a statement of the canon of the Judaic system of magic. The system that the Greeks called *Gematria* is employed to give numerical equivalents to words. The Hebrew letters are allotted certain numerical values, and each word or phrase has a definitive total value which bears an intricate relationship to the whole system. This rather unwieldy system was originated to cover the canon with a cryptographic umbrella intended to protect the 'secrets of the mystery' from the profane and the inevitable persecution that any closed heretical group is subjected to.

In essence, the whole Kabbala contains a psychological map, or chart, for the safe exploitation of the inner mind, or as I prefer to call it, the Overmind.

The Tree of Life, with its carefully plotted graph of ascending and descending paths to various areas of open contact with the collective unconscious, is a marvellous piece of imaginative scholarship, and *academically* it is a safe and rewarding study. Interlocked in the system are many safeguards to test the validity of each step – but it is a *life* study, for those of natural scholarship and, preferably, with informed Rabbinical guidance. Here again you play with these paths at your peril; and to mix the Kabbala with a drug-orientated method of operation is to guarantee disaster.

There are a number of reliable works on this subject. Authors such as William Gray, Dion Fortune and Bligh Bond have written works on the Kabbala and Gematria, and Watkins Bookshop at Cecil Court, WC2, is most helpful in these areas.

I have met several people who have been deeply into Kabbalism, and because they used this focus correctly they have come out of their studies unscathed and with considerably enhanced awareness and scholarship.

To sum up, in all the foci – from gazing at an ink-blot in the palm of the hand through Tattvas and the Flashing Colours, to water in a bowl, crystals, tealeaves, cards, cheiromancy and every other method that I have studied and seen practised, or even practised myself to a careful degree – I have seen the same pattern emerge. They are all a series of portals to a contact with the universal Overmind, your own Overmind, the collective unconsciousness, the Akashic Record or whatever area of the paranormal you may seek – via the survival mechanisms of *search* and *find* which have guided and maintained the entity of mankind through hundreds of thousands of years.

Do understand! You *play* with such areas of your normally dormant mind at great risk. Study them, be aware of them, treat them with humility and respect, and their careful examination is highly rewarding.

Of one thing you can be certain: you will receive no help and little encouragement – and a lot of ridicule – from the Establishment, be it scientific, religious or political, on that long and fascinating journey. Apart from loyal friends you will be completely on your own.

15 Dowsing, Temples and Gnostics

Through Colin Morris's BBC TV *Portrait of Michael
Bentine,* which I mentioned earlier, I became acquainted
with a group of experienced dowsers who had been
researching different fields of energy which they had found
to be apparently associated with ancient sacred sites. As our
casual relationship became friendship, I found myself
increasingly interested in their areas of experience and,
under their tuition and guidance, I soon became a practical
dowser myself.

The first supposition that emerged and that appeared to
be valid, was that everyone, to a greater or lesser extent, can
dowse.

'Dowsing' really means 'searching' and, to me, this
faculty – normally latent in the modern man of the
materially-orientated societies – is yet another facet of the
survival mechanism inherited from our earliest ancestors.
Children, whose uncluttered minds make them especially
suitable to searching without doubt, are extremely adept at
dowsing.

In my ignorance, I thought that dowsers only sought and
found water or minerals, gas pipes and electricity cables,
and I was most intrigued to find that one can dowse for
pretty well everything, from underground chambers to lost
contact lenses or even missing persons. The dowsing of
'fields of force' to determine their boundaries and characteristics, such as intensity, direction and flow, is the part of this
natural ability that intrigues me the most.

In discussing this phenomenon, and the probable methods by which it works, colleagues and friends such as Dr Stanley Rose and Dr Brian Houghton of Birmingham, Professor Eric Laithwaite and other accomplished and well-qualified scientific minds have evidenced a consensus of opinion which points to the possibility of dowsing being the result of 'abreactions' on the central nervous system. The implication seems to be that extremely low frequencies are involved, and the ability of man to transmit and receive on extremely long waves – as my father believed. This would certainly be the type of emanation that would be capable of penetrating layers of rock and earth; and as ELF is such an infant area of modern radio technology, there is not a great deal published about it. One reason for this is that of state security – both in the Soviet Union and the USA.

I should be most interested to see some detailed research carried out on dowsers in action with EEC (electro-encephalograph) equipment. Many of us suspect that the results would confirm that this faculty in man is yet another focus for entraining the 'Alpha' frequency range of the brain.

As yet no instrumentation – other than bio-instruments (i.e. Man himself) – has been able to pinpoint exactly when the Overmind comes into operation, as there appears to be no significant change in the brain patterns at the point of contact. (For that matter, we have, so far, no instrumental indication that the Overmind, or whatever you like to call it, exists at all.)

However, most quantum-leap advances in science are non-detectable on contemporary instrumentation, until special devices are built to detect the phenomenon hypothe-sized. It is still a question of the man who has come to read the gas meter saying, 'I don't believe in electricity because it doesn't register on my *gas* meter!'

A prime example of this 'lag' in instrumentation is the way in which it is necessary to build more and more huge cyclotronic types of   generator/detector apparatus to manifest hypothesized sub-nucleic particles. Oddly enough, these particles always seem to become detectable when the immensely complex and ultra-expensive equipment is finally brought into operation. Some researchers, for example that intriguing maverick Tom Bearden, a practical nuclear engineer turned philosopher, have suggested that this type of high-powered equipment not only successfully detects these particles but in some cases actually *creates* them!

Tom's line of reasoning is pure heresy in many ways, and gets conventional technologists of the I've-not-actually-done-any-original-thinking-but-I've-read-all-the-books type of approach to science well and truly riled. I heard one of them blow his top at the 'quasi-scientific nonsense', as he put it, promulgated by Tom Bearden. On asking for *his* qualifications to make such a judgement I was surprised to find that this young man's academic attainments were as fuzzy as my own. But he didn't have the excuse of the war having interrupted his studies.

The only claim that I have to being in any way aware of the paranormal is based on forty-five years of grass-root participation and observation - in a number of cases involving my own survival. That is why I am a little sceptical of technocrats bulldozing their way into a field of research which is largely unexplored and wholly heretical in the eyes of the Establishment. Contemporary techniques are only helpful as back up to original thinking and objective analysis, and cannot be taken as the final arbiter in such researches.

Learn the scales first and *then* criticize: surely that is fair if you are searching for truth! Otherwise the whole area becomes an internecine battleground between dogma and heresy. Science should be truth, not a bigoted religion.

In dowsing - lacking, as yet, although I understand that help is on the way, a valid set of basic electronic instruments - we are compelled to accept or reject anecdotal evidence, plus the observations that we can make ourselves during the operation.

However, most advances in science have started in the environment of a researcher's study; in the case of the great Tsilokovski, the pioneer Russian rocket engineer, in a cluttered bedroom. The instrumentation comes later. I was fortunate enough to gain my preliminary dowsing experience, over the past four years, with colleagues such as Colin Bloy, his brother David, Bob Cowley and other experienced practitioners. They were surprised to find that I already unconsciously used a form of dowsing, utilizing my 'body antennae', i.e. the ELF aerials that (I believe) are formed by the complex neuronal system of my whole body. Since childhood I have been able to detect 'centres of force' in buildings and 'generators of force' in the landscape by the feeling of intense cold and a prickling sensation that seems to run up my spine whenever I come into contact with an actual field of energy of this sort (a simple demonstration of a survival mechanism). This sensation can be quite unexpected and involuntary, or I can 'tune myself in' to receive it. On many occasions I have been with others, often children, who have without prompting confirmed a similar reaction to the environment, at the same time and in the same area.

However, this general 'area dowse' is obviously not accurate in defining the exact position and limits of such fields of energy and, therefore, dowsing them by more normal methods is the accepted mode of procedure. The movements of twigs, bent wire rods, spiral springs, whalebone 'vees', pendulums of various kinds and other simple mechanistic appliances, appear to be caused by very small involuntary muscular movements in the operators' hands.

These, to me, seem to be due to 'abreactions' – caused, possibly, by anomalies in the electro-magnetic field of the area being dowsed. The 'frequency' range of the dowsing seems to be determined by the mental attitude of the dowser during the operation.

As this is a partly telekinetic phenomenon, I would cite as an interesting area for experiment the ability of man to break up clouds by an effort of will. I have seen this done on a number of occasions by others and have performed the simple operation myself, being able to 'hit' a high percentage of times. Even sceptics have been somewhat surprised at finding themselves able to do the same! There is nothing even remotely mystical about it; everyone, possessed of a degree of will power and application, can do it. Try it for yourself.

I mention this because there is an apparent parallel here with dowsing. Both require the *elimination of doubt* - which, to me, is obviously a frequency block - being, in its own *negative* way, a frequency in itself.

It is a little like Dr R. V. Jones's splendid device for bending the 'Knickebein' radio beams of the German bombers' airborne radio equipment. (Indeed, if you are interested in intuitive thinking backed up by scientific discipline, do read *Most Secret War* by R. V. Jones.) One frequency can block or negate another - and dowsing has a definite frequency, hence the need for fine tuning when dowsing to remove or 'squelch' the confusing multi-echoes that seem to form a background to the operation.

Any apparatus that is eventually built and is portable enough to be used (probably incorporating chip technology) will have to be capable of fine tuning to very precise limits to parallel the dowsing ability in man's mind. For example, to find water, the dowser has to *think* 'water' in order to tune in to the frequency range required - in this case the frequency of *running* water, i.e. currents of force generated by the vortices created by underground streams. These could be in a water pipe or emanating from a spring, a fountain, an underground river, a sewage conduit or anything else of this nature; but it must be *moving* to be detectable, because it is *generating* force. To detect a static mass of water such as an underground reservoir is something quite different - for then only the *limits* of the liquid mass can be detected and determined as a shape and form.

Obviously the same set of rules applies if the dowser is searching for a buried gas main or an electrical cable – to tune into that frequency he thinks 'gas', or 'electricity'. In other words, he requires to formulate an image of what he is tuning in to in order to pick up the frequencies given off by the object for which he is searching.

It sounds ridiculously simple – or simply ridiculous! But then this is precisely what you do when looking for anything that has been mislaid in your own home surroundings. 'Where did I put it?' you ask, at the same time formulating the image of the missing article in your mind. 'Where was it when I last saw it?' 'Who had it last?' (This is a great favourite in my family!) 'When did I use it last?'

In your imagination you flip through various reconstructed scenes of previous actions, until: 'Ah, I remember now! I put it in that drawer.' That is really an everyday method of dowsing!

'Téléradiesthésie', as the French, rather ponderously, named the ability to dowse from maps and charts, is yet another fascinating focus of the mind of the dowser. In this case the map is scanned by using a pointer, held in one hand and passed over the whole area of the chart while, with the other hand, a pendulum is used to check a 'Yes/No' reaction to each different position that the pointer indicates.

I have seen it done, with remarkable accuracy, a number of times. In one case that I know of from a first-hand account, Colin and a colleague found a most interesting object of a crystal composition, pinpointing it to a position below the surface of the floor of a cave in the Pyrenees, on the border between France and Spain. They tracked this particular 'target' by using large-scale maps – from Britain, across to France and right down to the frontier cave site. All by téléradiesthésie! (Why they did it is another fascinating story, and one that is not mine to tell. Perhaps Colin might be persuaded to publish something of that strange tale.)

Another successful map dowsing of which I have heard involved the finding of the body of an unfortunate Belgian police officer who had been kidnapped by terrorists and tragically murdered. This was, apparently, dowsed by a British pendulum operator, using large-scale maps and charts provided by the Belgian police – and the dramatic result was the location of the body of the missing police officer in Belgium, in a culvert not far from the main road.

This sort of operation is connected, of course, with such parallel paranormal operations as psychometry, clair-voyance, clairaudience and similar forms of mental awareness. So, for me, dowsing falls into the focus category, and precisely the same rules apply to it as obtain with any of the other foci. In other words, as dowsing uses considerable amounts of mental energy and therefore draws on the nervous and physical energy reserves of the operator, *over-indulgence* in its performance, coupled with *over-reliance* on its results – unfiltered by rationale – can have harmful effects on the mental and physical state of the operator, leading to nervous exhaustion and physical collapse if carried to excess.

So, of course, could a fanatical over-indulgence in playing golf. You should balance your intuitive contact with down-to-earth common sense, or face the consequences!

The dowsing of standing stones, stone circles, ellipses and egg shapes, tumuli, barrows of various kinds, querns, quoits, stone avenues and alignments, dolmens, earth zodiacs or, for that matter, any of the ancient sites and monuments, leads me to the conclusion that the placement and siting of such objects was undertaken by intelligent and knowledge-able people who knew *exactly* what they were doing.

I am well aware of the controversy that exists, if not actually rages, over the question of ley-lines. These were originally brought to public attention in our era by Alfred Watkins, an intelligent and practical Herefordshire man who, incidentally, was an accomplished photographer and invented a light-exposure meter.

He was a brewer's representative by profession, which is a
down-to-earth base for reasoned thinking, and, one day,
while ruminating over the scene below him – the beautiful
Bradwardine valley – he 'saw', with his inner vision, a
complex pattern of glowing lines which seemed to inter-
connect various parts of the valley and its surrounding
landscape.

He eventually wrote an intriguing book, *The Old Straight
Track*, about his experiences, and his follow-up research
sparked off a fine old row among his contemporaries and
resulted in the formation of the Old Straight Track Club,
which only became extinct at the outbreak of the 1939–45
war.

Since then his theories – that ancient sites and marks cut
into or set up on the skyline are linked – have had many
faithful disciples and been the object of several bitter
attacks. Why these disclaimers should be so *bitter* is in itself
a mystery, but then I know only too well what Establishment reaction can be to any heresy.

Guy Underwood, a scholarly and serious-minded researcher, encouraged by Dr Allender Smith, the well-known
antiquarian and, incidentally, a leading member of the
British Society of Dowsers at the time, followed up
Watkins's ideas and applied dowsing techniques to his
researches.

The results you can read about in another fascinating
book, *Pattern of the Past*, written shortly before Guy
Underwood died in the early sixties. The content here is
concerned with the detection of intriguing patterns and
apparent lines of force, some of which Underwood described
as 'Blind Springs' and 'Aquastats'.

With my dowser friends, we found some interesting
patterns for ourselves connected with, and often emanating
from, Templar churches, ancient sacred sites and all the
stone and earth monuments and temples that I have listed
and actually dowsed. These were so consistently dowsed by
different operators, one after the other – each not knowing

the previous dowser's results and yet exactly duplicating them – that the results were, to us, as nearly empiric as you can get in this sort of exercise. These extraordinary results tallied exactly with Underwood's researches in other places and locations, such as Gothic cathedrals, ancient churches and temples, while as far as Stonehenge and Avebury were concerned, the patterns we obtained were identical to Underwood's.

The fascinating point, for me, was that, at that time I hadn't read Underwood's book; yet my results were so close as to make no difference. This occurred when I was very much a novice at these practices.

As I have, like my father, always been a devoted lover of things Chinese, inevitably I must compare the layout and landscaping of these beautiful islands of ours with the Chinese system of town and country planning called 'Feng Shui'.

Actually, Feng Shui is far more than this, though its basic principles have largely been incorporated into modern architectural planning and siting. Described as a pseudo-science, Feng Shui (literally 'Wind and Water') is really an art and has been the single most dominant factor in the laying out and geomantic development of China. Over hundreds of years, millions of marvellously busy Chinese people have moulded and shaped the landscapes of China so that it is completely harmonious.

The Feng Shui diviners used a flat, circular device based on a centrally placed magnetic compass. The disc was engraved in compartments marked with signs and hexagrams and resembled a long-playing record in size and shape. Each 'track' contained a number of divisions and, as each part of the site was carefully surveyed and aligned with distant marks on the landscape, the Feng Shui practitioner cross-checked his results by dowsing techniques.

A weighted piece of silken thread was laid across the Feng Shui compass as each alignment was taken. Then, by considering every facet of the proposed temple, building, tomb or garden in relation to the rest of the environment, and by taking due note of the dowsing reactions, the practitioner would make the executive decisions as to the best position and siting for each and every part of the project.

The results of some of these marvellous buildings are as impressive as the cathedrals of Europe, or the Pyramids and Colossi of Egypt and South America. The predominant factor in Feng Shui surveys was the effect that the construction might have on posterity, which is something that the Get-Rich-Quick clan who built so many of modern Britain's featureless monstrosities seem never to have considered at all.

As the main operational techniques of Feng Shui are determined by dowsing, it is self-evident to me that only when the extent and direction of the fields of force are given definitive parameters can the modification, the re-shaping and re-modelling of the landscape, be safely carried out. In other words, once you know the potential of your site and its relationship to its environment, you can go ahead with modifications in the light of the probable effects on posterity.

That is something that, up till now, has obviously been way down the list of priorities of those planners who have lumbered generations to come with their ugly brain-children. You can't build with cost/effectiveness as your sole guideline. Ugliness and monolithic bulk can only adversely affect the minds of those unfortunates who have to live in these uninspiring dwellings or under the shadow of their depressing domination.

In the case of the great British architects and landscapers, such as Vanbrugh, Hawksmoor, Capability Brown and Kent, Nash and Adams and, above them all, like a true colossus, Christopher Wren, each understood the prime importance of these things.

'All is shape, form and number,' the Pythagorean concept applies, manifestly, to the landscape.

Wren, Hawksmoor and Vanbrugh, along with the great Palladio, lived and worked in the early stages of the 'Age of Reason', when Newton's new and revolutionary theories had seized the imagination of men. Yet they employed principles in their architecture and landscaping that owed as much to the magical traditions of Egypt as they did to applied logic and contemporary scientific thought.

Count the number of times that Vanbrugh and Hawksmoor use pyramids, and Wren the octagonal form. The triangle, the cube, the double cube, the pyramid, the obelisk, the hexagon and the octagon dominate their marvellous creations. Mazes and long avenues, laid out to enhance the natural beauty of the landscape, abound in Brown's and Kent's glorious gardens.

Generations of people have enjoyed the fruit of the labours of these inspired men (all of whom, to my knowledge, were master masons and some of them Rosicrucians), and they were all well aware of the effect of shape, form and number on the minds of their fellow men and their descendants to come. Castle Howard, Stowe and Blenheim are just three examples which you can visit and examine for yourself. Wren's superb churches and his masterpiece, St Paul's Cathedral, were all based on the canon of proportion encapsulated in the Golden Mean.

To dowse them is a deeply thought-provoking experience. Presumably, in view of the feeling of cosmic order and latent power that each of these remarkable achievements radiates, the designers, builders and landscapers of these lovely estates must have been accomplished dowsers and practitioners of the general principles of Feng Shui.

These remarkable artists/masons/craftsmen/philosophers stated their credo in stone and brick, glass and wood, precisely as the Egyptians had once incorporated their gnosis into the enduring beauty of the Pyramids and the Templars had constructed their cathedrals and churches as sermons in stone. Analyse and closely study the forms and symbols involved in their construction, and you will be enchanted by the new vision that these sculpted truths will open up for you.

Since I was a child, I had wondered why certain parts of the landscape affected me so deeply and why different buildings and constructions held such a fascination. Now I begin to see the reasons, and the opening up of these new perspectives has given me enthralling pleasure, which I am now sharing with my family.

I can recommend this focus, without reserve, to anyone who will take the time and trouble to investigate these marvellous generators of cosmic order. Stonehenge, Avebury, the Rollright stones, Iona and countless other stone circles, ellipses, egg shapes and stone-avenue alignments are so well worth visiting, again and again; not just as a tourist chalking up a 'I've seen that' or a 'Here's Ethel and George, beside the Slaughter Stone', but with an open mind and an excited heart – feeling the long history of the place and absorbing the emanations which, surely, are being generated by these forms.

We know so little about the real purposes behind these marvellous constructions, built with such determination, ingenuity and pious care. Archaeologists sternly rejected Hawkins, Hoyle and Thom, three sound and highly intelligent scientifically-disciplined minds, just as they ridiculed Piazzi Smith, Lockyer and Petrie; yet archaeology is *not* an exact science by any means – rather it is a fine art.

It would seem that whenever a group of people, of scholarly and inspiring natures, gather together, drawn by the law of the mind 'like attracts like', the pool of their painfully-acquired knowledge forms the basis for a heretical school of philosophy. (It is heresy, of course, only in the eyes of whatever Establishment has gained temporary control of the status quo.) The school gains adherents and disciples until, after the passing of the founding fathers, the canon that has been established becomes dogmatized and, subsequently, obscured. The original simplicity of the basic principles involved at the inception of the radical heresy becomes lost as much in allegory and myth as in the complexities of endless analyses and critiques. The school of thought then decays into a hollow shell, by the natural process of entropy, and the power structure of its original truths is only maintained by force, either intellectual or actual. Inevitably it becomes the victim of its own hollow sham and crumbles, or is an easy mark to be destroyed and plundered by a rival and more powerful establishment.

This, of course, happened to the original builders of these great stone monuments. The circles, it would appear, were intended for or were adapted subsequently to a number of purposes. Whether as temples, astronomical observatories, power generators of the ethos or simply foci for the entrainment of the Overminds of the priesthood – their power is as obvious today as it must have been when they were built.

They affect the minds of men. That seems to be the object of the exercise.

One reason for this extraordinary continuity of efficacy and validity lies, I believe, in the composition and content of the actual stones used in their construction.

These megaliths contain a vast complex of crystalline substances. Many rocks include quartz crystals that are subject to piezo-electrical effects. This is the principle of a quartz watch – now understood by most schoolchildren.

A crystal with certain basic structural characteristics, such as tourmaline, for example, generates appreciable amounts of electrical current of quite high voltage when subjected to pressure at its opposite poles. Conversely, if an electric current is applied to the poles of these crystals a mechanical distortion is manifested.

Consider the possible power generation inherent in a group of stones with piezo-electric quartz inclusions arranged in a definite form around active springs and streams which are flowing in spiral vortices beneath their site. Being orientated with great care to match the diurnal movement of the earth (or the *apparent* movement of the

heavens above it), the great megaliths will contract in the
cold of the night and expand in the heat of the sun by day.
The resultant pressure puts stresses and strains on the quartz
inclusions which must be considerable.

A dowser can feel these radiations of detectable voltages
quite distinctly – even to the extent of being, in some cases,
somewhat melodramatically physically thrown to one side.
I have certainly felt vibration and tingling surface activity
on many of these great stones, and it seemed to vary with the
time of day and season of the year. Clearly no great mental
effort is required to imagine the possibility that in one of
their original purposes these structures were telekinetic
amplifiers.

Certainly they continue to affect the minds of men, in the
case of Stonehenge alone some four thousand or more years
after its contruction in its simplistic form, or some three
thousand since the trilithons were incorporated into its
structure.

Any society that could achieve such extraordinary
projects must have had a complex concept of the forces of
nature. From my own experience with the natural societies
of the Rain Forest and from long discussions with friends
who have lived in the Selvas of Peru I have learned that
extra-sensory perception and other paranormal abilities are
much more developed in these people than in our own
blunted awareness. Sacsahuaman, Machu Picchu and
other remarkable constructions that I have been able to
study convince me that the people who built them and
conceived their full purpose were possessed of very
advanced ability in constructional engineering and stone-
masonry. Lacking our materialistic technology, they
achieved amazing results by utilizing the full abilities of the
human mind.

A great deal of evidence of an advanced knowledge of the
paranormal extensions of man's everyday physical and
mental abilities is there to see – usually only a bus or train
ride away – in Great Britain. Go and touch, examine and

ponder on the achievements that we so glibly accept without
question. Great earth structures like Maiden Castle were
unlikely to have been built solely as fortifications, requir-
ing, I believe, by the latest estimate, close on half-a-million
defenders to hold it effectively with the weapons then
available, i.e. stones, slings, spears and short-range bows.

Read Professor Alexander Thom's splendid expanded
theses such as *Megalithic Lunar Observatories*, and think
about what other theories might be enunciated if the
Establishment was less inflexible.

The only worthwhile radicalism is in thought, with the
light of reason as its constant counterpoint. Revolution of
thinking – the only true and natural revolution – dictates
that we should think deeply about these matters, or
suffer intellectual stagnation and sterility in the mass of
technology which we have spawned.

Clever men – 'magicians' if you like – with knotted cords
and shadow wands, surveyed and laid out these structures
with immense ingenuity and care. Surely we can spare some
of our endlessly self-centred leisure time trying to find the
reasons for their actions.

One thing is certain: political motives (which some
demagogue recently stated were the only bases for thought)
had nothing whatsoever to do with it. Survival motives, yes!
The search for gnosis, yes! The achievement of self-
discipline, yes! The satisfaction of a remarkable accom-
plishment by group effort, yes! Politics, no!

Huge earth zodiacs were also laid out, such as the one at
Glastonbury, postulated by a Mrs Maltwood and set out in a
book called *Glastonbury's Temple of the Stars*. This
splendidly imaginative lady worked from aerial photographs, and the results are quite fascinating. Another
zodiac is being delineated at Kingston-upon-Thames; and
there are others apparently in Yorkshire, Lincolnshire and
Northumberland, as well as, of course, the famous markings
on the Plain of Nasca in Peru.

The outcry against vandals equipped with metal and

mineral detectors roaming the ancient sacred sites, has a valid basis for protest. These places are the sole remaining parts of this island's ethos. They are the true heritage of the people, and the archaeologists have only themselves to blame that they have kept their mystique too closely to themselves. Had they shared their art and encouraged its popularity at their digs instead of discouraging unskilled assistance, the sites would now be much more respected and more carefully nurtured than they are.

At least members of the Old Straight Track Club, ridiculed as they were, attempted to uncover and preserve the mark stones and clear the ancient pathways that criss-cross our land. 'Too much jaw and far too little fieldwork' was the valid complaint of such giants as the late much-missed Sir Mortimer Wheeler. I would like to see a proper co-operation, with mutual respect on both sides, between archaeologists and trained dowsers.

One summer, not so long ago, my family and I dowsed some intriguing patterns, in the Vicar's Close at Wells Cathedral, where we outlined a number of regular shapes and forms in what appeared to be a rectangular enclosure below the surface. The next year I came back to find it excavated – a *complete* and *hitherto unknown chapel* having been uncovered some six feet below the green lawn.

As our ancestors laid out the great earthworks and earth zodiacs without the benefit of modern surveyors' instruments or aerial photographic survey techniques, they must have been mainly guided by their foci. Dowsing was undoubtedly one of the portals through which their Overminds manifested.

The knowledge of foci or gnosis springs just as much from the intuitive survival-mechanism of man as from the acquired store of knowledge accumulated by the rational mind.

Part of this gnosis is the 'Canon', which appears and disappears throughout history as different gnostic groups rediscover it and are then suppressed by more materialist Establishments. The canon itself can take many forms, but in essence it is a statement of natural truths which can be utilized for the 'Great Work', as the alchemists would call it.

The gnostics can be anyone, from a valid witch doctor working his magic, through knowledge of mind-manipulation and telekinesis acquired by oral tradition, to the operators of global media based in Madison Avenue – or, for that matter, in Moscow.

Let us look at some of these gnostic groups in a little more detail. Taking as the cradle of civilization a combination of the Middle-East and China, via Chaldea and the silk route, we can detect an unbroken line of gnostic heritage that runs throughout history. Surfacing and diving below the ocean of man's development like a nuclear submarine, the gnostic entity sometimes lies submerged for long periods. Only the monuments and structures which are its physical manifestations remain visible – sometimes indecipherable for hundreds of years till some researcher starts to unlock their secrets. It is fascinating to think that, after all these centuries, we still do not know the why and the wherefore of either the Sphinx or the Pyramids. One thing is clear, though, that they still, after thousands of years, affect the minds of men. Is it too bold a supposition then, to state that *this* was their prime purpose? I don't think that statement is too wild for rational conjecture – mainly because it is so marvellously simple!

'My name is Ozymandias, king of kings: Look on my works, ye Mighty, and despair!' Shelley, who wrote that lovely rolling poem of man's arrogant folly, must have had a great awareness of the gnosis.

What fascinates me about the emergence and re-emergence of gnostic groups throughout history, is that there is worldwide evidence of the same thing happening, from China to Peru. Quite suddenly, historically speaking, a small group of inspired people – led by scholarly philosophers and practical engineers – discover or re-discover the

canon and put it to work – or the Great Work, if you like.
Sometimes, as in the case of the Essenes, these groups build
a long-lasting monument in the minds of posterity rather
than leaving their canon frozen into stone. Of the Essenic
Brethren's gnosis we have directly only fragments of the
Dead Sea Scrolls, but *Christianity* became their eventual
monument. They were magicians, gnostics, mind-manipu-
lators, media men, whatever you like to call them; but,
through the medium of John the Baptist, Jesus of Nazareth
and the disciples, they left a heritage which has lasted
nearly two thousand years.

The Jewish entity, scattered through many lands and
hideously persecuted many times, still retains its marvellous individuality though pressured and threatened by
some 250 million other people, surrounding the tiny heart of
its form of the gnosis – encapsulated in Israel.

The Cathars, the worshippers of the 'Abraxas' (which is
only another symbolic form of the gnosis) held the canon as
its guardians till they were wiped out, at Montségur in the
foothills of the Pyrenees, by Simon de Montfort.

The Albigenses, Waldenses and other gnostic group
entities were equally ravaged and pillaged – by the
Establishment: just as Hitler and the SS purged their
dreadful society of the dangerous heresies of the Jews and
the gypsies. Ask yourself – why the gypsies? The tragic
Jewish persecution could possibly have been brought about
by the need for the Nazis to centre their driving force – pure
unadulterated *hatred* – into a focus and to benefit
financially thereby through dispossessing a wealthy
segment of the German and European Jewish communities.
But why wipe out the gypsies unless the reason was a
mystical one, i.e. one magical system perverted to the
darkness clearing its territory of all other rival magical
systems?

It makes hideous sense, when you think about it – and if
you had seen what I saw, and experienced what I
experienced, you would have no doubt about the horrendous

purpose behind National Socialism.

The Templars, who were magi, inheriting their knowledge from a far older source – the Manichaean heresy – started with a tiny group of gnostics in the early twelfth century and rose to become the single most influential and wealthiest power in Europe, until they were wiped out by the treachery of Philip the Fair in the early part of the fourteenth century.

During my recent researches in Spain and France, I have visited many Templar sites – from abbeys to *commanderies, manoirs, granges* and *fermes*, all of which they set up and controlled along the routes of the pilgrims. I dowsed the ones that I was studying and, in every case, came up with the same interesting results. The patterns of the fields of force that all their sites seem to generate exactly bore out the results that the dowsers with whom I had worked had found in Britain.

What appears to be the truth of the matter is that one finds the same patterns and energy flows, in greater or lesser strengths, wherever the gnostic entity has taken root. Be the sites Chinese, Egyptian, Chaldean, Greek, Roman, Minoan, Cathari, Templar or, for that matter, Peruvian, Mexican or Hopi Indian, the dowsable patterns are identical.

If you accept dowsing, which I was forced to do, intellectually, after having researched it for some five years, backed by my own parallel experiences over the previous forty years, you find yourself looking at a historical pattern that is re-surfacing in our present era.

The Templars and their successors, the Freemasons, who re-emerged with their 'lodges' at the beginning of the eighteenth century, appear to have derived their knowledge and formulated their canon in line with the first magi whose minds opened to the truth in nature.

The Gothic era of church and cathedral architecture apparently sprang into being spontaneously, *after* the Templars returned from their studies in the Holy Land. The style has no connection with the Goths so where did the name come from?

Scholars with whom I have discussed this intriguing question have various explanations, but one interesting suggestion has continually been made: that 'Gothic' is a distortion (possibly deliberate) of the word 'Goetic', which means, simply, 'magical' (the study of the Goetia).

This would explain why the Templars, outwardly Christian, were in reality practitioners of the gnostic canon and dogma which originated long before the birth of Jesus of Nazareth. Their symbol was the cross, but then the Tau cross, and the Ankh, are far older than Christianity and trace their origin to the dawn of knowledge with Egyptian, Chaldean and Chinese connections. Their focus of worship was, outwardly, the Blessed Virgin – but actually 'Our Lady' in various forms – including Our Lady of Africa, the Black Virgin or, if you prefer another sacred name, Isis.

The symbol of an old man of wisdom – the head of a man with a beard – was regarded by the Templars as their prime logo, whereas the cross was their 'brand name'. They were, reputedly, worshippers of Baphomet, a nightmare creature in the minds of their persecutors, but actually an embodiment of the light. (Lucifer is, of course, another name for the Light bearer.)

That doesn't mean that they worshipped the Devil (Satan), far from it.

To find out more about the Templars read Louis Charpentier's splendid *Mystery of Chartres Cathedral* and *The Mysteries of the Templars*, published in French by Librairie Robert Laffont or, if you prefer, the first is translated into English, and the other, I understand, will shortly be translated into English as well.

I was shown the Templar sites in England by Colin and his colleagues, and then did my own examination of the European sites *before* reading Charpentier's books. (If possible, please do the same.) For me the books bore out the odd results that we had found ourselves.

The tomb of Philip the Fair (what a misnomer!) is located

in Granada cathedral, where he is interred, with his wife, Jeanne the Mad, and his in-laws, Ferdinand and Isabella, for whom El Cid conquered the Moors.

A visit to Granada and the beautiful Alhambra will satisfy anyone who is in the least bit sensitive to the depth and range of the gnostic knowledge of the Moors and Sephardic Jews. For over 700 years, Spain, under the Moors, who lived in amity with the Jews, practised mathematics, algebra, astronomy, architecture, music, medicine, surgery, chemistry and metallurgy, and a marvellous application of the gnosis – until the new Establishment, under Ferdinand and Isabella, nearly wiped them out and plunged Spain back into the darkness of the Middle Ages.

Philip the Fair treacherously destroyed the Templar entity and pillaged their swollen coffers, and once again the gnostics plunged below the surface of history – leaving behind the great monuments of the Gothic era, the soaring vaulted machines for the worship of God, portals through which to reach the universal Overmind.

Go to these monuments – whether you are Christian, Jewish, Buddhist, Muslim, Hindu, or agnostic – and you will find that, even filled with chairs and loud-speakers, these gigantic stone machines can still manipulate the minds of men.

My wife's family used to live in a lovely old manor house in Dorset, near Sherborne; and I have, from time to time, enjoyed its extraordinary ambience. It passed out of their hands, and was sold to some close friends, and then, later, was sold again to a family who lived in it for only a short time before they had some financial problems and, in turn, sold it to the present owners.

This manor lies within a few miles of Templecombe, a Templar stronghold, where a painting of that era shows a bearded head which is reputed to be the symbol of worship of Baphomet. The house itself I have always found to be 'lively', as far as its atmosphere is concerned, but never hostile in any way; however, the last owners-but-one, somewhat surprisingly, had it exorcized, or so the story goes.

I can't think why, because my family have always enjoyed its ambience and, apart from a somewhat disturbed area near the old secret priest-hole (where Royalists hid Roman Catholic priests from the persecutions of the Roundheads), the general feeling of attached memory patterns and shadow personalities was one of welcome and warmth. One could describe the passage on the upper floor, at night, as 'busy' but never malevolent or malignant.

The reason I mention this lovely building is that it was believed to be a Templar stronghold itself, and the presence of a moat and *étangs* (ponds) and the fact that it is on the site of a holy well and has strong springs underneath as well as a lengthy secret underground passage running some distance from the cellars, bears out its reputation as a Templar site. A dowsing carried out by a number of us quite recently also confirms, for us at least, that it has a great force and seems to generate a strong field of energy typical of Templar-held territory.

The whole point of this short résumé of gnostic and Templar activity is really to show you that throughout history, from the dawn of magic to the present day, the gnosis is alive and well and still very much with us as a stimulus to the searching mind. Freemasonry and the Illuminati in various forms, and their rites, have their basis in the gnosis; and the Temple of Solomon was only one step in that great flow of knowledge and contact with the universal Overmind.

Having been instructed, during the war, in the basic principles of Freemasonry, in order that I might better understand their invaluable service to the Resistance organizations throughout occupied Europe, I have a clear picture of this particular facet of the gnosis.

I have no doubt whatsoever, after forty-five years' involvement with paranormal research, that the gnosis is a valid fountainhead of wisdom. I have also no doubt in my mind that this knowledge is neutral and can just as easily be applied to destruction as to construction, to evil as well as to good.

I have attended many sales conferences as a front-man and presenter and have listened to the preliminary 'bull' sessions of a large number of massive industrial groups. Again and again I have heard high-powered executives propounding the psychological factors involved in marketing on a nationwide and even global scale. The psychology of overcoming sales resistance is always the name of the game.

Billions of dollars and pounds, and many other currencies, are invested in these 'war games' fought for the control of the minds of men and women; and the gigantic economic results fully justify the whole exercise, from their pragmatic point of view.

The system works; the 'logos' are all important; the 'pack shot' of the merchandise is given its ritual exposure on the TV commercials while the jingle invocations are blasted out as back-up on the audio side. Audio-visual presentation is simply applied *magical ritual*; and the degree of its effectiveness is in direct ratio to the amount of exposure that the public receive.

The magicians, the gnostics, the great totalitarian powers, or the vast commercial structures of industrialized capitalism, all employ the same basic élitist methods to capture and to manipulate the minds of the masses. As this world of ours plunges headlong towards the abyss and the final catharsis of the human race, it is only by seeing what is happening to each of us, and learning to control our exposure to these forces, by opening our own minds to the universal Overmind, that we can, by self-discipline and a combination of our survival mechanism and rationale, escape the ultimate holocaust.

16   *The Reckoning*

My involvement with paranormal phenomena has convinced me that the whole experience is simply an extension of our *natural* awareness and mental abilities. The phrase 'life after death' presupposes a following event, when it seems to me to be a parallel existence which is continual. The before, after and during is purely relative to the observer.

We mustn't forget that *we* invented time as we conceive it. We made the clocks and watches, the calendars and chronometers, and since then have tried to adjust them continually to keep them relative to the stream of true time.

This is, of course, space/time – a totally interdependent state of existence by which no event can occur in space without occupying time during which to occur, *nor* in time without occupying space. It is we who have departed from the natural appreciation of space/time that we experience in dreams or in a trance, and who have confused ourselves with our own artificial expertise.

It appears to me that we have three coexistent entities – the physical electro-chemical machine of the body; an intermediate astral body that serves as a linking medium; and the Overmind, a complex, many-faceted entity that incorporates all the effects of the lesser entities. This Overmind seems to combine the personality, the id, the ipse, the ego, the spirit, the mind entity, the unconscious, subconscious and supraconscious – and whatever other neatly-labelled compartment of mental experience you like to give it – into one individual set of experiences, i.e. you and me. Through the open experience of the Overmind we have total contact with the *collective* unconscious, the astral light, Akashic record, Samadhi state, etc., i.e. *us* – *all* of us (the universal Overmind).

The death-change separates the electro-chemical machine of the body – which has been either worn out or destroyed by accident or disease – from the astral or linking medium, but leaves it still attached to the Overmind or individual entity, which, in turn also, eventually separates from the astral body – rather like a three-stage rocket carrying a space-probe to the stars.

The booster – the massive, powerful take-off package of sheer brute force – is represented by the body; the second-stage booster is the intermediate power-package that pushes the command capsule into outer space, and the command module, which is the final space-ship, separates from it – leaving the second-stage booster to orbit the earth while the take-off package falls back into the sea below. The command capsule, with all the complex instrumentation, then sets course for the stars.

The main levels of communication between individuals also seem to be threefold. The purely animistic physical state, in which like is repelled by like and opposites attract, appears to be the first of these, and is subject to the laws of the physical universe.

The second or astral parallel state is that in which awareness is intuitive and is still mentally very much on the survival level – exactly like that of our early ancestors and still fully operative among the natural peoples of the earth, i.e. the Bushmen, Rain-Forest Indians, Aborigines and nomadic tribal societies and also among shepherds, deep-sea fishermen, mountain guides, hermits and other persons living close to nature. This state of mind-existence is what the Aborigines call the real life – as opposed to the dream life of our conscious experiences.

Lastly, there is the Overmind, the sum-total of awareness through experience and heredity, which survives the death change and exists in a parallel continuity to the universe of which we are a part.

The only academic point involved seems to be that, as we know energy cannot be destroyed but can only be changed in its form, does the individual Overmind continue as a separate entity or does it return to become part of the *universal* Overmind from which it must have originally come? It would seem to be a logical progression that, through the personal experiences and building-up of the will and knowledge of the Overmind in its individual forms, it eventually becomes the distilled essence of the other complex entities with which it coexists (i.e. all physical experiences and astral experiences impress their effects on the individual controlling Overmind in each case).

When this then discards in sequence the other two entities, they return to become component parts of the general fields of physical and astral forces which comprise the biosphere of earth. Logically, the Overmind will also eventually return to its original field of generative energy – the universal Overmind or, to use a conventionally acceptable term, God.

This is the concept of alchemy in its physical and mental sense, its spiritual sense if you prefer that word.

What the ultimate (if one can use such a finite term for a concept of infinity) purpose of this cycle of events may be is far beyond our incarnate state of mind to conceive – because it must, of necessity, be a totally discarnate experience in its final form (if there is a *final* form). In any case, it is so far beyond our thinking capacity to pin down the parameters of its existence as to be virtually unknowable at this stage in our individual or collective evolution.

The artist, the sensitive, the wholly natural man, those who have been the least affected by gross materialism and by all the mind-fetters of greed, fear, envy and lust for power, will inevitably have a wider and more effective contact with that universal Overmind.

It is equally obvious to me that, even with careful preparation and precaution, exposure to contact with the universal Overmind can only be *safely* experienced (while incarnate) for relatively short periods of time – because over-exposure causes excessive overloads on the astral and physical bodies and subsequent damage to both is inevitable. This explains to me the number of people whom I have known whose minds have 'blown' through having tried to do too much too soon. To me they have suffered the simple equivalent, on the astral plane, to a physical stroke on the earth plane.

I have talked to a number of people who have suffered such damage to their astral, with a parallel destruction of the physical brain circuit, from such over-exposures – often aggravated by the use of hallucinatory drugs and powerful alkaloids or even by simple over-exposure to intensely powerful fields of bio-energy which they have contacted during ritual magical practices ineptly and imperfectly carried out.

In each case I was aware of the presence of their Overminds – helplessly and terrifyingly trapped inside the web of the damaged complex of their physical and astral bodies. Each of them, also, gave me the strongest impression of an intense longing for release from that bondage.

I have also been present when someone was being kept alive only by artificial life support of their respiratory, renal and cardio-vascular systems. There the impression was of both the astral and the Overmind being locked into the bio-electrical and mechanical complex. It conjured up a vivid and dreadful image of Prometheus chained to the rock.

In my short experiences of the natural people of the Rain Forest I have been very impressed by their total acceptance of their coexistent entities. Obviously, in attempting to communicate such concepts, language, especially the lingua franca of the Selvas (Aymara) is so basic as to make translation very difficult. However, by signs, drawings and long discussions with colleagues, who have lived among the Indians for years, I have gathered quite a bit of information along these lines.

Firstly, it seems that life and death are as natural to them as breathing is to us. In certain tightly-knit communities, where there are, at most, 250 members of a group, each individual is completely a part of the *whole* tribal entity.

This is so much so that, at the moment of death of another member of the tribe, or at the instant of birth of a new life within the community, the experience is shared by *all* the tribe irrespective of distance or time.

The members of the community contain their hunting and fishing within distances of a few miles at most, so that they are all comparatively near to their base. But, in the Rain Forest, two hundred metres can be a very long way, so apparently distance is no barrier.

I myself have been fortunate enough to have been helped to develop some part of the awareness of my Overmind and to acquire a limited ability to make contact with the universal Overmind of collective unconscious by allowing my subjective clairvoyance (or vivid visual imagination) to release itself at will.

This I can, with practice, now bring into operation even in the crowded concourse of a railway station or air terminal. It has enabled me to work as a creative writer, and I am very grateful that I can gain a substantial living for my family by using this technique without consciously hurting anyone.

I really have little or no ambition, but I do try to be as professional as possible, even if I appear to be unconventional about it. I have no 'gag' files of other people's work; *all* the material I write and draw comes to me in the form of intensely vivid imagery. This is why, quite frequently, I have cut across an event that was *forthcoming*, for I have found it to be true – sometimes quite horribly – that coming events *do* cast their shadows before them.

In an appalling way I saw the coming death probability of my own son – just as I had during the war, with young air crew in the mess before an operation.

I had a similar odd experience when the children's programme that I had made over a year before about a battle in an embassy coincided, almost exactly, with the terrorist takeover of the Iranian embassy. It was scheduled to go out at 4.15 p.m. on the same day. I also, quite clearly, saw a facsimile of the American attempt to invade the Teheran US embassy – and was so impressed by the feeling of impending disaster that I wrote to an understanding friend in the House of Commons, whose mother had been a psychic, telling him about it. The letter arrived on his desk on the morning after the attempt had failed so disastrously. I still have his letter commenting on the remarkable coincidence. My letter had taken four or five days to reach him from Spain where I was staying.

What are the mathematical chances of that happening, I wonder. The letter described the main factors in the action and had been written about five days before it occurred; and, although it was not absolutely identical in detail, it delineated the combined ground and air attack and the employment of helicopters and C-130 Hercules transport aircraft landing some forty-five miles away in the desert. I said it would be a disaster!

This sort of thing has happened so often that a number of my old colleagues who have worked with me on TV and radio have remarked on the fact. I am not being immodest, because I do not believe that this situation is unusual – rather I believe that we *all* have the ability latent in us. The only credit that I allow myself is of having worked very hard, over a long period of time, to keep that ability alive and well and fully operational. It has certainly enriched my entire life, and I hope the lives of others in a small way; and I believe that the awakening of that particular 'sleeping dragon' is an important part of the destiny of man.

This faculty, or set of faculties, seems to be inherent in all of us, irrespective of race, colour, creed or religion; and if the credo and dogma of a person's religious convictions are open enough to allow and guide the *safe* development of these abilities without fear, suppression or damnation, I truly believe that each individual can, by his own and his helpers' efforts, enter the Aquarian age with greater understanding.

I firmly believe that at the opposite pole of our natural development lies the black hole of total dialectical material-ism, which confines, diminishes and, eventually, negates the individual Overmind and completely halts its natural progression. That path leads to destruction and chaos, as must be self-evident in the present appalling world situation.

Any religion or disciplined code of ethics based on the negation of self-gratification on the lowest material plane, and aiming at the distillation of the essence of the Overmind of the individual, must lead to cosmos, which is the true natural order of things. By those years of experience I am led to believe that guidance is a constant reality, but that it shows itself only when it becomes necessary in our lives - that is to say, when we have done everything that we can to bring about a progressive result.

Through gross materialism we seem to cut ourselves off from such aid, by blind worship of the pseudo-images of the man-gods. This is simply illustrated in the fanatical adoration of Lenin, Marx and Adolf Hitler - or, for that matter, Elvis Presley and the Beatles. In all these cases an almost religious hysteria is evident. The election of an American President is a case in point. By the time the struggle for possession of the media has been won, each of the candidates has achieved a near god-like status in the eyes of the most fanatical of their supporters. That is pure magical ritual.

Film super-stars, football heroes, some Trade Union leaders, even the Capo da Capo of the Mafia - given the full treatment, often achieve such a deification in the material world of their worshippers. So we become vulnerable to the ever-present destructive forces which would, joyfully, bring about chaos.

It is then that we lose our awareness of continuity, purpose and heredity - by fouling up the environment and halting the natural chain of events in the name of Power. If self-gratification is the sole end and purpose of man's life on earth, why bother about posterity at all? There would be no point in the continuity of the race-entity other than as an accidental result of indiscriminate sexual relations. Instead, we would substitute self-love for the love of family and children, lust for the love of a close companion, greed for need, hatred and envy for awareness and love of the universal consciousness. Power - raw personal power - would become the sole individual goal with the end of compassion (which would then be considered an expression of weakness) and the inevitable descent into the maelstrom of darkness, chaos and destruction. Fear and terror would become the instruments of temporal power, and tyranny the sole aim of man in his struggle to get to the top, by any means, and to stay there by any means (e.g. the Faustian Pact).

Such a choice, between opening up, with disciplined care, to the awareness of the universal Overmind, or embracing a totalitarian materialism, has always faced man - individually or *en masse*. Therefore, if the concept of the state becomes more important than the 'state' of the individual, it becomes monstrous and unnatural, and can only be sustained and maintained by force.

True freedom of the individual is *not* permissiveness without applied reason. Indeed, there seems to be no short or easy road to the opening and development of the individual Overmind - only a long and arduous way that requires great concentration, humility and compassion, as well as a genuine love of humanity, to complete the journey safely.

Tarot, I-Ching, pendulum dowsing, cheiromancy, numerology, gematria, Kabbalism, crystal gazing, mirror skrying, clairaudience, clairvoyance, psychometry, and all the many and various methods of contacting the field of universal consciousness (the Akashic record, or whatever label you wish) are all foci, paths, portals, etc., and should be treated as such with cautious respect. The motive for contact is the single most important guiding factor, which will determine whether the results are to be constructive or destructive, positive or negative, for the Light or for the Darkness. The whole of my life has been so far, and is still, a constant battleground on which these forces fight to gain the upper hand; and the first lesson that I have had to learn was to differentiate between the two.

By mental disciplines learnt over a long period, I can project my consciously controlled psyche (Overmind) through space/time - or imagine that I can - and bring back images from the past, present or future, irrespective of time or space, to use in my work.

I have witnessed, taken part in, and even induced, phenomena of different kinds which would be described as paranormal, in many seances, sittings, circles and experimental sessions and tests; and after so many such experiences I am convinced that the results were, in many cases, absolutely genuine and totally valid.

I am certain that there is now a growing awareness of the Overmind, certainly among the young, and that in the present state of parapsychological research we are now at the same crossroads that faced physics in 1939. That almost uncontrolled quantum leap of the 1940s across the unknown frontier of nuclear physics, nearly proved the undoing of man and could still lead to his destruction by his own unbridled ingenuity.

All the pressures that have been brought to bear on the individual have tended to inhibit his or her continued freedom of thought – in the face of the fear of nonconformity. My only advice to the young is, accept nothing until you have filtered the statements through *both* your instinct and your reason. Ask yourself: 'Does it feel right? Does it seem right? and Why?' Blind faith may be deemed a great virtue – but faith based on experience and careful selective thinking, coupled with intuitive reasoning, will endure in the face of the most extreme hardships. Such is my experience.

Above all I have learnt: '*Never* lose your sense of humour – for this will enable you to see some kind of perspective in this world of illusion.' To me that simple lifeline is my strongest hold on rational sanity.

Don't accept my word for it! Test it all with your own intuition, experience and rationale.

This is as honest a book as I can write, while relying on a fifty-eight-year-old memory of the events in which I have been involved.

Without those experiences and the help and guidance that I have received during my lifetime, I could never have opened my door marked summer.

Appendix I
Circuits, Diagrams, Rituals and Rhythms

During the 1930s my father built up a basic theory of the techniques probably involved in the manifestation of some of the paranormal phenomena that we witnessed.

The cumbersome physical method of table-turning bothered him and, as he didn't like the Ouija board, glass or planchette, he made some beautifully constructed communication devices of various kinds with the idea of combining telekinesis with direct communication. In other words, he wanted to eliminate as much of the subconscious as possible from the physical means of communication such as table-turning by removing the hand contact from the communicating device itself.

To this end he devised three pieces of physical apparatus, the first an ultra-sensitive adaptation of a Morse key, the second a delicately balanced seesaw to tap out a code and the third a complex and sensitive electrically-operated system of letters and numbers, which lit up when small wooden keys were depressed even slightly, i.e. telekinetically.

The object of each piece of apparatus was that actual physical contact with the apparatus was eliminated and only the table on which they were placed was touched by the hands of the sitters. We used a square table as the base for the devices and solemnly sat round them with much the same ritual that we used for the table. Nothing happened for six weeks. At the end of that time my mother suggested that we dispense with the square table and place the apparatus on the round one we normally used for sittings.

We exchanged the tables, repeated a short prayer and placed our hands on it. Immediately the *whole* table, apparatus and all, rose silently into the air.

Pop said: 'I think they are trying to tell us something.'

We returned to the tried and true method of table-turning - and the apparatus which Pop had so painstakingly produced went up into the attic.

It was as if 'anyone' or 'anything' could have operated Pop's apparatus and the clear message was: 'It's better our way.' So we stuck to it.

The content of the messages received through the table sittings was quite fascinating in its predictive accuracy and, though a lot of it was purely personal, we did get good evidential information for people outside the circle.

Here are some of the points of interest I have noticed during table sittings.

I have used an inorganic table (a stone one) for the same purpose and found it to be nowhere near as responsive as an organic wooden one. This may have been due to the weight involved and the subsequent increase in power required to move it and control it.

The presence of a high degree of electrostatic energy, such as is normally found on a hot dry summer night or during a cold dry winter or autumn evening, appears to increase the power available for paranormal phenomena such as table tilting. The cold vortex of energy that we all felt circling our ankles and rising to the bottom of the table seemed to be generated much more quickly when electrostatic was present.

How did we know that an abnormally strong electrostatic field was present? Simple! Both my mother and I had the same dry curly hair, and this instantly responded to electrostatic energy by standing on end, or becoming, at the least, hard to manage.

This affinity with electrostatic fields or electromagnetic fields becomes more apparent when you examine the processes of different forms of paranormal phenomena. As the power appears to be generated by the sitters and actually drawn from them and then manipulated, either consciously by them or some other intelligence, its nature must be electro-chemical in origin.

The affinity with electrostatic energies fascinated my father, for the transmutation of electrostatic into kinetic energy (energy capable of telekinetic operation) seemed to be through the medium present at the sitting. Pop, being a fully qualified electrical and mechanical engineer, had a clear picture of these forces in normal operation, and their paranormal manifestations and interplay became his main study in this research.

The relationship between mediumship and electrostatic fields seemed to him to be a link which had been recognized throughout the recorded history of man. The Biblical prophets went up into the mountains or out into the deserts to commune with their God; and these environments are just where electrostatic fields are manifested. The hot, dry air of the deserts and the cold dry atmosphere of the mountains seem to be the ideal environment for the prophet, the hermit, the wise men and the magi.

My father's reasoning went something like this. Man stands between heaven and earth, say the legends, myths and various bibles throughout recorded life. Furthermore, he stands bathed in a field of free electrons and ions, both positive and negative. This is the field of the ionospheric vault which lies between the earth's surface and the bottom layer of the ionosphere, fifty to eighty kilometres above our heads.

This thick layer, or rather layers, of ionized particles surrounds the earth, and the electrical potential within this vault, i.e. between its bottom layer and the earth's surface, increases in voltage at the rate of 200 volts every two feet or so in height: so that a man six feet tall at sea level is already being subjected to 600 volts at head height. As you go higher, the voltage is considerably increased, and the effect on the human entity is presumably more pronounced.

It appeared to my father that high-frequency currents are produced during mental mediumship such as clairvoyance and psychometry, and that, conversely, low frequency currents are present during mediumship of a physical nature. He explained to me that the source of these frequencies is the medium, and that the conductor is the ectoplasm exuded by the medium, which is of a coarse visible type if the medium is manifesting paranormal phenomena of a physical nature, and a fine, misty or invisible type (except to the infra-red camera or another medium) if the medium is practising non-physical, mental mediumship.

The increased power and efficiency of these phenomena in the presence of a significant increase in the electrostatic field, and the smell of ozone generated, implied to my father that the phenomenon was induced in the case of each medium, by the electro-chemical nature of their bodies. Therefore, the type of phenomenon manifested depended on the basic field force (i.e. an electrical field either electro-magnetic, electrostatic or a combination of both) in the electro-chemical make-up of the medium and the type of conductor, i.e. the ectoplasm, generated.

So far, so good – at least in theory – but now Pop attempted to devise instruments to measure these frequencies. He designed a number of highly sensitive meters and tunable oscillators to match the probable frequencies involved, but the cost of building the more sophisticated ones was beyond his resources. However, he reconstructed or adapted instruments which were currently available on the market, for Pop was a skilled amateur radio engineer and had spent a number of years designing and building powerful receiving sets.

The super-heterodyne valve had only just become commercially available; so our sets, though powerful, were fairly unsophisticated and quite massive in construction. I well remember my father co-opting my wondering assistance as he wound coils with a neat machine that he had devised for the purpose.

Most of the time the acrid smell of Baker's fluid and fluxite
hung over the garage/workshop and, occasionally, when
my mother was playing bridge and golf was off because of
lashing rain, around the kitchen table, where the heavy
ebonite chassis of some new receiver was being soldered up.
The tin of 'gunge' which Pop used bore the words:

> We're fluxite and solder
> the reliable pair
> famous for soldering,
> sold everywhere.

So my father turned his talent for building radio sets into
building instruments which he hoped would detect the
frequencies of the waves of energy generated by mediums of
various kinds.

Once again his work seemed to be in alignment with that
of Nicola Tesla, who had at one time experimented extensively with both high and low frequencies. In fact, I remember
Pop using both primary and secondary coils and large
oscillators of various types. Tesla also believed, and went on
record as saying, that man was affected, to a very great
extent, by the changes of electrical potential and by extremely low frequencies of the general order of 7.5 Hertz generated within the ionospheric field. He was also credited with
the discovery that the earth is a 'giant condenser' (now
called a capacitor) that, with its varying potentials for
generating ES and EM forces itself, affects man and his
environment. His discovery of the stationary waves of the
earth has paved the way to renewed research into extremely
low frequencies, for communication and to bring about
action at a distance.

Tesla, like Father, believed that man was directly affected
by sunspot activity and solar emanations, and that these
phenomena brought about tension, mental imbalance and
emotional disturbance. Research into these areas is now

being conducted by various foundations, with significant results, and nowhere more intensely than in Soviet Russia. In Professor Eric Laithwaite's words to me: 'In these areas of research, such as the paranormal, the Russians are twenty years ahead of us.'

Certainly Professor Kirlian and his late wife Valentina are the equivalent of the Curies in this field. Their breakthrough, in Kirlian photography, by which it is apparently possible to photograph the bio-energy emanations from organic and inorganic matter, exactly match the much ridiculed results of von Reichenbach's experiments with sensitives in the last century, when he was castigated by the Establishment for having investigated his supposed field of odic or odyle force. Similar results were gained by the use of Kilner screens in the early part of this century. An invention of a Dr Kilner at a famous London hospital, these screens, made of glass and coated with a dye, proved an excellent aid to the viewing of auras.

So far no scientist seems to have been able to give a better explanation for the remarkable Kirlian results. The photographs are taken without a conventional camera, by placing a sensitized emulsion-covered film or plate in a light-tight 'sandwich' with the object (for example, a leaf) and then pulsing high-frequency discharges of electricity through the package. The results are astonishing and postulate the possible existence of a human aura as a manifestation of a bio-energy, i.e. an electro-chemically generated field.

Let me remind you that Tesla was himself clairvoyant, though he didn't say so in so many words (in fact, he wasn't at all happy about 'spiritist practices'). Nevertheless he admitted, in a number of lectures and in his notes, that as a boy he was much 'inconvenienced' by vivid images which concretely (objectively) manifested in front of his eyes, causing actual interference with his normal vision.

These images were not the scotomata type of vibrating pattern so dreaded by migraine sufferers which my mother and I knew only too well, but three-dimensional, coloured images of actual machines and events and sometimes even people.

These clear-cut and definitive 'visions' or 'vivid imagination of a totally concrete kind' if you prefer, were the secret of his amazing prophetic pronouncements regarding man's technological progress; and their uncanny accuracy was demonstrated in his prediction of television, high-frequency therapy, ozone generation, hydro-electric turbines and his successful harnessing of Niagara Falls. And for the record, though Establishment science seems reluctant to admit it, by 1888 he held the original US patents on the alternating current induction motor, the polyphase current induction motor, high-frequency coils and high-tension transformers.

By 1889, with the backing of Pierpont Morgan, he had patented and developed a method of transmitting power – without cables, and with no appreciable attenuation in the power of the current – a distance of some twenty miles, and had actually succeeded in lighting a number of lamps with the aid of a tuned receiver.

All this happened before the turn of the century. By 1913 he had patented a 'teleautomaton', a small electrically-driven submarine which he controlled by radio waves from a distance, the signal being received on a coil wound round the midget submarine's hull. As I pointed out, by refusing the Nobel Prize in 1912, Tesla committed professional suicide on a par with rejecting Hollywood's Oscar, and the Establishment nearly wiped him out.

Such scientific colleagues as had previously respected my father's early work in aviation and electrical engineering did much the same thing to Pop when he asked for their opinions on his work on the paranormal. In a rather more restricted way my father became like Tesla, a scientific leprosy patient.

Today, both the Russians and the Americans use immensely powerful low-frequency transmitters, presumably to communicate with their huge submarine fleets, because frequencies of this ELF type can penetrate the whole earth. Submarines at depth cannot receive normal radio transmissions without the release of sonar-type buoys to the surface or by surfacing themselves; either way, they immediately give away their position to searching airborne radar.

When the Russian ELF transmitters went on the air in late 1976, there was a flood of complaints from commercial and amateur radio interests who found their own transmission/reception wiped out. The Russian stations started operating at Riga, on the Baltic coast, then at Gomel, some hundreds of miles to the south. Semi-Palatinsk, beyond the Urals, then went on the air and subsequently stations at Novosibirsk and as far away as Yarkutsk started operating.

These immensely powerful ELF transmissions were of the order of power, peak to peak, of from 4 to 40 megawatts in signal strength – that means from 4,000,000 to 40,000,000 watts, built up to maximum output over periods of twelve hours.

The American naval transmitter at Wisconsin had, up till then, been operating at around $2\frac{1}{2}$ megawatts at full power, which gives some idea of the potential of the Russian transmitters. The fascinating side-effects of such transmissions, experienced by Tesla with his own pioneering work, range from the creation of standing waves in the atmosphere to possible weather pattern modification. Whether these areas of operational manipulation are in fact being used is a subject for informed conjecture.

Tesla's small portable oscillators could disintegrate a solid steel link from an anchor-chain in ten minutes. When he attached the larger one to the unclad steel structure of a New York building, he virtually had to stop the oscillator within twenty minutes or bring the whole thing down! If those oscillators were scaled up and their oscillations beamed, using a TMT (Tesla magnifying transmitter) as the carrier wave and modulating the signal, who knows what results might be achieved in the path of the tracked signals?

There is no doubt that Russia has an extensive research programme into the paranormal, from which we could, at one time, extract useful research information. Some of this information concerned the work of Dr Pavlita of Czechoslovakia and his self-styled psychotronic generators, bio-instruments in which he included the human mind into his circuitry to generate telekinetic force. Today, that information, and any other such research information and material connected with paranormal research behind the Iron Curtain, is totally restricted, and Professor Naumov, the scholarly Jewish academic who once headed one of the top research teams, has been in a prison camp.

Vladimir Bukovsky told me that Shcharansky, who was sent to prison for dissidence and on other charges, had been deeply interested in parapsychological research.

A Soviet researcher, Petukhov, was roughly handled by the KGB within the last couple of years for, apparently, passing state security secrets to Robert Toth of the *Los Angeles Times*. Toth claims, and he is a fine journalist and an honest, open-minded one as well, that Petukhov was merely giving him some information regarding advances in the field of paranormal research. One wonders what aspect of the paranormal is now considered to be of such vital interest to the defence of the Soviet Union?

I am led to the belief that there is a possible connection between ELF transmission and paranormal phenomena, in the light of my father's experiments and conclusions which, considerably simplified, he told me about in the late thirties.

My father's second line of inquiry, pursued diligently at this time, dealt with the effects of different levels of electrostatic force and their relationship to the phenomena manifested.

Using the techniques of ritual magic, he found that telekinesis (action at a distance) was possible by applied willpower summoned up by ritual conditioning.

Incantation, ritual dances, hyperventilation, increased metabolic rates, and the increased flow of adrenalin brought on by these practices, when stripped of all the mumbo jumbo resolved themselves into well-thought-out methods of summoning up the potential of will normally dormant in man.

These experiments were carried out in a scholarly manner and under careful control, and with the sole motive of research into their mechanistic techniques and not to acquire power or sensation for its own sake. The results were surprising and most effective. Once again the frequencies involved during these transmissions of willpower or, if you prefer it, of a directed electro-chemically generated signal of extremely low frequency but reasonably high amplitude, gave my father and the one or two interested and loyal colleagues who stayed the course an insight into the electrostatic fields – low and high frequencies – in mental transmissions producing various forms of paranormal phenomena.

The main barrier to the general acceptance of the part played by the ELF frequencies (from .05 Hertz – i.e., .05 cycles per second – to 100 Hertz is the accepted range of extremely low frequency) is that the human body would require an aerial of gigantic length to receive or transmit such signals.

Acoustically (by sound waves), it can be shown that these ELF frequencies affect the human mind and body drastically. Furthermore, when a flickering and powerful light (such as a discotheque stroboscopic lamp) is set to operate at frequencies within the ELF range, various dramatic changes in the mental patterns can be made, even to frequencies that cause epilepsy and *petit mal* in susceptible subjects.

Could it be that the neuronal system of the human body acts as the aerial? My father believed that this incredibly complex system of billions of nerve cells, with their interconnecting mass of axons and dendrites and, where they cross each other, the synapses, could well serve as a compact aerial and would more than fulfil the requirements of minimum length (which is around 40,000 km for ELF).

Why then cannot the whole human nervous system (to make it simple) be itself a gigantic aerial which can, and in fact does produce low frequencies in this extreme range, as my father concluded from his own experiments during some ten years of research? Conversely, cannot the human body antenna *receive* such frequencies as well?

The electro-encephalograph (EEG) is the machine developed to detect, locate and measure the patterns of the electric currents that pass through the brain.

These have been categorized roughly as:

> 0.5 Hz to 3.0 Hz (Delta waves)
> 4.0 Hz to 7.0 Hz (Theta waves)
> 8.0 Hz to 13.0 Hz (Alpha waves)
> 14.0 Hz to 30.0 Hz (Beta waves)

Theta, i.e. 4 Hz to 7 Hz or 4 to 7 cycles a second, is now believed to be the frequency connected with enhanced mental activity, and creative thinking is believed to occur in this general range. It is thought to be the spectrum of frequencies allied to mental imagery and artistic imagination.

Alpha, 8 Hz to 13 Hz, is believed to be a meditative state and induces a feeling of well-being and relaxed mental attitudes.

Beta, 14 Hz to 30 Hz, is the range of frequencies which is probably used for logic and rationalization (i.e. the analytical state of the brain).

The lower the range, the more 'depressive' and inactive the mind's environment, the higher the range, the more excited the mind becomes.

This machine (the EEC) was in its infant state during the thirties, and was still being developed at that time, yet my father seems to have been on the right lines with his theories of frequencies in different modes of mediumship.

To give an example or two of what this all seems to signify. Consider yourself part of the *Last Night of the Proms*, whether present at the Albert Hall or watching at home (though there is a further entrainment factor in TV, which I went into in Chapter 12). You listen to great music, brilliantly executed by fine musicians, and find yourself being carried away by the music, the atmosphere and the enthusiastic response of the young promenaders. You don't have to be an acoustic engineer or to utilize advanced laboratory equipment to find yourself agreeing with this concept of entrainment of the human mind by sound frequencies.

Why then are there still sceptics, their minds closed to the idea that the same effect might be achieved by radio or electro-magnetic waves?

The same principle of entrainment applies to Tibetan Lamas, chanting mantras such as 'Om Mani Padme Om' at a regular tempo, with the consequent resonating effect this has on the bones of the face and cranial vault. Once again, the brain is entrained into a meditative state, or a creative state, by varying the frequency of the incantation.

The same techniques are used by magicians performing rituals, which are all designed to entrain the mind into different frequencies. The war dances of the American Indians, the tribal dances of the African Zulus, the whirling gyrations of the Dervishes or the Maori Harkas, were all carefully developed over centuries to arouse the fighting spirit of the participants or induce a meditative or exalted state of mind. In these dances drumming and rhythmically shaken metal ornaments and jewellery contribute to the entrainment of the mind by the vital generation of acoustic frequencies.

'The beat is everything, man!' say the young. Having been, at one time, a professional drummer in a small jazz outfit, I totally agree with them. Rock and Roll and its insistent beat has an all too obvious effect, whether in concert in vast stadiums or on recordings blaring out at some terrific wattage and decibel reading. I am not 'knocking the Rock', I'm merely citing it as a prime example of frequency entrainment of the mind.

As contrast to the uplifting and highly enjoyable

experiences of a promenade concert, or to the sheer animalistic enjoyment and sexual stimulation of the hard rock pop scene, let us examine the demonstrable effects of manipulated political rallies such as those conducted by the Nazis at Nuremberg. Here mass mind manipulation produced appalling hatred and hysteria and resulted in dreadful suffering.

To listen to recordings of Hitler's speeches at Nuremberg Stadium in these terms is a revelation. They are diabolic in their evil. The negative generation of power, still lingering in the cadence of that ranting, grating voice crosses the barriers of language. The pulsing hatred which flows in a dark stream from that fountain of evil still has an effect across the years.

First there are the preparatory pulsations of the massed drummers, hypnotically beating out the military cadence that throbs, at low frequencies, into the mind. The stamping of thousands of jackbooted feet and the roaring choruses echoing the words '*Ein Volk - Ein Reich - Ein Führer!*' punctuates the ranting stream of invective railing against the Jews and the foetid flow of hatred against the world, amid hysterical screams of '*Sieg Heil! Sieg Heil! Sieg Heil!*' It is all pure nightmare, just as we listened to it in half-understood horror on the radio or in newsreels in the mid-1930s.

John Buchan (Lord Tweedsmuir) the author and scholar and at that time Governor of Canada, agreed that the Hitlerian Nazi regime was satanic and utilized the techniques of mass mind manipulation and perverted rituals to twist the ethos of Germany (the *Kultur* and *Volk* spirit) into a terrifying, evil force. This imaginative and practical Scotsman, whose books (*The Thirty Nine Steps* and the other 'Richard Hannay' novels being probably the best known) were immensely popular, had a deep understanding, as a scholar of magic and the whole concept of ethos and *Volkgeist* - the inherited spirit of the people; not the flag-waving jingoism but the actual inherited race memories – and he knew how it applied to these small islands.

Another painstaking researcher was Air Vice-Marshal Dowding (later Air Marshal Lord Dowding), a remarkable and highly intelligent scholar and, though he was the last person to admit it, the architect of the Battle of Britain to come. He became acquainted with Pop at various meetings, and they exchanged views on the progress of their researches. He was also convinced that the Nazis were using diabolic practices and, when I interviewed this highly respected and kindly philosopher many years after the war, he agreed, once again, that the Nazi hierarchy, had, knowingly, utilized these dark principles and indulged in black magic to gain their dreadful ends.

His treatment at the hands of the Establishment, after he had won the Battle of Britain with the RAF's slender resources in fine pilots and fine aeroplanes, plus the co-operation of everyone associated with Fighter Command, was shameful. Only at the very end of his life was full restitution made; he was at least buried as a Marshal of the Royal Air Force. My admiration and affection for that great man and his fine determined mind was shared by just about everyone who served under him – whether they agreed with his strategy and tactics or not. He, undoubtedly, knew the vital role played by the ethos of this island people and wasn't afraid to risk his professional reputation by saying so.

In their day so did Blake and Wordsworth, Stukeley and Inigo Jones, Wren, Hawksmoor, Vanbrugh and many other wise men and women, such as Queen Elizabeth I. She *knew* that her half-starved people could take on the might of Spain, which, at that time in history, so closely resembled Nazi Germany in its lust for world domination.

The Nazi message, which was supposed to be a ritual of light, 'Strength through Joy', was really directed at the lowest of human emotions, hatred, greed, lust for power and the basic hunting instinct of man.

Top initiates of the Nazi power structure were known

practitioners of ritual magic, for example Rudolf Hess (a disciple of Guido von List, Germany's Aleister Crowley) and General Karl Haushofer, Professor of Oriental Studies at the University of Munich, a member of the Japanese Green Dragon Society and a recognized authority on magical practices. Heinrich Himmler, the ineffectual little mob follower who, in the first *Putsch*, had his revolver taken from him as he cowered unresisting, became the single most feared man in Europe as Head of the 'Black Knights' (his description of the Gestapo). Joseph Goebbels, who had made a deep study of magical manipulation techniques, hypnosis and the ritual entrainment methods of cult groups and covens, understood above all of them the significance of the 'Logo', the twisted cross (swastika) which he turned from a symbol of light to the encapsulation of terror and evil.

All the wealth of evidence that, half understanding, I, and others who were skilled in their knowledge of German, could scarcely believe, all that written evidence of ritual: 'Devil's Diaries', 'Satan's Bibles', whatever you like to call the meticulous Teutonic records of incarnate evil that, in their panic, the SS and Gestapo only partially destroyed. Why was it never brought out at the Nuremberg trials? I will explain that later, and I have every confidence in the source of that explanation.

Meanwhile, let us examine the insane course of events that suddenly overtook the minds of the German people.

Why was a Bavarian/Austrian obsessed by pure Aryanism as the symbol of the 'hyperborean' German archetype? What earthly (I use the term advisedly) connection of natural interests could this semi-literate painter of water-colours, a badly wounded corporal who held an Iron Cross for bravery, have in common with Haushofer, the super-literate scholar and academic Professor cum General of pure Prussian descent?

Why should Rudolf Hess, a gallant officer of the First World War *Luftflotte*, Germany's chivalrous 'Knights of the Air', a well educated and scholarly student of ancient philosophies, join forces with Hitler and become his deputy?

The eccentric bon viveur and dilettante Goering, the meticulous scholarly perverted Alfred Rosenberg, the brilliant yet twisted Joseph Goebbels were all clever, well read, well informed men. What drew them to succour, mould, initiate and finally worship the manic-depressive, unbalanced mind of a half-starved visionary to whom no one had listened in the pre-war café society in Vienna?

None of this could have happened unless they were formed together in some unholy alliance, based on *unreason*; it was the mutual recognition of these chaotic forces, masquerading as the 'New Order', that drew them together irresistibly. Like attracts like.

The *Thule Gesellschaft* and *Germanen Orden* were the foci for their dreadful weapon of darkness. These pseudo-mystical/political societies, with their mating of ritual and political credo and dogma, cloaked in the Parsifal allegories, were the spawning ground of the Nazi evil.

Poets such as Dietrich Eckhardt, and scholar/politicos such as Otto von Sebottendorf (whose real name was Glauer; he was actually a Turk) and Lanz von Lebenfels, a Cistercian monk who had great knowledge of magical rituals and practices, were the originators and developers of the credo and dogma from which National Socialism grew into the full horrific entity of the Nazi party.

There was widespread use of the *Protocols of Zion*, a forgery purporting to unveil the 'World Jewish Plot' for the take-over of civilization by a cabal of Jewish financier/magicians so effectively used by the 'Okhrana', the Tsarist secret police, in the late nineteenth-century pogroms.

These dreadful persecutions were carried out by the Cossack regiments against the Ashkenazi Jewish people, who lived in the Baltic States, Poland and the western parts of Russia, and had been instrumental in depriving them of all their possessions and their countries.

So with the Nazis, *The Protocols of Zion* were resurrected and their wild unsubstantiated lies were, once more, promulgated to those only too eager to believe. 'The bigger the lie, the more people believe' was one of Joseph Goebbels' favourite maxims.

As we were warned by the messages coming through to us in the 1930s, the evil inside Germany perverted the truth, promulgated the dogma of hatred and oppression by force and spread wide the credo of *Ein Volk, Ein Reich, Ein Führer!* to the eager millions of believers. It was all applied ritual magic, according to the same principles of the creation of the god/king followed by the Egyptians, the Persians, the Chaldeans and the Greek Dionysian cults.

Frazer had said it all, in that monumental work *The Golden Bough*, copies of which were carefully and minutely studied in the hierarchy of Nazidom.

As I have already pointed out, the practice of ritual itself is no more evil or destructive than a cockpit drill to ensure the safe operation of a jet airliner. It is the motive that determines everything in the end.

Freemasonry – that world-wide universal system of brotherhood based on the principles of Faith, Hope and Charity and employing the impressive rituals and grading of the magical structure of its 'Temple' by steady application and guidance had been in existence long before its resuscitation of re-emergence into open recognition and acceptance in the early eighteenth century (1717). My (British) grandfather – and three of his sons were Masons, and good ones at that, and they all worked for the 'Light'.

All social activities have a ritual of some sort – you only have to see a Cup Final and hear the community hymn singing and ritual massed chanting of slogans and catch-phrases to realize that. It is how the 'group force' is applied, once it has been generated, that is the determining factor between good and evil – positive and negative – the difference between a 'good natured crowd' (so beloved of radio commentators) and a mob, howling for blood.

All the great religions are, of course, objectively speaking, pure applied ritual, with the object of individual and mass mind-manipulation – *for the light*. Let us take Christianity, and Catholicism in particular; and please do not think that I am being blasphemous in this simple demonstration of objective thinking. First suppose that you are a Christian – a Catholic – and are trying to explain to me, a heathen, what happens when you go to Mass.

You would start by saying something on these lines: 'We hold our meetings in a temple – a tall building, usually with a vaulted roof, which is normally orientated north, south, east and west and with the altar in the east. This building is decorated with images and symbols of our saints and our Trinity of deities, and often has rose-shaped windows and a squared floor, in black and white stones. Sometimes a labyrinthine design is featured, and there are many geometrical shapes built into the walls and furnishings, such as an octagonal pulpit and font. At the altar there is a large cross of wood, with the figure of our Lord and Master, a half-naked crucified man held by nails to the wooden cross, hammered through hands and feet; and he is wearing a crown of thorns.

The hierophant, or priest, speaks a language long dead (if the Tridentine Mass is observed), and the worshippers genuflect and give ritual responses during the Mass. A censer of burning aromatic herbs (the thurible) is swung ritually to fumigate the cardinal points of the church's orientation; and a bell is rung and ritual knocks are given with a sacred staff of office.

The culmination of this rite of worship occurs when *only* the *initiates* go forward, to kneel before the hierophant and partake of the mystical ritual of eating and drinking the *body* and *blood* of their Lord.'

Once again let me state that I am *not* being blasphemous; for the Mass is a most beautiful and deeply moving and uplifting ritual when considered *subjectively*. But would you be surprised if a simple pagan, confronted by such an *objective* description, said: 'But that is pure ritual magic.'

A great cathedral Mass, the Nuremberg Rally, The Fourth

of July in the United States, Quatorze Juillet in France – or, for that matter, the Russian May Day parade, all are as ritualistic as the 'Rites of Eleusis' or the 'Invocation to Astarte'. Only in their all-important subjective *motive* are they different. All of them are designed to have the maximum effect on the minds of the participants for whatever purpose is intended.

As I stood years later in the ruins of Germany and confronted the dark practices of the Nazis so accurately predicted in our simple 'home circle' in the thirties; as I walked aghast through the revealed hell of Belsen, I realized to what sub-bestial levels the human spirit could sink. It was all pure horror, Dark Satanic Horror.

I once asked the late, brutally murdered Colonel Airey Neave why none of this clear evidence of the Nazis' practice of black magic and diabolic rituals had been exposed to the world during the Nuremberg Trials.

This honest and scholarly man replied: 'It's really quite simple. If we had, as the prosecuting team, brought such hard evidence of these practices to the courts, the Defence would undoubtedly have used it as evidence of their clients' insanity. The war criminals would have been acquitted on grounds of diminished responsibility.'

Let the last words on that subject rest with this good man.

Appendix II

Ectoplasm

The question of ectoplasm and its different types for different phenomena is an interesting one.

Apparently, when analysed by chemists, coarse types of ectoplasm, used for physical phenomena, has often proved to be mucosal in origin: an excretion of the mucous membrane tissues of the medium. The points of exudation were, at different times, the nostrils, the mouth from the base of the throat and the solar plexus – and the sex organs.

Ectoplasm seems to be altogether remarkable stuff. In an invisible form it manifests as a 'chill' form of energy; and in the case of the table-turnings in which I was a sitter, it appeared to generate as a rising spiral of force forming around our ankles and feet.

The point of exudation of this type of ectoplasm was probably our solar plexi, hence the yawning. Only Ma, Tony and I yawned uncontrollably during this 'draining off' of power. Obviously we were being used as the physical mediums.

An interesting side effect was the distinct smell of ozone, which was most apparent during physical phenomena I experienced later in materialization, direct voice and transfiguration tests. This suggests discharges of electrical power such as a Tesla ozone producer would give. Many other investigators have come up with a similar deduction. As we are electro-chemical by nature, it isn't all that surprising.

Most physical phenomena require coarse fully materialized ectoplasm (a term invented by a Dr Richet for this
protoplasmic substance), which is exuded from the solar
plexus, though I have also seen the substance being
extruded from the nostrils and partially covering the
medium's face like a veil. This type of situation, where the
ectoplasm will be used to build up into a face or even a fully
materialized body of life size, is subject to certain limita-
tion. For instance, the phenomenon should take place in total
darkness, although I have seen it occur in infra-red light. It
seems that light is harmful to the substance in this form.

However, it can be argued that these conditions of total
darkness are conducive to, if not ideal for, fake illusions and
trick materializations. Undoubtedly they have been used
for such nefarious purposes on numerous occasions. But if
the researchers are experienced and resourceful, there are
plenty of ways of ensuring that the ectoplasmic exudations
are not just regurgitated mutton cloth or thin gauze hung
over light wire collapsible frameworks.

Luminous slates, painted with a suitable fluorescent
substance, will give enough light to allow at least some
monitoring of the manifestations, and infra-red film can be
safely used to take a series of photographs during the
proceedings, all with the knowledge and permission of the
medium. Serious physical injury could result in the sudden
application of light, just as it would cause injury to eyes
which have been bandaged after ophthalmic surgery. So
never try sudden clever tricks to 'expose' a medium. If you
are at all doubtful, sound commonsense will be your best
protection against fraud.

Manifestations of direct-voice, materialization and transfiguration without corroboratory evidence are only demonstrations of telekinesis of one form or another. The
instant recognition of the manifesting entity or a piece of
spoken or written evidence that could *only* be known to the
sitter and the communicant is the best insurance that the
whole sitting has not been a waste of time.

Your best yardstick for determining fake mediumship is
your own instinct. Never go into a research test of a medium
with your mind previously made up. Keep your wits about
you and listen to that 'still small voice' inside you that says
'Yes' or 'No' and you will not go far wrong.

The type of energy which is contained by the lighter kind of
ectoplasm used for simpler phenomena such as table-turning
and the levitation of objects of low weight can be and has been
photographed many times. It appears as *rods*, which act as
fulcrums and levers, and often as a swirling mist such as the
vortex of power that moved our table. Had we conducted the
sittings in full darkness, this energy field would have
appeared eventually, as our eyes became accustomed to the
dark; or we could have used infra-red light and film sensitive
to it to take pictures. But as the phenomenon worked
extremely well in subdued light and firelight, and this
condition reassured me in particular, there was no point in
blacking out the room.

The 'message' was the object of the exercise and those
results were remarkable. Whether we had established a
rapport with a number of discarnate entities or had somehow
contacted the latent forces of levitation and prophecy in our
own Overminds (or, if you prefer, supra-conscious) is once
again a question of personal conviction.